Meeting the Needs of Students with Diverse Backgrounds

Also available from Continuum

Class Talk, Rosemary Sage
Inclusion in Schools, Rosemary Sage
Lend Us Your Ears, Rosemary Sage

Meeting the Needs of Students with Diverse Backgrounds

Edited by
Rosemary Sage

continuum

Continuum International Publishing Group

The Tower Building   80 Maiden Lane
11 York Road   Suite 704
London SE1 7NX   New York, NY 10038

www.continuumbooks.com

British Library Cataloguing-in-Publication Data
A catalogue record for this book is available from the British Library.

ISBN: 978-1-85539-468-1 (paperback)

Library of Congress Cataloging-in-Publication Data
Meeting the needs of students with diverse backgrounds / [edited by] Rosemary Sage.
p. cm.
Includes index.
ISBN: 978-1-85539-468-1
1. Minorities–Education–Cross-cultural studies. 2. Multicultural education–
Cross-cultural studies. 3. Inclusive education–Cross-cultural studies. I. Sage, Rosemary
(Rosemary Joy Wysall Beaton) II. Title.

LC3715.M44 2009
371.829–dc22

2009035016

Typeset by Newgen Imaging Systems Pvt Ltd, Chennai, India
Printed and bound in Great Britain by CPI Antony Rowe, Chippenham, Wiltshire

This book is dedicated to the many special people whose stories feature in this book. We, the authors, hope that as a result of this publication, people will reflect on their attitudes and actions, because some of the people you will read about endure lives blighted by discrimination and exclusion. We hope that one day, like the phoenix, they will rise, shine and glow in the beauty of their undeniable uniqueness.

Contents

Preface

I am delighted to present this book to you, as it represents the views and scholarship of a very special group of friends and colleagues with very different experiences of diversity and inclusion. The book is for anyone who wants to reflect on this subject in some depth. The 12 chapters are crafted to give the reader knowledge and understanding as well as focusing on the skills that are needed to cope with diversity and inclusion in the context that is relevant for them. To make diversity and inclusion a successful reality, education is an important factor and so many of the authors are professionals in this field. The book is very suitable for those studying the subject, either at undergraduate or postgraduate level, and will appeal to those in educational, medical and social work fields. However, the general reader will find much to interest them within the chapters. The narratives tell compelling stories from around the world and I have learnt a great deal in the process of editing these chapters. Do enjoy your read and celebrate the vibrancy of the society we live in, due to the many fascinating differences that exist between us. The aim of the book is to make us more aware and informed about the issues that help or hinder the acceptance of diversity. The goal, for all of us, is a society in which each of us is valued equally and given the respect their uniqueness deserves.

Rosemary Sage, Professor of Education
The College of Teachers

An introduction to diversity: Meeting the needs of students from diverse backgrounds

Rosemary Sage

These are interesting times. The world has gone 'global', with its people economically and politically dependent on each other as never before, resulting in unprecedented movements of people across national boundaries. In Britain, this means that English is a minority language in 1,500 schools with approaching 50 of these having no indigenous children on their rolls (National Office for Statistics, 2010). The one million immigrant children account for one-sixth of the school population. In some London boroughs, only one-fifth of the children speak English as a first language costing the Government around a quarter of a billion in support for them. Such a phenomenon brings challenges but also benefits. Immigrants introduce different views, values, cultures and customs, appreciating education more than us. The British tend to dismiss academics and dream of celebrities with Paris Hilton and David Beckham the main career models for children (Brettingham, 2008). This situation is evidenced in the Trends of the International Mathematics and Science Study across 60 countries and involving 400,000 pupils (Gonzales et al., TIMSS, 2008). British schoolchildren lag academically well behind those from the Far East and are overtaken by countries such as Kazakhstan.

The present challenge is the development of a successful multi-cultural society in a country no longer sure of its identity and direction. Confusion is greater, however, than national, ethnic and religious issues. Reactions to the recent war in Iraq displayed sharp divisions regarding our attitudes to past history. When the UK government engaged in battle, was it acting in an imperialist role, or as protector of oil exports, or deliverer from evil or perhaps just a supporter of the United States' desire for reprisals following earlier skirmishes?

Over centuries, Britain has evolved a society that has been relatively free, fair, peaceful, prosperous and distinctive for its democratic principles. It pioneered a more civilized, less-violent society than most because of a jury system of law and order. This model was exported successfully throughout the vast British Empire, involving nearly one-third of the world's people, so that it no longer seems our invention and the United Kingdom no longer different from other nations (Bingham, 2007). He points out that it is not just Britain that was made great as a result of such development but also the rest of the world. From law and order to the Industrial Revolution and mass education, the British have made an immense contribution to world progress even though 'our national identity has been dented in the process' (Bingham, 2007). This experience has made us very used to living and working with those of diverse colours and creeds over a significant period of our history. We have shared our principles of democratic government and have benefited from the help of others in supporting these politically and economically.

Britain has been renowned as a liberal, tolerant, polite society but many believe that it has recently become fragmented, irresponsible and degenerate. Children are thugs, workers ill-educated and decision makers incompetent and greedy (Bingham 2007). He cites that when a newspaper asked readers for a new British coin design one respondent wrote: 'How about a couple of yobs dancing on a car bonnet or a trio of legless ladettes in the gutter?' Such impressions have led the Islam4UK group to set out its vision of how Britain should be run, involving the dismissal of our jury system and trial by an Islamic judge to avoid miscarriages of justice. They believe that people have lived in oppression with man-made laws resulting in a society rife with crime and a government struggling to tackle it. With nearly 100 Sharia courts operating in the United Kingdom, we can expect great changes in our traditional society over the course of the present century but must be aware of what they mean for us.

It is against this background that the book is written and the more we discuss our views and examine our differences the safer and more successful we will be as a society. I remember as a child of around 9 years of age playing on Brighton beach when a much older girl of 13 joined in. When asked what religion I was and replying 'Church of England', the older girl suggested that Catholics and Protestants were equivalent to 'good' and 'evil', respectively. I felt, at the time, that this was what she had been told to say to those she met. In retrospect, one is struck by the credulity of this teenager who was prey to manipulation by influential hate-mongers. The more we can share and understand each other's beliefs, customs and lifestyles the less we will imbue them with the demon qualities held by bigots. The Church of England Synod has recently strongly argued for the right of members to express and openly admit to their faith. They have cited examples of them treated as pariahs in a society, which is traditionally and officially Christian (e.g. workers threatened with the sack for wearing crosses, etc.). What is lost in such confusion and cowardice is the sense of humanity and understanding that might guide us through such situations more sensibly with appreciation of our history and tradition.

In a world of constantly shifting circumstances and a variety of viewpoints, our children are reared and educated. Differences amongst us are in gender, race, social class, culture, ethnicity, personality, ability and education. It is a combination of race, gender and class that are the key determinants of educational achievement with the former making the biggest difference (Marley, 2008). This issue is complex as Platt (2009) describes the shift towards a mixed-race Britain as 'dramatic'. She paints a picture of the United Kingdom where Caribbean, African, Chinese, Indian and White British are more likely to marry and have children with those of other races. The fact that President Obama of the United States is of both black and white parentage gives great impetus to such development.

The Platt study shows that 9 per cent of UK children are of 'mixed or multiple heritage', living with parents of different ethnic groups and themselves of mixed ethnicity. Over the past 14 years, those of Caribbean background with a white parent have risen from 39 to 49 per cent and for the Chinese from 15 to 35 per cent. In the Indian population the increase is from 3–11 per cent and for Pakistanis from 1 to 4 per cent. Pakistanis and Bangladeshis are entering mixed-race relationships at a lower rate than others probably because they are mostly Muslim and live in more enclosed communities. Some feel that history and distinctive culture are being lost in mixed-race unions with the playwright and actor Kwame Kwei-Armah lamenting this publicly. He points out that most Premier League footballers who are black have white partners, signalling that when you are successful you date outside your community.

We are all likely to belong to several, different societal groups and people have 'complex identities and multiple roles so labels can be misleading' (Sage, 2004, p. 10). Discrimination against groups and individuals can often be detected in processes, attitudes and behaviours, as the following chapters will reveal. I remember being discriminated against and bullied at primary school because my father was the local vicar and another pupil the same because hers was the neighbourhood policeman. Reared in a middle class home with well-educated parents, however, my sister and I were socially and academically advantaged and were the first ever in our area to pass the eleven plus exam for grammar school. Such factors suggest that we must become better acquainted with what helps people succeed in a diverse society and this book will give a glimpse of what is deemed important.

Underpinning success is an understanding of others and acceptance of their views and habits, which enhances our ability to interact successfully with them.

As examples of other customs, the Japanese regard nose blowing and wearing shoes indoors as disgusting but talking constantly in lessons as necessary for thinking and communicating. Africans only eat with the right hand as the left is reserved for a related function. Middle Easterners do not believe in targets as only God knows the future and males may not want to talk to female teachers and encourage their boys not to do so. Indians are not allowed to look you in the eye when admonished. Knowing these and other conventions aids communication, understanding and effective learning. If we can stop making judgments on things we are unable to change and focus on those we can, the better we will achieve a tolerant, civilized society.

I consider myself to be one of the lucky generation. To be middle aged and middle class in middle England has been largely pleasant, comfortable, secure and free. However, this golden age is now over with public finances in dire straits and the International Monetary Fund (IMF) cracking down on our state insolvency. The nation will no longer be able to afford the full panoply of tax-funded services and amenities that it has enjoyed in the past. An age of austerity has dawned in which the world will be less cushioned and more hostile. There is a danger of social disintegration with current government and banker bashing a sign of this. However, we can turn resentment for others into respect, creating a greater sense of community which counts for more than envy and greed. The present book is most timely in this context as it will help us all reflect more deeply and hopefully inspire us to work for peace and a moderate prosperity for us all.

This reflection depends on us recognizing the lessons of history so that we are not beguiled by false opinions. The four most important words, according to Sir John Templeton, the stock market guru, are 'it's different this time', applying to all spheres of life. We can identify issues and probabilities but if we do nothing about them they will invariably bite us. As a nation we have espoused the view that self-interest would guard against reckless behaviour. Laws of probability teach us that the longer a trend goes on, the more it is likely to be interrupted. Psychology, however, works in the opposite way; the longer something continues the more followers it attracts and the more remote are memories of anything different. Misplaced faith in the self-serving model at the expense of a collegiate one is now defined by the abdication of individual and organizational responsibility and a society beset by economic, social and emotional problems.

There is what is known as the '40-year rule', which says that crisis happens as soon as those who remember the last one retire! No one can predict the future with precision but we can identify risks and act accordingly. People are resilient and resourceful so there is hope that we can resolve our present differences and difficulties if we focus on the similarities that bind us and goals that are common. Then diversity will be a blessing and not a curse and we will all benefit from a deeper, wider view of the world and its people.

Stories about diversity

A synopsis of the chapters

Chapter 1 – Narrating the stories of others – *Rosemary Sage*

Rosemary Sage is the Editor of this book and her qualifications and working background in speech and language therapy, psychology and teaching has brought her into close contact with the many issues of diversity in human experience. In this chapter, she goes into the tricky problem of writing about the lives and activities of others and reveals how truth can so easily get distorted to fit a certain philosophy and practice. This has a very devastating impact on the people concerned. Using a real case study of a boy that she was involved with, as a practising clinician, Rosemary looks at how this has coloured people's perception of him and considerably hindered his progress through school and now work.

Chapter 2 – Inclusion from exclusion: Cultures and communities seen through the eyes of a Muslim – *Yaasmin Mubarak*

Yaasmin moved to this country from Kenya when she was eight years old. Her parents are from a Yemeni heritage and her moving and compelling story opens our eyes to the problems of settlers from other lands and cultures. Yaasmin has been determined to develop her education and recently gained a BSc degree in Inclusion Studies, under the expert guidance of Dr Christine Bold, who has written Chapter 6. Now, Yaasmin is working at a senior level in a private school. Her story of struggle and success is so inspiring and revealing that readers will not fail to be moved by the narrative of her life. Yaasmin's first school in the United Kingdom was a Catholic one, practising many ritual ceremonies, such as Mass, that are part of their faith. She tells us of her puzzlement and fear that resulted from such novel, strange experiences in her school life. As an example of courage and perseverance against a mountain of odds, this story is a powerful reminder of what one can achieve if realistic and positive about life events.

Chapter 3 – Diversity versus adversity: Included or excluded? Issues emerging from teaching in state and private schools – *Diane Macarthur*

Diane is a very experienced senior school teacher, who has worked in both the state and private sectors, and has interesting and important comparisons to make about both these systems. She has also brought up four boys single-handedly and understands the challenges of having to cope with earning a living and raising a family. As a teacher, she has become very aware of the difficulties of children from diverse cultures and backgrounds and understands their feelings of isolation and problems of identity. She presents a picture of *diversity* and *adversity* by first describing a typical school day and teasing out the issues that emerge. As the most excluded group in UK society, Diane then brings in her knowledge of the Traveller communities, who are never in one place for any length of time to make relationships outside their own group. She describes, discusses and evaluates the subject of *diversity* and *adversity* with examples from her professional and personal life and has powerful points to make on salient issues.

Chapter 4 – 'Now he has a label we can cope!': Parent perceptions of attention deficit hyperactivity disorder – *Lynne Kendall*

Lynne is a very experienced primary school teacher, who has worked at a senior level in mainstream and special schools, and is now a university lecturer in the special needs and early years' fields. She completed her Masters thesis in the area of *parent perceptions of their children with special needs* and has a particular interest in the family situation. In this chapter, she focuses on the distressing condition of ADHD *(attention deficit and hyperactivity disorder),* which appears to be an increasing societal problem linked to biological and environmental factors. The condition is described and causation discussed, as a prelude to four case studies of two children and two young adults, in order to understand the difficulties that emerge for them and their families over time.

Chapter 5 – Working with diversity in a primary school: Experiences of a special needs co-ordinator – *Gill Dixon*

Gill is a very experienced teacher, who trained in Physical Education, and initially worked in the senior sector before specializing in children with special needs in a rural, primary school. She has been particularly successful with a range of problems that children experience with their learning, according to feedback from colleagues and parents. Gill has been committed to further study both at Northampton and Sheffield universities and this has been crucial in widening and deepening her knowledge and skills for teaching children requiring a different approach to learning. Dealing with a wide range of problems across the school, as well as taking responsibility for a class, is a continual challenge and the normal remit of staff working in the primary sector. Gill shares her experiences of coping with a range of diversity which gives us an opportunity to reflect on this with regard to our own practice.

Chapter 6 – The diverse and changing roles of teaching assistants: Supporting diversity in schools – *Christine Bold*

Christine is an experienced teacher of Mathematics in senior schools and has been a principal lecturer in a university, who has pioneered undergraduate courses in Inclusion, and knows first hand the challenges of preparing professionals to work with issues of diversity. She has an interest in the changing role of Teaching Assistants, who are rapidly becoming the experts in education regarding diversity and inclusion. The graduates in this field take their degree studies in this topic and so are able to take leading roles in implementing various types of learning support in schools. Christine describes and discusses the issues that have emerged with the development of this professional group alongside teachers in schools.

Chapter 7 – My diverse and very modern family – *Julie Crofts*

Julie has a very typical modern family. She has been married twice and had to cope with being a stepmother to children very much older than her own. Her own daughter has a bi-cultural heritage and the family has been swept into the effects of globalization as her present husband, daughter and herself have lived, worked and studied abroad. Julia has much enjoyed the life of the ex-pat in China, finding settling back into the United Kingdom, without a coterie of servants, extremely difficult! Nevertheless, she has coped with her challenges with great equanimity and her attitudes to others and creative problem-solving capacity is a lesson to us all. Julie is a great communicator and this is undoubtedly a key to her success. She has worked as an administrator, in the Psychology department of a hospital, and so has first-hand experiences of children and adults who struggle with the diverse issues that face them in very complex, difficult lives. She is an author of a recently published book reflecting ex-pat lives.

Chapter 8 – Issues for living and working in a foreign culture: Discussions with Miki Nishimori from Japan – *Rosemary Sage*

Miki is Japanese and came to Britain to study for her Masters in Education at the University of Cambridge. She has specialized in early Japanese education and now lectures in this subject area at Shugin University, Kyoto. Miki has been the international co-ordinator at the Women's University, Nara – one of two famous and prestigious female establishments in the Japanese Higher Education system. Therefore, she has travelled the world in her university role and has become very adaptable to and knowledgeable about foreign cultures. Some of the linguistic and cultural problems of living and studying outside one's own birth place are brought out in this chapter and are the result of talking with Miki over a four-year period in the *Dialogue, Innovation, Achievement and Learning (DIAL)* projects, an initiative between the United Kingdom and Japan to prepare students for working and living in the twenty-first century.

Chapter 9 – A call to arms: Developing diverse students through service learning – *John Patterson* and *Alison Patterson*

John and Alison are both inspiring, charismatic teachers who have worked at a senior level in primary schools (John was a deputy head teacher) and now are university lecturers in a School of Education. This chapter explores *diversity* within the context of *student volunteerism*. It describes a cross-curricular arts and citizenship project, in a City Primary School, managed by teacher students and evaluated by those involved. This *Service Learning Model* helps educators gain insight into local communities, surrounding schools, and develops teacher and learner practical skills of communicating and relating to people with different backgrounds and abilities. It is considered a value-added tool for the new *Professional Standards Framework for Teaching and Learning in Higher Education,* while balancing the present academic National Curriculum (NC) with opportunities for personal and academic teacher and learner development.

Chapter 10 – The role of charities in supporting diversity and inclusion: The Selective Mutism Information and Research Association (SMIRA) – *Alice Sluckin* and *Lindsay Whittingham*

Alice is quite one of the most inspiring people one is likely to meet, writing this chapter in collaboration with Lindsay Whittingham the co-founder of SMIRA. She is the only survivor of a Czech and Polish family who were all tragically murdered by the Nazis, so her life is one of supreme courage in the face of deep sadness. Alice was a senior psychiatric social worker and collaborated with Rosemary Sage (then head of Speech and Language Services in Leicester and Leicestershire) in developing parent and child communication groups. Alice's husband was a famous, international academic, known for his work on artificial intelligence and imprinting, who, as Professor of Psychology, headed a department at the University of Leicester, previously working at Durham and Cambridge. As the Chair of the Selective Mutism Information and Research Association (SMIRA), Alice shows how charities reach the parts that are impossible for the statutory services to do so, playing a vital role in supporting diversity and inclusion. She has been awarded an OBE in the 2010 Honours List for her pioneering work with Selective Mutism and this is long overdue and well deserved.

Chapter 11 – International perspectives regarding inclusion: Comparing Cyprus and the United Kingdom – *Panayiota Christodoulidou*

Panayiota completed an MA in Inclusive Education at the University of Leicester and her tutor was Professor Rosemary Sage. She completed her thesis in *International Special Needs Education*, tracing how this has evolved in her native Cyprus and contrasting this with the United Kingdom and elsewhere. Cyprus has a great commitment to the post-graduate studies of their teachers and Panayiota is one of many who have studied at the University of Leicester. Although progress towards inclusion of all students learning together, in mainstream, is slower than many would like, there have been huge changes in the last 20 years. Now attitudes are much more positive about creating opportunities for those with specific difficulties, to develop their potential and contribute to their communities. Panayiota looks at these policy changes and their implementation. She evaluates them, in the light of experiences, making well-considered suggestions for future development that are useful for policy makers, professionals and parents.

Chapter 12 – Succeeding in diversity – *Rosemary Sage*

Rosemary Sage is a Professor of Communication, now working at London University as consultant to the Medical Schools at the Kent, Sussex and Surrey Post-Graduate Deanery. She is the first female professor at the College of Teachers based at the London Institute for Education. In this chapter she brings together the main message of the authors of this book and reflects on these for future consideration. People with diverse backgrounds often have difficulties or disabilities, which are broadly organized as learning, social/emotional behavioural or physical/medical problems. Using case studies, as well as personal experiences of the authors, to show how positive and negative experiences of diversity shape people's lives, we challenge assumptions about those labelled as '*different*' and frequently question the truth of expert opinion.

Appendices 1–5

These provide definitions and descriptions of the main divisions of diversity in the United Kingdom:

Appendix 1: Religious diversity
Appendix 2: Terms used for minority ethnic communities
Appendix 3: Examples of how people are named
Appendix 4: Families and diversity
Appendix 5: Glossary of disability and social exclusion

The book addresses the needs of personal and professional development at undergraduate and postgraduate level that are relevant for educational management, health promotion and youth and community work. The stories of the authors familiarize readers with the vocabulary and terms of discussion; provide a concise overview of recent research and current debates and convey a sense of future direction, growth and change. The overall message is that success for children and adults is the result of positive interactions and experiences at home, school and work, so that they can move confidently between social worlds, cultures and languages in their daily lives. The fundamental issue of *effective communication* needs greater emphasis, if succeeding with diversity is to become a consistent reality. This factor has been stressed by each of the authors of this book as being the *most important* but also the *most neglected* aspect of education and training for diversity and inclusion.

References

Bingham, H. (2007) *How One Small Country Changed the Modern World*, London: HarperCollins.

Brettingham, M. (2008) *How we're evolving*. London: *The Times* Educational Supplement Magazine, 18 July 2008.

Gonzales, J., Williams, Jocelyn, L., Roey, S., Kaotberg, D. & Brenwall, S. (2008) *The Trends in International Mathematics and Science Study (TIMSS): 4th and 8th Grade Students in the International Context*. U.S. Department of Education, Institute of Educational Sciences, pub. NCES 2009001.

Marley, D. (2008) *Mind the performance gaps: he combined impact of gender, race and class*. London: A series challenging education stereotypes. *The Times* Educational Supplement. 30 May 2008.

National Office of Statistics (accessed 20 April 2010) http://www.statistics.gov.uk/ default.asp

Platt, L. (2009) *Multicultural Britain.* University of Essex. Research commissioned by the Equality and Human Rights Commission.

Sage, R. (2004) *Inclusion in Schools,* Stafford: Network Educational Press.

1 Narrating the stories of others

Rosemary Sage

Overview

This chapter introduces questions that arise when writing about others whose lives may be very different to our own. Experts, educated and trained to deal with human diversity become defined by activities that must operate within the strict bureaucratic controls of today's workplaces. Therefore, when reporting on the lives of others, truth may be distorted to fit a certain philosophy and practice. It is important, therefore, not only to consider what we say about others but also the power relations which influence our views. We need awareness of the processes which can separate someone from their own life history and unwittingly slow progress. Encouraging others to retain ownership of their experiences, as well as our own, keeps them in mind to support self knowledge and self development. Communication between us all is crucial if we are to work for some common identity and purpose that accounts for individual differences and needs in our society. This sharing of information has become more difficult since the shift from an oral to a literate culture, so we must recognize this and seek opportunities to engage with one another in patient, persistent dialogue.

Introduction

This book presents stories about *diversity* and there has never been a greater need to take stock of the feelings and views of our many neighbours. Today's mobility of people around the world is unprecedented. In a recent trip to our local supermarket, I heard 15 different languages being spoken, and then stopped counting! There was also a blind lady and a gentleman in a wheelchair, receiving shopping assistance by store employees. These daily events demand awareness of others and an enhanced ability to communicate across a myriad of differences for better understanding of individual values and needs. This comes at a time of increased income dispersion over the past decades due to continued mechanization and globalization and a decline for less skilled workers. Where those in power are, through higher incomes, divorced from the experiences of those who are economically poorer, they are unlikely to seek income redistribution. Political choices can lead to a rise in inequality and a focus on the negative issues of diversity such as less ability and less money (Goodman et al., 1997). These are issues that must be acknowledged and addressed. First, we will consider the nature of diversity.

A definition of diversity

The definition of diversity stresses the idea of people being of different kinds, both in nature and qualities. It is only within the last 30 years that Human Rights Law has tackled inequalities between abilities, sexes, social classes and nations. Segregating people has been common practice but integrating and including them all in daily life has been promoted by world agreements, such as Salamanca (1994) and Jomtein (2000). Now, we use the word '*diversity*', with its emphasis on *variety*, to recognize our differences and understand how we can live and work together. Inclusion of everybody in everything and in everyway, however, has not always been appropriate or effective. For example, including *all* children in one national curriculum has been against the needs and interests of increasing numbers, as evidenced by SENDIST (the special educational needs tribunal system) and the hundreds of cases they cope with each year. However, exclusion from the established system effectively prevents their full social and economic involvement later on in life. Many think that the expansion of an elite, academic education, originally devised for those entering legal, medical and teaching professions, and made available to the masses, devalues practical intelligences. This results in exclusion from rather than inclusion in learning activities for a significant number of children (Sage, 2004). Countries, like Cuba, high in UNESCO health and education tables, have sought education within *universal* rather than *inclusive* principles, based on knowledge of child development as well as national needs. The goal is relevant learning for everyone rather than a one-size-fits-all system (Sage, 2009).

It is within this ethos that we relate the stories of those whose lives are different from our own, but in so doing we must account for assumptions made when reporting about others, as well as consider the interpretative and communicative theories regarding aspects outside spoken and written words. As teachers, social workers, health professionals, psychologists or others, our practices depend on communicative exchanges, in which we can easily miss their variability and complexity. Communication involves many individual separation and exclusion possibilities, involving the following issues, which are marginalized in education and practice:

- The move from oral-based cultures to literate ones with the consequent drive for mass education and universal literacy being only 100 plus years old (Education Acts of 1870, 1944 and 1981);
- The transition from non-verbal to verbal communication in human development and then to literate forms, which are basic to effective education;
- A life behind and between spoken and written words, establishing the meaning of the communicative exchange in not what is said or read but inferred.

Four *communicative aspects* are reported in the literature, expanding on these issues:

1. *Expressive*: Words and actions can represent feelings and be uttered for our benefit (Bion, 1962).
2. *Informative*: Words and actions can explain our feelings, ideas and views to others or respond to theirs (Vygotsky, 1986).
3. *Material*: Words and actions are *matter*, moving in relation to other things through time and space (Lacan, 1977).
4. *Making meaning*: Words and actions help us make sense of our lives (Newman and Holzman, 1993).

We are generally unconscious of the above aspects so our reasons for claiming truth in our views about people require reflection. Regarding the accuracy of professional stories about others, examples are provided of the way words become government acts and written reports used to justify separation and exclusion. Analyses that account for narrative talk and text complexity facilitate observations and their interpretations and are reviewed in the next section.

Communicating objectively

In our expert role we use words continuously to represent people with whom we work. How important are the ideas and beliefs that lie in and outside the words we use? Discourse analyses does not just focus on a speaker's words, mind and manner but on the meaning of the event from the context, roles of the participants and non-verbal elements of voice and gesture, which are inferred rather than observed in written text. Professionals are trained to be objective and emotionally detached from events. Practices, however, are in danger of separating people from their experiences, by claiming greater professional knowledge and truth. Nagel (1984, p. 4) mentions this limitation: 'Realism underlines the claims of objectivity and detachment but supports them only up to a point'. Aristotle (1976, p. 210) expands on this, suggesting: 'The maker of the work exists, in a sense, through his activity'.

Awareness and understanding is made conscious through sharing views and core to cultures such as Japanese.

People tell stories in words and actions to themselves and others to make sense of their lives, but in a literate culture first hand narratives are rarer. Benjamin (1992, p. 83) suggests that: 'the act of storytelling is coming to an end – it is as if something that seemed inalienable to us (was) taken from us: the ability to exchange experiences'. In oral cultures, people retained ownership of their history with Genette (1980) defining narrative types:

- Events recounted by someone: the act of narrating (traditional definition)
- Oral or written discourse relating an event
- Real/fictitious events that provide the subject of the discourse.

The traditional definition of narrative regards the activity and way of retelling events as equally important, encouraging analyses of both. Authors in this book experience in their accounts not others' reality but their own activity of writing about them, although some chapters are autobiographical. So, we hope to present a reliable method of recording. Reconnecting with our activities is not introspection as 'self-understanding is at the heart of objectivity' (Nagel, 1979, p. 78), which is demonstrated in the story below:

The Story of Jim

Several years ago I was asked to see an 11-year-old boy who was transferring to mainstream secondary school from a special unit for children with speech and language difficulties. My professional background, as a speech and language therapist, psychologist and teacher, meant that clients were referred to me who had cognitive, communicative, linguistic and phonetic problems. Teachers told me that Jim's language and behaviour were unacceptable in some situations. For example, his form tutor was killed in a car crash whilst three months pregnant, and Jim appeared to find this amusing – laughing and joking about the event. Staff held views about Jim's past, in a language unit, which affected their attitudes and tolerance of his presence in school. They referred to the low performance of those in specialist provision, ignoring Jim's good general knowledge and life experience, excellent family support and exceptionable expertise on the computer.

My first meeting with Jim was at home and lasted one hour. I learnt that he had been adopted as a baby and experienced considerable problems with speech and language development and socializing with others. From examination, he presented with a very high-arched palate and small articulators in relation to his physical size. He had problems

---

in a number of communicative areas with speaking clearly, fluently and appropriately. Jim chattered away, and was generally understood when reminded to talk slowly. He recalled anxieties linked to bullying in school and teachers' lack of interest. 'I think I am too complicated to bother with', he said. Our meeting indicated that social and cognitive profiles were not significant given his history. I spoke to both parents after seeing Jim and they did not attempt to 'medicalise' his situation. They were aware of early problems and anxious for him to achieve his potential, suggesting that a lack of close, communicative relationships with peers would be a major handicap.

Over the years, Jim attended a once weekly Communication Opportunity Group Scheme (COGS, Sage, 2000a) in the village where he lived and made great progress, interacting with others and practising informal and formal talk. Now, aged 21, Jim lives alone in a flat and has had a variety of jobs. He socializes mainly at the pub and is able to stand up for himself but lacks confidence in new situations. Presently, he is having investigations for anxiety problems and has been undermined by two break-ins at his flat and assaults by gangs in the town that have resulted in hospital treatment.

Beyond words

Our spoken narratives help us to retain ownership of our experiences and resist the alienating effect of events as, for example, contact with others at home, school or work. Depending on the tales we hear, spoken words may sow seeds of separation and disintegration. In reconstructing histories, we employ and share the *material* elements of speaking, with language helping us to own experience and consider things beyond this. To what extent can I share events that Jim told me and his feelings about their importance? Could I use his words to re-experience these exactly?

Such understanding and empathy is unlikely and imprecision in saying what we mean questions the exactness of words and what lies beyond them. For speaker and listener, the *material* of language and its *representations* and *meanings* will be different. The real, affective message lies in *how* and *where* it is performed and the roles and relationships of those interacting. Words, therefore, are the basis of miscommunications between us. Experts constantly raise questions concerning their precision and reliability, but as Humpty Dumpty reminds us in *Alice and Wonderland*, they mean what ever we want them to with the 500 common words having at least 15,000 meanings (Sage, 2000b).

Although language is now of greater concern in a society where many different ones are spoken, Vygotsky (1986, p. 5) suggests that 'word meaning has been lost in the ocean of all other aspects of consciousness'. Discourse analysis promotes meaning in spite of a traditional focus on fragmented specializations and so resists a reductionist theory of communication. Varying viewpoints can be integrated in this verbal and non-verbal process, subject to strong personal and interpersonal influences. If communication and its meaning are functions of both verbal and non-verbal language we must understand how they use symbols for this.

Communicating with symbols

From an early age, symbol formation allows us to represent our internal and external experiences to our selves and others. It demonstrates unconscious knowledge of things and representations of them consciously, as well as the separation within us and between us and our environment. Qualitative and economic aspects of separating and splitting processes are involved in identity formation. Lacan (1977) makes *splitting* the fundamental developmental one, motivating studies in how children separate from their mothers. What exists for a child pre-linguistically and pre-symbolically is 'la langue', or maternal language *(words and actions),* from which their own signifying system develops.

Jim's identity formation

Jim split from his birth mother who disappeared when he was adopted. This loss of *'her'* (babies recognize mother's voice at 14 weeks *in utero*) is like a sudden *'death'*. The experience required symbolism for which he was developmentally incapable. The loss of his mother (inseparable from himself) probably felt permanent but Jim lacked the symbolic language to explain it. 'The symbol of experiences is used not to deny but to overcome loss' (Frosh, 1987, p. 138).

Jim's experience encouraged me to maintain contact with him over several years. Through this, I gained some understanding of his adoptive family, allowing me to form a view of his reality. As professionals in a bureaucracy, however, our thoughts on someone are recorded in written reports. Do these words belong to the *writer*, the *subject* or the *authority* requiring them? Berger (1992) suggests that written words belong to writing, so where is the writer and the person recorded? To what extent can they be true? Two views are available in the literature:

- Writing is speech for an absent person without the interlocutor present with both possibly having different views on the subject (Vygotsky, 1986, pp. 182, 240).
- Texts speak in the absence of the speaker, 'meaning detached from local contexts of interpretation' (Smith, 1988, p. 40)

So, a report allows the *invisibility* of the writer with selected words having theoretical and practical significance. Narrative definitions, discussed earlier, have temporal complexities – the time of the thing told and the time of the narrative, with opposition between story and narrative time (Genette, 1980, p. 33). Professional reports 'pathologize' a person, defining the power relations in which they can be separated and excluded. Examples are seen in my report on Jim and one from school:

Written reports on Jim

My report said: 'Jim is a young person whose thinking, communication and academic performance are within an expected range given his background. Difficulties in adapting to mainstream education result from attendance at a special school and his sensitivity about this'.

The school report took a 'pathological' perspective, placing Jim hierarchically:

'Jim is a student of low average ability with basic skills in line with this'.

The report written by me failed to mention *'ability'* or *'achievement'*. Also, I referred to Jim as a *'young person,'* contrasting with the school labelling him a *'student'*, defining him as a *'learner'* rather than a *'human being'*. The idea that Jim had feelings about his previous education was ignored, suggesting that pupils are only granted the sensibilities allowed by authority figures. Such examples show how written reports reflect the terms of professional work references – mine in the Health Service and the School in Education. To blame individuals, however, conceals the nature of bureaucratic control.

It may be viewed that reports do not belong to the subject or claim to be true to their life. A report's power is 'statutory' as in a legal statement of educational needs, assuming truth because of this fact. The power relations in which it is produced should be considered. Analyses by Billington et al. (2000) were concerned with the language of the discourse and the power at work in the position of people when not speaking. Parker (Burman and Parker, 1993, p. 158) says: 'power relations endure when the text stops'. 'Political regimes thus conduct a silent war for the control of symbols and rites of belonging to the human race within their frontiers, not least through their control of the public school system' (Hobsbawm, 1987, p. 106). The following questions are thus relevant to the information in this text:

- What can be reasonably known of the person/s reported?
- Does an account written by someone else contain this knowledge?
- What part of this account can be considered 'expert' and what as 'truth'?

Other questions spring to mind. How do you (the reader) relate to this *knowledge*? Do you possess the *knowledge* of the expert? How do you relate to the *knowledge*?

Do you accept or reject this *knowledge?* Truth can exist but the problem is reducing it to be understood by others.

Through your reading you will have formed ideas from the information about Jim. Facts are interpreted by me but you judge them from your own experiences of people or from what you have read previously on the subject. Accuracy, reliability or validity of the account is not the main issue here but reflection on the reasons and consequences of reporting about other people. Some of us regularly report on the life of others, justifying this because people like Jim are *'different'* in some respect and greater awareness of this will assist in their needs being met.

Jim's evidence did not have the power of professional accounts and was not used for his educational plan. This could only be achieved *through* an adult or professional as he was judged as lacking self-knowledge, even though his comment about teachers regarding him as too complicated reveals that he does. He was referred to me because of inappropriate communication, which was an issue in a mainstream school.

Jim's parents were unable to manage the situation alone, revealing academic, social and economic constraints. These were active in the initial referral and throughout his education with experts assessing Jim's ability to reach academic targets and providing assistance. When he was reviewed for inclusion in or exclusion from school activities is important. This could lead to exclusion from certain levels of economic activity later, which occurred as he was not given opportunity to gain qualifications to help job prospects. At the moment, he survives on a succession of temporary jobs for unskilled labour, although intellectually capable of more than this. He says: 'I know I'm bright, but school never saw this and denied me the help I needed to get on well.'

Policy, therefore, is introduced not necessarily to meet child needs but to control labour markets. Attention is deflected from the fact that schools are the means for this by legal processes in place for children with special needs. Although we focus on the problems people face because of differences we must understand the processes controlling their lives by regulating education. As Jim had difficulties complying with the *social* demands of school, he was effectively excluded from access to appropriate aspects of academic and now economic life. This was managed through expert assessments that gave him pathological labels to justify his management. The law states that Jim's needs must be considered and not the school ones, but is this the case? Assessment depended not upon his psychological and educational needs but on the following:

- Use of school resources greater than for other students
- Support requirements that could disadvantage his peers
- Expensive specialist input required inside or outside school.

Therefore, people are often excluded for economic reasons affecting the quality of decision-making. The process is eased with protocol justifying exclusion. Allocating Jim a particular pathology separated him from others with representations of him driven by economic rather than real needs.

Review

In this chapter, Jim's story is based on evidence with narrative representations supported by theories: 'When we conceive of the minds of others, we cannot abandon the essential factor of a point of view; instead we must generalize it and think of ourselves as one point of view among others (Nagel, 1986, p. 20).

This promises a more scientific approach than would be possible for me as a speech and language therapist, psychologist or teacher, working within a prescriptive system. Jim's story is my own interpretation with reflections backed by literature. Although written language provides possibilities for other ways of *'knowing'* the following quote shows how our separations can be anchored in writing. 'In the school there, I learnt to look at words like something written on a blackboard. When a man swears, the words come out of his body like shit. As kids we talk like that all the time. I leant that words belonged to writing. We used them; yet they were never entirely our own' (Berger, 1989, p. 123).

Sessions with Jim helped him review earlier experiences, exploring feelings and ideas safely without judgement. Jim had become separated from his history by professional and institutional opinions over the years, as problems with speaking and behaving kept him within their orbit. His medical problems meant that professionals had low expectations of him, a fact mentioned by Croll and Moses (1985). Aristotle's (1976) concept of a wisdom, which can accommodate both intuition and science is relevant here but Benjamin (1992, p. 86) reminds us we have a fading ability to access these links because the 'epic side of truth and wisdom is dying out' as the act of story-telling reaches its end. This wisdom knows instinctively that 'with words everything can happen, yet never change what has happened' (Berger, 1990, p. 190).

We must be aware of what can separate a person from their life history and prevent self-awareness, self-confidence, self-communication and self-control. As professionals, we should encourage others to retain ownership of their experiences, as well as our own: 'to preserve promises and potentialities which are betrayed and even outlawed by the mature, civilised individual and which are never entirely forgotten (Marcuse, 1966, p. 18).

Although a diverse society, we are not always conscious of the fact that inclusive policies and practices are socially and economically excluding for some people, setting them apart from others. The more diversity we have the more we need choices but a *common culture* whereby everyone can communicate effectively. People must talk with those who are made to feel they have no place in society. Professionals must listen more, talking and advising less. Those with special needs may need *extra* and not just *equal* opportunities for independence and fulfilment. It is hoped that you enjoy dipping between the pages to consider some of the existing issues of diversity, so that you look at the myriad of human faces and listen to their voices with new interest.

Suggestions for classroom practice

Think carefully when writing a report on a pupil and be aware of the natural prejudices we all have about other human beings. Learning to listen to others and holding back from making judgments until a full picture is obtained about a child or situation will mean a more successful outcome for everyone.

Main points

- Diversity encapsulates the idea of people being of different kinds, both in nature and qualities, so requiring flexible approaches and choices in their living, learning and working arrangements.
- Writing about others who are different than us poses problems regarding how we represent them, as the bureaucratic controls that constrain us may work against meeting their real needs.
- Professionals need awareness of the processes, which separate a person from their life history and how policies and practices of inclusion can, in fact, operate to exclude people socially and economically.
- We need to achieve regular dialogue with those who feel they have no place in society, talking and advising less but listening more.

Discussion point

Have a look at some reports written about someone you know. How do the words represent them and how might this influence their opportunities?

References

Aristotle (1976) *Ethics,* Tredennick, H. (ed.), London: Penguin Classics.

Benjamin, W. (1992) *Illuminations,* Arendt, H. (ed. and trans.), London: Fontana Press.

Berger, J. (1990) *Lilac and Flag,* London: Granta Books.

Berger, J. (1992) *Pig Earth,* London: Chatto & Windus.

Billington, T. (2000) *Separating, Losing and Excluding Children,* London: Routledge Falmer.

Bion, W. (1962) *Learning from Experience,* London: Karnac Books.

Burman, E. and Parker, I. (eds) (1993) *Discourse Analytic Research: Repertoires and Readings of Texts in Action,* London: Routledge.

Croll, P. and Moses, D. (1985) *One in Five: The Assessment and Incidence of Special Educational Needs,* London: Routledge and Kegan Paul.

Goodman, A., Johnson, P. and Webb, S. (1997) *Inequality in the UK,* Oxford: Oxford University Press.

Lacan, J. (1977) *Ecrits,* London: Routledge.

Marcuse, H. (1966) *Eros and Civilization,* Boston: Beacon Press.

Nagel, T. (1986) *The View from Nowhere,* Oxford: Oxford University Press.

Newman, F. and Holzman, L. (1993) *Lev Vygotsky: Revolutionary Scientist,* London: Routledge.

Sage, R. (2000a) *The Communication Opportunity Group Scheme.* Leicester: University of Leicester.

Sage, R. (2000b) *Class Talk,* Stafford: Network Educational Press.

Sage, R. (2004) *Inclusion in Schools,* London: Network-Continuum.

Sage, R. (2009) What can we learn from Education in Cuba? *Journal of the College of Teachers: Education Today,* Summer.

Smith, D. (1988) *Femininity as discourse.* In Roman, L. G., Christian-Smith, L. K. with Ellsworth, E., *Becoming Feminine: The Politics of Popular Culture,* Sussex: Falmer Press.

Vygotsky, L. S. (1986) *Thought and Language,* Cambridge, MA: Harvard University Press.

Inclusion from exclusion: Cultures and communities seen through the eyes of a Muslim

2

Yaasmin Mubarak

Overview

This chapter focuses on differences in religion and values. It reveals my story, as a Muslim girl, grappling with living in various cultures and communities with different views and lifestyles to the one in which I was born. At a time when we are adapting to living and working in close proximity with those originating from countries holding alternative ways of thinking, communicating and existing, it is important to express our feelings about this experience. By becoming more aware of others and the basis on which they live their lives, we have a better chance of communicating, collaborating and cooperating for the overall good of the community. Issues that help and hinder the inclusion of others are highlighted in this account.

Definition of diversity

Diversity, in the Oxford Dictionary, has various meanings according to its contextual use. These include diversity in multiculturalism, politics, business and biodiversity (*Oxford Dictionary*, 2004). Throughout this chapter are references to multiculturalism and business contexts.

My background

I was born on 7 January 1968, in a remote town called Nakuru, near the Rift Valley in Kenya, which borders the East African region. It is the fourth largest town in Kenya and home to Lake Nakuru, packed and a flame with pink flamingo. Nakuru, in

Masai language, means 'dust or dusty place', which describes the area perfectly. Kenya, in the 1950s, was undergoing a state of emergency arising from the Mau Mau rebellion against the British colonial rule (Anderson, 2005). In May 1963, Jomo Kenyatta was elected President of the Kenya African National Union (KANU), which was the newly formed political party. During December 1963, Kenya achieved its independence with Jomo Kenyatta becoming the President. The following year, the nation became a republic (Anderson, 2005). It has seen many rebellions, with one party ruling the country and very little democracy practised.

Both my parents are descendents of the Yemeni people. The invasion of Yemen, by the Ottoman Empire during the late 1830s, ultimately led to the occupation of Sanaa, which became the capital in 1872. During this period, there was the opening of the Suez Canal. This helped the increase of traffic on the Red Sea route to India, increasing military and commercial interest in Yemen (Korotayev, 1995). It gave the Yemeni people an opportunity to migrate from the eastern protectorate of Hadhramaut states to India and my descendants were part of that movement. My great-great-great-great grandfather then continued the journey into Africa, when fleets of cargo shipments crossed the Red Sea. At first, these were just business trips, lasting for six months, but due to the vast demand for exported goods, my fore-fathers eventually settled there. Some of the children married into African families and others into Arab ones, from their homeland in Yemen and India. This is how the diverse integration within my family came about. It has been an exciting and challenging event.

Early life in Kenya

Growing up in Kenya during the first eight years of my life, in the rebellious times of the late 1960s and early 1970s, I remember little about friends and school life. Vivid memories remain of our home in Kibera, Nairobi, opposite to the Vice-President Daniel Arap Moi (Prime Minister of Kenya from 1978 to 1997). Our dwelling was a large bungalow, with about three acres of surrounding land and detached servants quarters, enclosed within a high security wooden fence. Kibera was an area in Nairobi where highly educated, important dignitaries lived, such as the Sudanese ambassador and the Ethiopian captain. In addition, there were solicitors, business-men, local members of parliament, scientists, immigration and excise officers, teachers from the local Jamuree University and an English artist. All these people had young families with whom my brothers, sisters and I played. Although we were a multicultural neighbourhood, our commonality was living in the same area and speaking Kis-swahili (Kenyan native language).

At this point, I have no recollection of exclusion, racism, prejudice or any form of hatred towards one another. Integration was easy despite a diversity of experience, home practices and upbringing and this situation is noted by Heath (1983). These important and highly educated families had nannies looking after their children, who all attended private, specialist schools and had individual bodyguards. In contrast, we went to a state school and my mother cared for us with the help of two servants – a male one who did the physical, hard work at home and a female, who carried out the domestic chores. My father was a telephone engineer, working with the East African Telecommunications Company, and we were an average, middle-class family. Included within my father's working contract was the house, company car and certain paid expenses. Before Kenya's independence in 1964, the majority of the population consisted of British citizens, as Kenya was a British colony. After Independence, the population was given the option of becoming Kenyan citizens or remaining British. My parents decided to stay as British nationals. For our education and better future prospects, they decided to migrate to England on 6 June 1976.

My move to England

My first memory of arriving in England was the cleanliness of the place, with the air fresh and clear. It was so unlike the dust bath of Lake Nakuru. I also remember being cold, although that first year was the hottest recorded summer, known as 'the year of the ladybird' (Whittaker, 1977). My uncle's house was our temporary accommodation, until my parents could find a home of their own. Our neighbours were a mixture of white, Guajarati (mainly from India), Pakistani and a few Moroccans. Meeting and greeting these neighbours proved to be very different experience in comparison with the Nairobi people. As previously mentioned, living in the same place and speaking the same language created an instant bond between us. These two factors are vital in enabling effective communication, integration and inclusion from my own experiences.

In Britain, due to my limited ability to speak English, Guajarati, Punjabi or Arabic, 50 per cent of common ground was lost with the people I was living amongst. After six months, we moved to another area, where there were more Guajarati and Pakistani speaking neighbours. My parents and all of my brothers and sisters were very fluent in these languages as they had friends in Nairobi schools who spoke them. I was the youngest of eight children, which had its positives and negatives, with language being the biggest problem in my early life.

Attending English schools

The local primary school was approximately one-and-half miles away from our home and my youngest brother travelled there by bus. This bus was also used by the older secondary students from the West Indian community. Although these students had similar physical features to my friends back in Nairobi, I quickly realized that their personalities and characters were very different. They interacted very loudly, with energetic body movements and gestures, whilst talking. Speaking with such a very pronounced beat and rhythm was strange to me. I remember a phrase that one West Indian girl always started her conversation with: 'That nincompoop . . ' This idiomatic language really confused me. I thought that it was normal talk and assumed that this girl was an expert, fluent speaker. It was only later, when the class teacher became infuriated with her speaking and corrected her that I realized otherwise. As this was a Catholic school, with practices strange to me, such as Mass and Saints' days, I was often confused and afraid.

During my junior schooling, I had the tremendous task of learning to read and one of my best friends was an English girl called Ruth, who supported me with my literacy skills. Ruth would listen to my reading and help me with the pronunciation of words. When writing, she would correct my spelling mistakes. As already discussed, I had great difficulty interacting with the Gujarati and Pakistani children, due to the language barrier and the differences in culture and tradition. It was easier to mix with English children, as they were not so quick to judge my dress code or hair style. I had always worn dresses without trousers and had short hair. The Gujarati and Pakistani girls wore trousers and because of these differences, I felt singled out, excluded and isolated. These issues were never discussed and I hoped they would soon pass. I spent some of my earlier school years trying to become like the Guajarati and Pakistani girls by wearing similar clothes to theirs, copying their hair styles and following them around the classroom and playground, in order to be accepted as 'one of them' or 'perceived similarly' (Champers, 1995).

It soon became apparent that I should not change my personality to suit others. I was a considerate, kind, gentle girl, whilst my perception of them was that they were arrogant, selfish and snobbish. I was being treated as an outsider and an outcast. At this point, I realized that language differences did not play a big part in my exclusion, as my communication improved, but the barriers were still there. School reports made positive remarks about my excellent behaviour, outstanding creative skills and ability in arts and crafts. Reading, however, was always an issue. All my teachers were excellent role models, who motivated and encouraged me by giving rewards, smiles, extra support and one-to-one reading opportunities. In Kenya, we were taught to have total respect for all teachers and other adults, but this was not evident in British schools and public places. I found this quite shocking. For example, in Kenya when a teacher entered the class or was seen outside the school premises, speaking to them and greeting politely was considered very important. This marked our respect for them. Also, a young person was expected to get up on a public bus for an adult.

Secondary school, however, changed my view of peer acceptance and tolerance to differences. Compared to my junior school, the secondary school was four times larger, with five times the number of students. The school had a wide mix of multi-cultural students. The diverse students, with whom I had contact, were Indians, Pakistani, West Indians, Chinese, Bangladeshi, Afghanistanis and Kenyans. Although some of these Kenyans were from my adopted community, Kutchi (originally from a remote town in India called Kutch), their culture, traditions and language were very different. Their general attitude to life was very casual with low academic aspiration, motivation and an indifferent value for a good education. This slowly rippled through my community, as a result of frequent social gatherings, when these attitudes were reinforced through comments. There were regular meetings, with mundane conversation and chat about various cultural rituals that were frustrating and stressful. I now understand that everyday conversation is important in bringing about a sense of belonging and unity within a community. By sharing views, one comes to understand the nature of people's differences.

As our family was different to others in the neighbourhood, our closest friends were the Kutchi, as they were mostly from Kenya, but yet again our perspectives were very different. Although I had very few memories of my friends and neighbours back in Nairobi, my parent's circle came from a variety of backgrounds and experiences. Mixing and talking with them brought about new understandings and a knowledge of others, which was openly discussed and reflected upon afterwards within the family. I found these family talks, and the rapport that resulted, very useful when interacting with my peers. I could understand what Diwali was, why Sikhs wore the five 'K's, the significance of 'raksha bandhan' and the reason for Pakistani and Guajarati families behaving differently with each other because of where they came from. (Appendix 1–4 gives detailed information about religious and racial differences.)

An example was a Pakistani family, originating in Pakistan, and being very different to ones from Kenya. This family from Pakistan were withdrawn and kept to themselves, never meeting the neighbours or integrating within the community. In contrast, a family from Kenya were outgoing, attending community functions, helping neighbours with weddings, births, sickness and even death. Although it was always taboo to ask questions on why these friends' beliefs were very different to ours, my parents taught us tolerance and respect for everyone at all times.

I remember one occasion during Eid-Ul-Adha, the festival of sacrifice, held in the Islamic 12th month of Zil-Hijja. My parents' friend and his family visited our house.

They were Hindus and regarded the cow as a sacred animal. We all knew not to mention anything about our celebration and the importance it held within our lives, as this would upset them and make us look uncaring and insensitive. We had to consider others, no matter how difficult or inconvenient it might be for us. Sometimes, it is a problem to understand and accept other people's actions, motivations and beliefs, but as long as they are not harmful to others then respect and tolerance should always be practised. This is what I was taught by my parents, which I would like to instil in my own children, and hopefully they will teach the future generations, so this legacy of respect may continue. During my study of religions, I realized that every faith emphasizes total respect and tolerance to one another, together with not harming or hurting any living creatures unnecessarily. Therefore, every human being walks a different path in order to lead a fulfilling life, but the goal of pleasing our Creator and abiding by his rules is the same.

Growing up

As I grew up, my circle of friends changed, developing my personality, character and most importantly my beliefs, so building on the foundations of my parents' teaching. One very close student, who I befriended, was a Gujarati girl who lived nearby. She was nothing like those I had encountered during my primary school. Her personality was gentle and timid and she had very strong religious convictions. She and her family taught me how tightly knit the Gujarati community was and during the early 1960s they established places of religious worship, by converting small derelict houses into makeshift mosques. The teachers were a few dedicated local fathers, who worked during the day and voluntarily taught Islamic studies in the evenings. These families worked tremendously hard, with little financial support, to run these establishments, continuing the legacy of their forefathers.

This friendship made me realize how a community worked to provide opportunities for its future generations. The majority of this Gujarati community had sacrificed the luxury of having good food, better housing conditions, designer clothes, top model cars, private schooling and most importantly a better livelihood, in order for the next generation to go through life with fewer problems. Not only did they look after families, here, in England, but financial support was given to extended families back in India. By contrast, today's generation want everything, but they do not want to sacrifice anything. The motives are the same but ways to achieve these are very different. I see this trend in my own life. My parents sacrificed everything in order for us to have a good education, better job prospects and a safe environment to live. I want my children to have even better. Each generation needs to give up something, in order for the next to gain, but the older ones appear to have sacrificed the most. As mentioned before, the secondary school helped me realize this and to live a life that is as fulfilling as possible. The motivation and encouragement I gained, through my friendships, played a big part in my life and still does. I was taught to respect not only others but also myself and seek what was good for me, my education, parents, siblings, children and future. Most importantly, I was encouraged to live my life according to my beliefs.

Leaving school

Leaving school and entering into the big, wide world was scary yet exciting. Two months after my last term I travelled with my parents to make a pilgrimage to Mecca and this changed my life dramatically. The trip gave me a new perspective regarding my existence and I began to question numerous things. Finding answers proved to be difficult, yet enlightening, and I began to understand more as the laws and obligations of my faith began to make sense. I will always remember the contentment and the feeling of belonging, when I first saw the Kaa'ba (house of Allah {SWT} in Mecca). People from many parts of the world had gathered there in millions. We felt united in our white clothes, following the same rituals and prayers. This was the largest community I had ever belonged to and it felt amazing. I went again the following year and the feelings grew even stronger. I then made a promise to return with my family again in the very near future.

The world of work

My first working experience was in a Youth Training Scheme (YTS) within the Social Services Department where staff there came from many backgrounds. The head of department was decisive and effective. The deputy head had worked her way up the career ladder, from a junior to a senior social worker, then to be deputy head. She was a calm, collected, cautious person and took her time to make decisions, assembling relevant information in order to do so. Other staff had varying personalities and there is one who I especially remember. She had very strong orthodox beliefs, yet through conversation she thought beyond these, which I found intriguing. Working in a Social Services Department can, sometimes, be contradictory to some religious beliefs. An example is the issue of abortion. This lady was able to separate her work from her religious convictions. I do not think I can do this, as following my religion and its guidance is very important to me. Working in Social Services brings regular contact with the public and this gave me first hand experience of people's multiformity (*Oxford Dictionary*, 2004). At times, I found it very strange that people were so open about their personal lives and were willing to discuss these with total strangers. I prefer to keep personal details between one or two close friends, who I can trust.

I then moved on to become a clerical assistant in a foundry making ball bearings. I was one of 10 women working there and the only coloured lady out of 360 employees, but I never once felt degraded, humiliated or out-numbered as I was always given total respect. Again, this was an opportunity to understand and work with people from different backgrounds, upbringing, culture, practices and religion. As a clerical worker, my job dealt with employees' personal records. I had close contact with all the workers and learnt that all the high-ranking jobs were held by Whites. Manual and labouring jobs were carried out predominately by Indians, Pakistani and Punjabis. Many of these Asian employees spoke very little English and communicated through the common language of Urdu. Whilst acting as their translator, I found many were very unhappy in their jobs, as it was hard, dirty, monotonous and anti-social work.

As none of these employees socialized inside or outside work, they found it difficult to find any common ground, apart from their jobs. Even I found it difficult to socialize with my work colleagues, as after work, or during weekends, they would be 'clubbing and 'pubbing', which is not allowed in my religion. I felt like a messenger between the White and non-White groups and it was very difficult to interpret information, especially when it was mentioned in confidence. I felt in the middle and sometimes there would be friction between myself and these two factions. The people, in the workshop, knew I could communicate with the management as well as the workers and vice versa, so the foundry was using my skills effectively. During this employment, I was given the opportunity to enter higher education with great encouragement from my boss, to whom I will always be grateful. He taught me to value education, reach my potential, always aim high and never give up. These words of wisdom I carry as my motto to this day. Through determination, I gained my BTEC National in Business and Finance, which was a route I strongly wanted to follow. Very soon after gaining this qualification, I married a man that I knew very little about and had met only a few times, and this involved me moving to another town. It was an arranged marriage with full consent from both parties.

My marriages

My husband was from the Kutchi community and he believed in total male domination within the household, with females in subservient positions. Within my own family, my mother has equal rights in everything and my sisters were treated exactly the same as my brothers. Becoming a new member of this family, with differing views and values to my own, made me confused and scared. I could not comprehend that such people existed and sometimes wondered which faith they followed, as this certainly was not the teaching of Islam. I questioned how such behaviour, in this day and age, could be accepted. What surprised me more was the scale of tolerance of this behaviour by other people. This marriage lasted just under eight years and I eventually left my husband with my four children. I lived as a lone parent for about five years, developing a strong personality, with the support of caring professionals, such as my health visitor.

I kept busy, by taking part in my children's school activities, becoming a member of a private Arabic School, of which I am now Manager and Chairperson. I completed many short courses, to help build my self-esteem and prepare for the future. Eventually, I continued with my higher education studies, not in Business and Finance, but within the education field. I also became a parent governor and voluntarily worked in a school for over four years, which gave me first hand experience of dealing with teachers, support staff, outside agencies, parents, but most importantly the children who we were there to support. Sometimes, I felt I had to wear different 'hats' in order to liaise with such a variety of people. During my Foundation degree, I got married again to a man who professed to be loyal, truthful and eligible. After attaining my BA (Hons) degree in Inclusive Education, four years later, problems began to occur within my second marriage. These were possibly due to my growing independence, with less reliance on my husband. There were other difficulties, but past experience taught me the importance of maintaining stability within the home, for my children's sake. My marital problems were eroding this stability, which I could not allow to happen. So we went our separate ways.

During my eight years away from my immediate family, the Kutchi community had developed their lifestyle and broadened their attitudes, with regard to socializing and achieving academic and professional recognition. Today's generation have many qualifications and are entering into professional jobs, as solicitors, doctors, accountants and financial advisors. Education seems to be at the top of their agendas, with even the older generation enrolling for part-time courses and attending on-the-job training. This community have also set up their own women's group, known as the Kutchi Women Group (Hasham, 2006), where activities such as 'lads and dads' and 'mums and girls', 'health and wellbeing', 'community cohesion', and other such initiatives are being introduced. I have also seen the changes, within the Pakistani and Gujarati communities, with the new generation integrating through marriage and friendship. They are now trying to see beyond their differences and concentrate on similarities between them. The older generation is not happy with this, as they feel that there are too many differences to cope with, causing a great strain on their relationships and consequently having a negative effect on others. I feel that there will always be differences between any two individuals but tolerance, respect, understanding and sympathetic dialogue should overcome these. It is a lack of these attributes that makes co-existing so difficult.

In 2005, I fulfilled the promise to take my children to Mecca with my parents. This was their first holiday abroad and they certainly did not forget the heat, humidity and the buzz of people around the Kaa'ba. They compared the number of people there to *Camelot* or *Alton Towers*, during school trips. The feeling we all shared was a sense of belonging without any discrimination. The children felt safe, but an occasional commando style conversation with some guards made them a little intimidated. Once they started putting their Arabic language into practice, however, they very soon picked up the colloquial jargon. We visited many wonderful places of worship that enabled us to understand their religious significance. Examples were the battle field, the place where the Prophet Ibrahim went to sacrifice his son, Ismail, the Masjid and tomb of the Prophet Muhammad (SAW) and most importantly, the Kaa'ba, known in Arabic as Baitullah (the house of Allah {SWT}). This was the most exciting and rewarding holiday of my life, with important quality time spent with my parents and children.

Revisiting my birthplace

When I revisited Kenya after 31 years with my children in July 2007, meeting my relatives and the local community was overwhelming. I began to speak a little of the kis-Swahili, that I had previously practised with my brother, making me realize that we were automatically accommodating to their way of speaking as well as merging with local tradition and culture. I found it easier to adapt and conform to diverse groups, which resulted in less confusion and confrontation with other people. It also stopped me from having unrealistic expectations of myself and others as well as understanding, accepting and respecting our differences. Boundaries and limits were understood, and I did not go beyond them or compromise my beliefs. I remember integrating with every community, even the Arabs, but not feeling as if I fully belonged to any one of these. Today, I understand that this is what 'community cohesion' is all about, when individuals accept and respect the differences that exist in others. I feel that I am making my personal identity richer, as I share knowledge, understanding and views with the wider community.

Review

Integration and inclusion do not happen naturally and do not have to be verbal. A great example is when I went on the antiwar protest for Iraq, in London.

Approximately 18,000 people came, from many backgrounds, and we were all there for one reason, giving us a great sense of unity and common purpose. I believe that interaction and integration are very valuable, producing an enriched, diverse community with greater understanding and empathy for each other. Not only does it widen acknowledgement of differences, but it also gives an opportunity for a greater choice of lifestyle. Diverse, in this sense, does not mean only differences in religion, culture or tradition, nor does it mean differences in lifestyles. It has a wider and deeper understanding and meaning. These differences can be within thinking, communicating, attitude, personal characteristics, routine practices, general manner and behaviour along with emotional, psychological and physical reactions.

All my life, I have seen and been involved in the process of integration, diversity and inclusion, and in order to belong, one does not have to ditch one's own identity but to accept, respect and tolerate that of others. In my experience, different communities and societies have their own criteria for acceptance and, in order to feel included, an individual has to personally work hard to achieve this. As life became more challenging, I began to feel less sorry for myself and to think positively. I started to voice my opinions and views with confidence so gaining wider understanding and knowledge of my true self. You do not know what you think and believe until you communicate this to others. As Sage (2004) states: 'To make inclusion a reality, we must enjoy the challenge of change'.

Due to my ,open mindedness and experience of integrating with different multicultural communities, I feel confident socializing with mixed groups and approach any unknown individual, if the need arises, without any conscious awareness of differences. I believe this is very important, especially as research by Bell (2007, p. 9) suggests that 'there is a growth of service industry jobs . . . greater interaction among people from diverse backgrounds . . . travel around the world interacting with people from different cultures . . . who often speak different languages.' The future is taking us to all corners of the world and integration between multicultural societies is developing much faster and has proved to be fundamental to personal, academic and economic success.

The education sector in England is recognizing this need for 'community cohesion' (DfCSF, 2007) and has introduced many changes in the curriculum to accommodate this. Examples include Personal, Social and Health Education (PSHE) and Citizenship Education, with strands brought together in a coherent national framework in 2002 within primary and secondary education. The aim of these subjects is to help children learn about differences, how to interact with others, be independent, behave responsibly, tolerate and respect others in order to become the good citizens of tomorrow. Individual initiatives, such as local, national and international school twinning, where the cohort is very different, together with exchanges of school practices, are also contributing to these aims. In order to include the wider public, diversity training, seminars and cohesion tours (Naylor, 2008) are regularly carried out by local authorities. So far, there is limited improvement in community integration but hopefully 'change' will accelerate when the new black president in America, Barack Obama (BBC News, 2008), provides a strong focus and impetus to solve the problems of diversity. Change for any of us is painful but there is great pleasure to be gained from developing greater peace and harmony amongst us all.

Suggestions for classroom practice

Group discussion is essential for shared understanding. The Communication Opportunity Group Strategy (COGS) (Sage, 2000, 2006) has been particularly successful in helping people to express themselves better and facilitate better understanding. In this scheme, participants choose their own content giving opportunities to share information, promote interest and develop knowledge. A particularly successful activity, with a recent class, involved groups of three having a newspaper and six pins to create a fashion object which they then had to model and sell to the audience. The activity proved hilarious and in the review precipitated discussion about different fashions, customs and dress and what they symbolized. On another occasion, members of the COGS had to bring a national dish and explain how it was made. Such sharing helps to understand differences and develops tolerance and respect for others.

Main points

- Living in different cultures and learning something of their language and customs brings greater understanding and acceptance of differences between people.
- Enjoying the challenge of interacting with others makes pleasure out of the pain and sweeps away the fear we have of those that are different from us in substantial ways.
- Developing our skills in communicating, across cultures, is vital in our mobile societies.
- Valuing education and developing our knowledge and skills gives us confidence to communicate and share our views and competence to manage diverse relationships.

Discussion point

What practical ways can you think of to engage more fully with others who are different from you?

Acknowledgements

I would like to take this opportunity to thank my relatives and friends who have helped me tremendously in compiling this chapter, especially my father and mother who helped me remember my Yemeni roots and life during my younger days. I would also like to thank my wonderful children, whom I love dearly, for their kind patience. Please remember that this chapter is based on my personal experience, thoughts and perception of the diverse people within my life. It does not in any way or form create a stereotypical understanding of individuals, communities or societies.

Glossary

(SWA) This transliteration in the Arabic language stands for Sallallahu-Alaihi-Wasallam and means May the Blessings and Peace of Allah be upon him (Prophet Muhammad)

{SWT} This transliteration in the Arabic language stands for Subhanahu-Wa-Ta'ala and means Glorious and Exalted is He (Allah)

References

Anderson, D. (2005) *Histories of the Hanged*, England: Weidenfeld and Nicolson.

Bell, M. (2007) *Diversity in Organizations*, Indiana: R. R . Donnelley.

Champers (1995) *Diversity in Organizations, New Perspective for Changing Workplace*, New York: Sage.

Department for Children, Schools and Families DfCSF (2004) *PSHE in Practice (Primary & Secondary)*, London: DfCSF.

DfCSF (2007) *Guidance on the Duty to Promote Community Cohesion*, London: DfCSF.

Dresch, P. (1989) *Tribes, Government and History in Yemen*, Oxford: Clarendon Press.

Heath, S. (1983) *Ways with Words, Language, Life and Work in Communities and Class-rooms*, Cambridge: Cambridge University Press.

Korotayev, A. (1995) *Ancient Yemen*, Oxford: Oxford University Press.

Naylor, G. (2008) *Diversity Training & Cohesion Tour*, Blackburn: Blackburn with Darwen (BWD) CVS, BWD Services CIC.

Oxford Dictionary (2004) Oxford: Oxford University Press.

Sage, R. (2000) *The Communication Opportunity Group Scheme*, Leicester: University of Leicester.

Sage, R. (2004) *A World of Difference, Tackling Inclusion in Schools.* London: Network-Continuum.

Whittaker, J. (1977) *Whitaker Almanack,* London: William Clowes and Sons Ltd.

Internet

BBC News (2008) Profile: Barack Obama, 26 November 2008.

Hasham R. (2006) www.kwg.org.uk, 25 November 2008.

Diversity versus adversity: Included or excluded? Issues emerging from teaching in state and private schools

3

Diane Macarthur

Overview

Britain is a kaleidoscopic populace of different colours, shapes and forms that is ever changing. This diversity can be intriguing, exciting and intellectually stimulating. The cultures, life-styles, appearances and personalities of the people around us add vibrancy and interest to life. Formed naturally by default, perpetuated historically and presently manufactured for political and economic reasons, diversity is essential to our progress and our personal identity as a unique and free thinking being but is closely linked to adversity. Our differences can have posi tive or negative effects on others and attitudes change according to time and circumstance. I believe that any efforts to manipulate society against the natural order must be explained to each generation and the feelings that are generated must be acknowledged. We cannot assume that we can live, learn, work and play together naturally without knowledge and understand-ing of each other. In this chapter we begin with a story about a school day and from this tease out issues that demonstrate positive and negative sides to diversity. A study of the Travellers is presented as one of the most excluded groups in our society and most educationally unsuccessful but as an oral culture they have much to teach us about communicating and sharing understanding.

My background and views on diversity

My view of diversity and adversity arises mainly from experiences and observations of school life, spanning 50 years, first as a pupil and now as a teacher. Reflection on classroom management, as it operates today, begs the questions: Is current thinking about managing diversity in schools too controlling and misguided? What are the consequences of this approach? Has it all gone too far?

A rationale regarding diversity

We do not live in isolation and our happiness, welfare and well-being depend upon the views and actions of others around us. I call this 'the piggy effect' as described in the *Lord of the Flies* (Golding, 2002). Any diversity from the accepted norm in a community can be accommodated with clear thinking, compassion and empathy as long as we are secure in our *own* identity. When faced with bigotry and ignorance, diversity creates fear and then poses a threat with a host of problems manifesting themselves. These include physical and verbal bullying, discrimination and exclusion and the Travelling communities in the United Kingdom are the minority groups that most suffer in this way. Qualities of understanding and tolerance are required for the cohesion of diverse peoples and this is being undermined by legislation and governmental interference that makes it more difficult to live together peacefully and productively.

A scene from the real world

Here is a picture of a typical day in my life as a teacher in a Design and Technology department of a rural comprehensive school of about 1,500 pupils. As you will see, *adversity* creeps in, in all sorts of ways and the community's *diversity* brings constant challenges.

7.45 am. I arrive, somewhat harassed, having followed a school bus and witnessed wild behaviour from pupils at the back. I pull up alongside the bus, and make humble apologies to the driver, who is silently seething, and then speak to the pupils concerned. Oh no, this means a report of events to be written later! Why did I get involved? I then struggle to find a parking place near to the department to be able to unload a mountain of paperwork and resources. Some teachers have resorted to small trolleys or wheeled suitcases to shuttle their stuff from home to car to work and back again. I just stagger with my mammoth armful and collapse at my desk. A quick 'good morning' to colleagues is followed by a dash to my classroom. I smile and wish a 'good morning' to pupils en route but receive only grunts or glares in return. Are they just expressing their lack of enthusiasm for the day ahead?

8.00 am. I laboriously write the aims and objectives for the first lesson on the board, spelling out the National Curriculum (NC) targets for levels 4, 5 and 6 and obeying, to the letter, the latest government dictat. The next few minutes fly by: preparing tools and equipment, getting out students' work folders and laying out pre-prepared samples for demonstration of the design task ahead. I grab the technician (before anyone else whips her off) to help with these tasks and then rush to photocopy sheets for homework and find resources that should be in the room but are missing!

It is then a quick flick through the Quality Log for an overview of the pupils that I am going to teach and their work to date. Lesson plans and schemes of work for all the day's lessons were studied last night and again over breakfast so that my mind was fully prepared for the long day ahead.

8.15 am. I log on to the computer and check emails. Oh no! There are at least 40 urgent ones! They consist of changes to the day, illness, absenteeism, parental concerns, new and existing IEPs to complete, events, meetings, cover lessons, notice to move a car, the 'thought for the day' to name just a few of the items! The case of a Traveller's child, who has absconded from school, preys on my mind! I have a real bond with him and we have a very deep communication. I can empathize with the fact that he finds school such a strait-jacket after the freedom of home-life.

8.30 am. A full staff meeting is called: reporting on the day before, the day ahead and the next day. I then walk back to the department (or rather run) reminding pupils to tuck shirts in, straighten ties, turn around and go to the correct 'up' stair-case. Chivvying along those hanging around to avoid registration and stopping to find out why someone is crying is an extra stress with so much to do before lessons start. I throw a laptop into the IT office (it's not working again) and beg for urgent attention.

8.45 am. I complete a cover registration of 32 pupils in a year 10 group for an absent tutor. They remain huddled in groups, mostly with their backs to me, standing, sitting, lying and lolling, sprawling on desks, the floor and over each other! Chairs and tables are strewn about and the blackout curtains are ripped and hanging off their hooks. It proves impossible to quieten them so I resort to selecting a responsible looking pupil to run through the list of names with me. I attempt to make the day's announcements but few seem bothered to listen. Then it's the loud tones of the lesson bell. No one moves initially. I spell out the urgency to get going to reach their lesson on time. As they leave, I reinforce rules about uniform again, in line with the latest directives. There are spot checks to make sure that teachers are carrying out this duty. As they leave the room, I hold up the bin for the disposal of kilos of chewing gum and make sure that indiscreet jewellery and nail varnish is removed, makeup washed off and girls have buttoned up their blouses.

9.05 am to 3.30 pm. During the day, I am faced with around 125 pupils (400 in the week) in groups of between 20 and 30 boys and girls of mixed ability who are 7–11 years old. These include a large number of pupils with Asperger syndrome, attention deficit and hyperactivity disorder (ADHD), disruptive and aggressive behaviour, special educational needs, dyslexia, the gifted and talented as well as previously excluded pupils. One of these is from the Travelling communities who has received little schooling and just cannot settle down to our very prescriptive routines. His lifestyle and attitudes are about freedom and doing what you want when you want. All these pupils' individual education plans (IEPs) have to be read and added to. In addition, various allergies and health problems, all too numerous to mention, have to be considered but will include pupils on crutches, in wheelchairs and the sight and sound impaired.

Reviewing the issues of the day

Teaching assistants (TAs) are allocated to certain individuals and at times there are as many as four adults in a classroom. TAs are not always present, depending on the demands of their timetable, and often the child does not want them nearby as it makes them feel different. TAs vary in their knowledge, understanding, ability and skills and their presence makes classroom management more complex and difficult. They are a developing resource but need a relevant education and training and the personal skills to be effective members of the education team.

Social problems are an increasing phenomena and it is necessary to have an awareness of them and know how to deal with the girl spaced out on drugs, the distressed state of a child abused at home or bullied at school, the shy one who does not interact or the travelling child whose free life does not fit fixed routines. We need much more time within the school structure to discuss these problems and work out how to overcome them in the classroom.

Portable technology such as mobile phones and I pods are a massive problem in the classroom and trying to confiscate items, so that the lesson is not constantly disrupted, reminds me of a *tiny tots tantrum* on a much bigger scale. It is akin to taking a dummy away from a baby! Can you hear the screams and howls of protest?

Moving classrooms hugely adds to my stresses. I have to change classrooms four times and subject teaching three times during an average day. Two of the classrooms are open-plan and used as a thoroughfare to access other rooms. One is too small for the numbers present and squashing teenagers together like sardines in a tin is asking for trouble. None of us likes being crowded and for those with communication and social problems this situation spells disaster.

Teaching outside your specialist area is now normal practice and this presents problems. It is not only that you will not have studied the topics in depth at university and grasped their complexity, but also may not have any real interest in the subject to convey it with the necessary enthusiasm. There are regular *learning walks* carried out by senior management, which include observations, work scrutiny and outside visitors. Is it any wonder that we feel like canon fodder, given instructions by those who could not possibly carry them out successfully themselves? It is akin to be sent to the frontline to be torn to pieces!

Covering for absent colleagues means any free lessons are taken for cover or used for giving assistance to an inexperienced NQT. Breaks and lunchtimes are filled with detentions, general duties, extra curricular activities and mentoring.

3.30 pm. There is no point in trying to leave the premises promptly as your way out is blocked by school buses, pupils and parents. In any case, the next two hours are relatively peaceful and the time to respond to emails, write reports, mark work, etc. In term time, there is plenty to occupy a teacher until bedtime and it is wise not to go out unless you want to be permanently exhausted.

Comment

All this begs the question: 'Where is the teaching and where is the learning?' However, rest assured this does happen somewhere along the line, in spite of adverse conditions that hinder the process. Teachers, on the whole, are a professional, determined bunch, dedicated to the task of preparing the next generation for their life's challenges. Nevertheless, today's pupils often do not have the skills of thinking and communicating at the level that is needed to underpin learning. We have produced a system that many are unable to cope with and need to 'walk the talk' and have the freedom to create an environment that all children can access.

We can see, from the above account, that teachers are expected to be saints and angels rolled into one and ready and willing to cure the ills of society. They do so in difficult conditions, coping with a huge range of pupil diversity with many struggling with severe and continuing adversity in their lives, whether it is disability, instability or poverty. Both the diversity and the adversity of pupils is the responsibility of teachers whilst in the classroom. Can you imagine a greater challenge than this? The case of the Travelling communities reveals these challenges in greater detail and is reviewed in the next section.

An example of adversity: The Travelling communities

Although not much historical research has been carried out on Traveller life, there are references to nomadic groups in the twelfth century who were craftsmen, fortune-tellers, entertainers, message carriers and tinsmiths, engaged in buying and selling goods or services. The Traveller identity is marked by common features such as their oral tradition, own language (Cant, Gammon or Shelta) and value for a nomadic way of life. When you get to know them you will find them great storytellers. They are known by several names such as *travellers, gypsies or Roma.*

Roma are a minority ethnic group whose recent origins are Eastern and Central European. The word 'Rom' is the singular for one person. Dispersal is central to Roma history and although of common lineage, their migrations over time have produced many distinct communities and dialects. Gypsies are believed to have originated in India, gradually migrating to the near East and Western Europe, reaching Scotland in the early sixteenth century. The Commission for Racial Equality (CRE) launched a consultation on a new strategy for gypsies and travellers in October, 2003 with the following facts emerging from the report.

Roma Gypsies and Irish Travellers are currently recognized racial groups under the 1976 Race Relations Act. There are also other groups of travellers with ethnic or national origins that could come within the definition of a racial group. Although there are no official figures on the size of this population, the CRE have estimated it as around 300,000 from various sources of information. There is little systematic monitoring of key areas affecting Roma and Travellers, which makes it difficult to analyse their needs and experiences. However, many Gypsies and Travellers have deep rooted fears about revealing their ethnic identity. The CRE noted in a 2002 document:

> Hostile and racist attitudes towards Gypsies and Travellers are common amongst the general public. In a recent representative poll (Mori).more than a third of respondents – which equates to about 14 million adults in England – admitted being prejudiced against Gypsies and Travellers. Gypsies and Travellers Strategy, CRE (2002)

Travellers are often called cheats and it is assumed that they choose to live in dirty conditions because they do not respect their surroundings or others around them. These misunderstandings promote racism and discrimination.

Evidence has revealed that the most disadvantaged group within the education system are Roma Gypsy children and children of Travellers of Irish Heritage (*Raising the attainment of Ethnic Minority Pupils*). For those actually enrolled in schools, the average attendance rate for Traveller pupils is around 75 per cent. This is well below the national average and the lowest attendance profile of all the minority ethnic groups in the United Kingdom (*Provision and support for Traveller pupils*).

With regard to healthcare, an indicator is that the mortality rate of Traveller children up to aged 10 years is ten times that of the population as a whole. Only 10 per cent of the Traveller population are over 40 years old and only 1 per cent over 65.

Obviously, the housing needs for Travellers and Roma Gypsies are very different from those of the settled community. Research indicates that local authorities are reluctant to provide sites for this group for fear of attracting more Travellers to their area and upsetting the locals who perceive them as messy and noisy. This has resulted in an estimated 3,000 unauthorized sites. Travellers came within the statutory definition of homelessness if they are without an authorized place to stop. Roma Gypsies and Travellers without permanent sites for their caravans face considerable problems in accessing health and education services. This is a major factor in their over-representation in most indices of deprivation and social exclusion. In addition, many Travellers have limited access to basic amenities such as running water, electricity and sanitation. This also includes some Travellers living on serviced sites (Final Report of the Promoting Social Inclusion Working Group, Belfast, 2002) at www.newtsnni.gov.uk. Concerns that have been raised are:

- A high number of racist incidents in which the Travellers are blamed
- A low level of trust in police handling of Gypsy and Traveller cases
- Concerns regarding sentencing and stop and search
- Disproportionate rates of death of those in custody
- Use of powers of eviction and lack of sensitive police handling of these cases
- A tendency to label all Gypsies and Travellers as criminals.

The Scrutiny Report on Access to Education for Gypsy/Traveller Children (2004) demonstrated how the systems that we rely upon to assist pupils through the educational process may sometimes unwittingly create difficulties for some families. We cannot assume that people have the skills to fit in with our systems and we need to adapt them so that learning can be accessed. Good practice needs communicating more widely and is identified in the report as:

- Strong leadership and a welcoming attitude from the head teacher
- Well-informed staff with a knowledge of the Traveller culture and values
- Flexible approaches to including Traveller pupils in school activities
- Open acknowledgement with displays about Traveller culture in school corridors
- Willingness to consider new ideas to engage reluctant pupils and retain their interest.

Learning activities that were based on Traveller life, such as building and practical, survival skills, were the most successful in winning over reluctant pupils and we can learn from this experience and generalize this to other disengaged students.

Facing adversity and managing diversity

In the 1950s and 1960s, it seemed a relatively simple task to categorize the British population according to their health, wealth, education, employment and family background. Individuals were rich or poor; healthy or sick; grammar school or secondary modern school educated; academic or practical; quick or slow learners; university graduates with good prospects or factory operatives with low expectations.

Analysis of these differences, in tune with the attitudes of the time, was to classify the former in each of these examples as *middle class* and the latter as *working class*. Physical appearance, clothes, accent, personality, constitution and manner were clear indicators of class divisions. These factors, combined with background, led to admiring or ridiculing these attributes. There were individuals who fell between the two class groups for various reasons such as misfortune.

Diversity from the norm was a parochial issue and handled locally within a tightly-knit community. It was a time of limited social and spatial mobility and with people more static there was a feeling of belonging to a neighbourhood and being known, valued and understood by everyone within it. Life was safe and relatively stable and people knew and understood their neighbours well and, therefore, had no fear of them. The closeness and cohesion of this situation offered security and acceptance of differences between people. Could it be that communication and relationships were more effective because we lived and worked in a tight social group with a great deal of shared meaning between us? Anyone new to the neighbourhood was regarded with fascination and intrigue and warmly welcomed and integrated. The first Pakistani pupil at my school was like a celebrity and everyone wanted to be his friend. There was an air of discovery and wanting to be informed about other worlds. Today, anyone new is treated with suspicion and as an intruder. It is no longer enough to just 'be'. Is this because we now have too many different peoples amongst us so that we feel swamped and getting to know them and inducting them into our customs is much more of a problem?

Review

In an ordinary town, within middle England in the 1950s, where I lived and attended school, there was a balanced cross-section of society and a strong sense of community. There were the same areas of personal and social adversity that can be identified in comparable socio-economic groups today with the difference being there were far fewer people experiencing problems then. It was only the most serious cases that received any special attention and most people learnt to deal with their difficulties in their own way. Many specific problems, such as autism, were unknown and people with difficulties that were outside the norm were just accepted as 'odd'. Ignorance was bliss as there was not so much anxiety generated by strange conditions and people responded instinctively to those suffering them in a natural, kindly way.

The structure of education, at this time, supported the class system and perpetuated exclusion. Though not impossible to overcome, there were barriers making it difficult to migrate between the classes. Fulfilment of aspirations and deferred gratification could, with fortitude and determination, champion a path beset with adversity due to position at birth. Diversity could be challenged in simple ways such as an improved accent, cleanliness and aspirations to be upwardly mobile. However, the education system in place was divisive and prevailing prejudices and notions of accepting your lot were key to managing the workforce and hence the economy. It was my naive belief, at that time, that education was undertaken for its own sake and for the enhancement and enrichment of the individual, not just to prepare a workforce to improve the economic position of the United Kingdom. As a student in the 1960s, my essays were intensely political and one-sided. I wrote passionately about the inequities of society and the education system of that time and wholeheartedly embraced the ideology of the 'comprehensive' and the causes of the proletariat.

These essays were, quite rightly, criticized by my tutor who told me that I needed to produce a balanced argument. I now have the opportunity to write the second half of that particular essay nearly 40 years later. My views now benefit from a lifetime of seeing diversity and adversity in action and the transition each has undergone to reach the present state of total inclusion for better or for worse. It is a personal journey through a dramatically changed society. My views now balance the advantages and disadvantages of inclusion, from my frontline experience of working with inclusion in the comprehensive system. I can write with first hand knowledge of twenty-first century diversity, with all its complexities within the myriad of adversity that is faced in life, and set against a historical backdrop.

Changes in how children relate to others

As a teacher and a mother I have observed that children today lack compassion and empathy, which are such important attributes for accepting differences in others. Since the introduction of the National Curriculum, in 1989, we have had two decades of prescriptive learning and children's personal development has been marginalized with the consequences just noted. Although communication and empathy are written into the curriculum, can they be enforced or should they occur naturally? Does this come from home experiences and are children lacking the talk and discussion opportunities that are necessary for such development?

Sage (2004) suggests that only 15 per cent of what we learn takes place in formal ways and that learning by example is our most common and effective method. Most of what we understand comes from observing others. All adults who work with children must have the skills of compassion, empathy and communication as models for the younger generation. However, Sage (2003) (in a study of teachers in a city comprehensive school) found that 63 per cent of the staff felt they did not have the skills to communicate effectively with the diverse pupils they had to manage. No wonder that we have such problems with learning and discipline in our schools? Children need to experience good and bad as well as right and wrong to be able to compare and make judgements. It is our ability to communicate with them, in a way they can comprehend and then express their feeling, views and knowledge, that brings about this understanding. This is a fundamental issue now in schools with the many different communication patterns and customs of both teachers and students. I have found this issue is given more attention in the independent schools and has to be one reason why they are academically more successful.

I have taught children with plenty of cash in their pocket but filthy feet, neck, hands, nits, ill-fitting, shabby clothes and trainers two sizes too big. Has the whole thing gone too far in the wrong direction now and the only route is to self destruct? Think about what happened to the Romans in past history. They lapsed into decadence and then a rapid decline, from being the most powerful nation in the ancient world. We were the most powerful nation a century ago with an Empire that extended to a third of the world. We have now lost this and our position in the world has been quickly eroded, both educationally and economically. There are certainly many examples of decadence in classroom anarchy. I have witnessed classes out of control and behaving like a pack of animals. If you talk to any teacher they will have had this experience and often on a regular basis. This is very different to the well-ordered classrooms of my school days.

The present education system is like a conveyor belt with pupils dropping off the other end either fit for work or not. Jobs are directed and controlled by government and commercial forces that have succeeded in killing off creativity and natural enterprise with stringent regulations and restrictions. Integrity and ingenuity barely exist in our present society, as revealed through our media stories. Do we blame television, computer games, dysfunctional family life, bad parenting or poor teaching? Could it be that power and control has been handed to people who do not have the knowledge, understanding or skills to handle it? They actually need to be controlled and directed to lead ordered, successful lives? Education, therefore, maybe on the wrong track. In my specialist field of Design and Technology, lessons are no longer for pleasure and to build practical skills and confidence. The curriculum now aims to teach pupils to recognize markets and design products to sell, but the majority of them have no interest in this narrow, functional approach. Should entrepreneurship be approached and taught in this forced and artificial way?

The populace has been equipped with a set of tools but no instruction manual. My fear for the future is that the United Kingdom will have an inappropriately educated, dissatisfied and disaffected population that can only lead to the breakdown of a decent society. My conclusion is that a culture of 'me' has been promoted and nurtured and the culture of 'us' has not moved beyond the rhetoric. In an ideal world there would be resources to cope with the ever growing demand for services and support but in practice, inclusion is not ideal for everyone and the burden upon society is too great.

We should not be trying to over-legislate for inclusion and leave room for people to cope with their diverse needs in a way that is right and relevant for them. To believe that a 'one-size-fits-all' academically focused curriculum will meet the needs of everyone actually denies diversity and its requirement for a flexible approach to living and learning to suit different needs. An interfering nanny state cannot be right. It may help some but certainly not others.

Each generation has to learn from scratch as understanding is not automatically or naturally carried forward. We learn from our own kind and although there is a continuing debate regarding the balance of *nature* and *nurture*, there is no doubt that our genetic inheritance has a powerful influence regarding our attitudes and values. In the animal world it is natural to keep with your own kind. As human beings we are drawn towards like-minded people and tend not to mix with those who think and operate differently to us. Those in the minority group/s will always stand out and the majority will be wary of them because their values and lifestyle will conflict with their own. Anyone 'different' in the slightest way is easily identified and will always be picked on by those who feel threatened in some way or lack understanding of others' condition or position.

Being exposed to knowledge does not automatically lead to its comprehension. It is probably dangerous to be made aware of something without the powers of reasoning that evolve from our thinking and expression. This ability is fundamental to personal and academic success but is mostly lacking in today's learners, at every level, although in my experience of teaching in the private system, this is thoroughly addressed. If we are to treat everyone with respect and do no one intentional harm we have to give attention to personal development before academic achievement is possible. There is an analogy, here, with Design and Technology. If you learn the basic skills and practice set standard pieces of work then you will easily be able to design and make original things, without guidance, that will extend your imagination, understanding and initiative.

There is very little research on how minority groups view the majority. It is a sensitive subject and truth will be difficult to obtain from respondents, as they will not want to give their opinion in case it is used against them. The drive towards inclusion is based on conformity to the majority norm. We want everyone to perform in the same way and reach a standard level. Because large numbers are not doing this we must ask ourselves whether it is better to abandon the present single education super-highway and develop more interesting paths, for those that desire them, that can be travelled on in a more natural, enjoyable way so that the journey is ultimately successful.

Suggestions for classroom practice

Children have to talk together to understand each other. Some come from backgrounds that value education but others do not. Sharing and caring helps everyone appreciate that education is the route out of poverty and the antidote to adversity. Giving equal value to personal as well as academic development is the way to build self goals, determination, persistence and stamina necessary to cope with diverse and adverse challenges.

Main points

- Diversity has a positive and negative face. It provides a variety of culture and creeds for a more vibrant and interesting society but the differences between people can prove unacceptable.
- Over the last 50 years, life has become more complex and demanding. The stresses this has created could make us less tolerant of others as we strive to make our way in a competitive society.
- The key to inclusion and acceptance of others is the opportunity to communicate together and acknowledge the feelings that living in a diverse society generates.
- Education has to have personal development at its heart as it is the ability to think and communicate that produces understanding and the prerequisite of peaceful co-existence.
- We need more opportunities to learn in depth about other cultures and the way they think and communicate. The Travelling communities are the most prejudiced against in our society and the less academically successful. Their history and customs are based on a broad knowledge of the world and we have much to learn from their oral tradition.

Discussion point

In society we belong to many groups – family, gender, religious, work, leisure etc. In some of these you may well have suffered discrimination of exclusion. Can you identify these and evaluate how these circumstances might have influenced you?

References

Bowling, Ben (1998) *Violent Racism: Victimisation Policing and Social Context*, Clarendon Studies in Criminology, Oxford: Oxford University Press.

Chief Inspector of Education (2001) *Raising the attainment of ethnic minority pupils* (School and LEA responses to the Ofsted Report, 2001).

Derrington, C. and Kendall, S. (2004) *Gypsy Traveller Pupils in English Secondary Schools: A Longitudinal Study*, London: Nuffield Foundation.

Education and Training Inspectorate (ETI) *Survey of Provision for the Inclusion of Traveller Children into Mainstream Education in Northern Ireland*, Belfast, Northern Ireland 2002, 20 June. ETI.

Essex County Council, England (2004) *Final Scrutiny Report on Access to Education for Gypsy/Traveller Children*. Essex County Council publications.

Golding W. (2002) *The Lord of the Flies*, London: Faber & Faber.

Parekh, B. et al. (2000) *The Future of Multi-Ethnic Britain*, London: Runneymede Trust.

Sage, R. (2003) *ESCalate Project: School-based CPD*, Leicester: University of Leicester.

Sage, R. (2004) *Inclusion in Schools*, London and New York: Network-Continuum.

Stonewall (2003) *Profiles of Prejudice: The Nature of Prejudice in England*, London: Stonewall/Citizenship 21 Project.

'Now he has a label, we can cope!': Parent perceptions of attention deficit hyperactivity disorder

4

Lynne Kendall

Overview

One of today's most pressing problems is the sharp rise in both child and adult anti-social behaviour that adversely affects families, schools and workplaces. This chapter considers the diverse nature of such problems and after setting the context and defining the issues, takes a glimpse of these through the eyes of children and young adults, examining the views and feelings of their families. The aim is to answer four major questions:

- *How does the individual with the problem see themselves?*
- *What affect does a behaviour problem have upon the family?*
- *What is in place to support the individual and the family by various agencies?*
- *How effective are the interventions employed by the family?*

At the end of the chapter, the reader will have gained a more complete picture of behaviour and its diversity and be acquainted with some of the successful management interventions can be employed to alleviate problems.

Introduction: Setting the context

Within every educational establishment, there are learners who show erratic work performance. They fail to reach their potential, despite average or above intellectual abilities, and are perceived by others as lazy, rebellious, lacking in motivation and disinterested. In schools, these pupils present as disruptive and aggressive and may be hyperactive, leading to their exclusion from mainstream education. They are viewed as problem pupils, who struggle to make friends with their peers, being at risk of underachievement and exclusion because of attention deficit hyperactivity disorder (ADHD). This condition may cause friction between parents and school, with both camps critical of each other. Although not generally said openly by professionals, poor parenting is perceived as the root of the problem. Parents, in turn, see the school as not understanding their child's needs. Feeling isolated and unable to cope, they experience stress from the break-down of home–school relationships.

My own experience

During my years as a mainstream school teacher, subsequently responsible for students with special education needs, I became very aware of the problems that families encounter because of anti-social behaviours. It was not uncommon for discussions to occur amongst teaching staff regarding students exhibiting extreme behaviours. Sometimes blame was apportioned to the parents. It was felt that if they were stricter with their offspring, then behaviour would improve. I felt, after meeting the parents of these pupils, that this was not generally the answer to this growing problem in schools. What I witnessed were parents who loved their children very much, but felt that they were 'out of control' and did not know who to turn to for support. These parents were blamed for their child's behaviour by health and education professionals and their own families considered they had 'poor parenting skills.' Through discussion with parents (and subsequent research) the effects of this complex disorder upon families and schools became evident. This chapter gives the reader an insight into the condition, from the parental perspective, through real case studies. We consider parental thoughts, opinions and concerns for children with ADHD for greater awareness and reflection for those coping with such difficult, diverse behaviours.

Definitions of bad behaviour

Children can be hyperactive, impulsive and inattentive and certainly will misbehave sometimes at home and school. This does not mean, however, that the child has attention deficit hyperactivity disorder (ADHD). Inappropriate behaviours are not considered to be a problem if they remain isolated events, but if frequent will have an effect upon others so that the child who does them is perceived as problematic and disruptive. ADHD is a medical diagnosis for children and adults who experience significant cognitive and behavioural difficulties in emotional and social growth.

ADHD is often described as a developmental disorder although discussion abounds as to its exact causes and whether it actually exists (Soan, 2004).

The ADHD label is often viewed as an excuse for poor behaviour or poor parenting skills. However, evidence shows that there are children whose impulsivity and hyperactivity are substantially more severe and certainly different from other groups of children (Singh, 2007). Cooper (1994) takes a different slant on the labelling process by suggesting that ADHD is slapped on children who do not comply with the rigid constraints placed upon them by society. They may be biologically and temperamentally different from their peers and only termed 'disordered' because this is regarded as undesirable. Interviews with adults who still suffer from these behaviour problems show that their bodies will not obey their brains, suggesting some disconnection between thought and action. Thus, ADHD is publicly recognized as a disability and covered by the SEN and Disability Act 2001 (also known as SENDA), which was implemented in September 2002 by an amendment in the Disability Discrimination Act, 1995. Children with ADHD may have been diagnosed with the condition by experts and demonstrate similar core symptoms (described later) but are likely to differ in the number of problem behaviours and their relative severity. It is a condition that does not only affect children but also adults and is viewed as a life-long issue with symptoms changing from childhood to adolescence and then to adulthood. Some individuals are not identified until they begin to fail at school during early adolescence (Montague and Castro, 2005).

Diagnosis

There is no blood test that will establish a diagnosis of ADHD although magnetic nuclear resonance (MRI) scans have been used by researchers in studies conducted into brain activity and ADHD. However, MRI scans are not routinely used in diagnosis (Munden and Arcelus, 1999). This can be a complicated matter requiring input from a range of different sources, including teachers, doctors, therapists, parents, psychologists and others, defined by Ayers and Prytys (2002) as a multidimensional assessment. Behaviours need to be observed within different settings that include home and school. ADHD is defined, by experts, using ICD-10 or DSM IV criteria. The diagnostic criteria employed in the United Kingdom are based on the International Classification of Diseases, version 10 (known as ICD 10) and devised by the World Health Authority. ICD 10 does not include a definition of ADHD and uses the term 'hyperkinetic syndrome', which is more rigidly described. Although there are similarities between these two diagnostic criteria, there are also differences. In ICD 10, hyperactivity and impulsivity are separate aspects, whereas in the DSM IV criteria both are placed together. This means that when using ICD 10, only the most severe cases will be diagnosed. Many UK clinicians now use the U.S. version, DSM IV and its latest revision DSM IV TR to identify children and adults with ADHD within three subtypes:

- ADHD – predominantly hyperactive-impulsive type
- ADHD – predominantly inattentive type
- ADHD – combined type

There are three core features of ADHD, which are inattention, hyperactivity and impulsivity. Inattention defines those who make mistakes in work or other activities. For a diagnosis, individuals must display at least six of the symptoms associated with inattention, hyperactivity or impulsivity. The criteria of the DSM-IV state that symptoms must have been present for at least six months to a developmentally inappropriate degree and present before age seven years. Pierangelo and Giuliani (2008) say that the DSM-IV-TR suggests that clinicians should disregard the possibility of ADHD if they see pervasive developmental disorder (PDD), schizophrenia or other psychoses.

The cause of ADHD

The cause of ADHD remains unclear but is viewed by some as a medical condition with neurological dysfunction having a genetic element. The dysfunction is thought to be in the neurotransmitters of the brain's frontal lobes (Cooper and Ideus, 1996) This brain area controls short-term memory, attention, reflection, social cognition and communication. An immature neurotransmitter, in those with ADHD, results in smaller amounts of dopamine and/or norepinephrine in the synaptic mechanism transmitting nerve signals, so preventing messages from travelling from one cell to another. The result is poor concentration and short-term memory.

Sage (1998), in a review of treatment at the Oxford Institute of Psychiatry, Warneford Hospital, explains how emotions created by the amygdala (a small almond-shaped structure at the base of the brain) can overwhelm thinking. She discusses studies by Professor La Doux, at the Center for Neural Science at New York University, into communication and behaviour disorders and the new drug therapies that are being evolved to control biochemical movements. As Pierangelo and Giuliani (2008) acknowledge, ADHD is not, as has previously been assumed, a disorder of attention but is a developmental failure in the area of the brain that monitors self control and inhibition. These activities, as Sage (2004) suggests, depend on the ability to communicate effectively with oneself and others (intra and interpersonal communication). ADHD is familial, particularly amongst close male members.

Hughes and Cooper (2007) say that there is no one single cause that is responsible for ADHD but suggest that it is genetic with workings of the brain and psychosocial factors impacting upon behaviour.

Characteristics of ADHD

The history of some children with ADHD can be unremarkable whilst others experience difficulties from an early age with feeding, sleeping and responding to physical affection. By the time a child with ADHD is walking their behavioural problems become more evident. They may be very active but have difficulty playing constructively, communicating and socializing with others. It is often when they begin formal education and have to communicate and conform in a disciplined manner that ADHD becomes evident. The school experiences a pupil who will not settle to work and is often non-compliant.

All pupils can show inconsistency in their school performance due to health, social and environmental factors that interfere with concentration. Some children, because of their outgoing personalities, are more disruptive than others but their misbehaviour, in class, is not severe enough to warrant serious attention. This is usually temporary due to anxiety in carrying out a task, especially one not previously attempted. Often the child with ADHD displays inattention, which is one of the three core features (the other two being hyperactivity and impulsivity), resulting in them not completing tasks. There may be short-term memory difficulties as instructions are easily forgotten. Some with ADHD are constantly on the go with the degree of overactivity differing from child to child. On the other hand, they may not be unusually active but complain of feeling restless with inability to fully relax. Those who are not hyperactive may have the inattentive type of ADHD and are more likely to go unnoticed and undiagnosed. There are some with a severe form of overactivity who are never still, leading to injuries because of a limited concept of how to keep safe as well as insatiability resulting in not knowing when to stop. These children find it difficult to calm down and can become excessively defiant, which causes problems at home and school.

Disorders that occur with ADHD

ADHD is a complex disorder that often co-occurs with other behavioural, emotional and learning problems (Cooper and O'Regan, 2001). This co-existence is known as co-morbidity of disorders. Difficulties associated with ADHD are dyspraxia, dyslexia, communication and specific language disorders. Often their existence is masked by

ADHD. Research by Dykman and Ackerman (1991) as well as Richards (1994) explores the correlation between ADHD and dyslexia, suggesting that children should be screened for both problems. Sage (2000) cites studies of a link between ADHD and spoken communication problems whilst O'Regan (2007) suggests that specific learning difficulties, such as dyslexia and dyspraxia, occur in approximately 40 per cent of children with ADHD. The La Doux studies, referred to by Sage (1998), suggest that all these disorders arise from regulating problems in the amygdala of the brain.

There is also some evidence to suggest a correlation between ADHD and autism (Gillberg, 1990). Arnold (2000) discusses the rare co-morbidity of Tourette's syndrome (TS) and ADHD, suggesting that about 1–2 per cent of people have this combination with ADHD preceding TS by 2–4 years. Arnold says that children who have ADHD should be monitored for the development of any tics. The co-morbidity of the two conditions has implications for any medication. However, Montague and Castro (2005) highlight that the concept and validity of co-morbidity have been questioned in regard to DSM-IV-TR diagnostic categories.

Children with ADHD often have very low self-esteem (Travell and Visser, 2006) and are never satisfied even when they succeed. This low self-esteem may manifest itself in different behaviours such as aggression, feelings of being threatened and discouragement, leading to withdrawal. As the child matures, feelings and problems associated with low self-esteem may give rise to suicidal tendencies. Pliszka (1992) suggests that in clinical studies, a quarter of the ADHD population have experienced an anxiety disorder. This is supported by O'Regan (2007) who writes that about 30 per cent of children/adults with ADHD have anxiety disorders. These are manifested in many ways with symptoms including being restless, feeling fatigued, difficulty with concentration, irritability and sleep disturbances. There are many differing types of depression and dysthymia is often associated with ADHD. The individual may experience a depressed mood over a period of time, over or under eating, sleep disturbance (sleeping for too short a long a period), limited energy and low self-esteem (Pierangelo and Giuliani, 2008).

The most common disorder associated with ADHD is oppositional/defiant disorder (ODD) showing angry, resentful, spiteful and vindictive behaviours often accompanied by swearing or obscene language. ODD may evolve into a conduct disorder (CD), which has some of the features of ODD but extends to far more serious antisocial behaviours such as bullying, physical cruelty to animals, stealing, arson, forcing someone into sexual activity, destroying property, truancy, lying and stealing. Conduct disorders may be seen in up to 50 per cent of individuals who have ADHD (O'Regan, 2007). Arnold (2000) makes it clear that aggression is not a diagnostic criterion for ADHD although it is often wrongly associated with this condition. Any presentation of the above symptoms would suggest either ODD or CD rather than ADHD.

Management of ADHD

At present, there is no known 'cure' for ADHD and because of the very complex nature of the disorder the child may well have a variety of behavioural, academic, social and family issues that require addressing. There are various interventions offered, including the following.

Family therapy

Family therapy may help a child and his/her siblings and parents come to terms with and develop a better understanding of the condition, leading to a more suitable home environment. The child with ADHD requires different parenting techniques to the norm. As previously stated, poor parenting can cause poor behaviours but this is not often the case with the child who has ADHD. Parents can feel that they are to 'blame' (incorrectly) for the behaviours of their child and can be hurt by the derogatory comments of others. They can feel anxiety regarding the social and academic future of their child. Family therapy sessions offer stress management courses and advice on dealing with difficult situations. This involves several sessions with parents, other siblings and child, trying to resolve their conflicts, and ideally should compliment other forms of treatment.

Behaviour management

In this approach three assumptions are made:

- That all behaviour is learned
- That all behaviour can be changed
- That factors in the environment can be engineered to determine which behaviours will be rewarded and which will be punished

The child can learn acceptable behaviours through imitation of good role models. With younger ones having ADHD, behaviour modification can be successful if rewards are frequent and immediate and regular reinforcement is given. Children thrive on attention even if this is negative, so parents have to control their natural responses to situations. In some cases, providing the behaviour is not dangerous, the best course of action is to ignore it. 'Time out' is a technique that is often used in a behaviour modification plan. The child is removed from where he/she is demonstrating unreasonable, inappropriate behaviour to a calmer place, for a short time, until this subsides. Behaviours that are desired are rewarded and those deemed undesirable are met with negative reinforcement. This type of therapy works short-term in contexts where it is regularly used, such as school. However, the desired behaviour may not generalize to other settings so may not be the best long-term solution.

Cognitive behaviour therapy

Cognitive therapy allows the child to talk through his/her problems and develop supportive strategies. The child works on a one-to-one basis with a skilled therapist who facilitates ways that will help him/her stop and think before they act. Cognitive therapy aims to teach the child self control and manage impulsive actions. This 'talking therapy' has been found to produce the best long-term results as communicating with others develops the thought processes that are the basis of self-control (Sage, 2000).

Diet

There has been conjecture that diet can alter the symptoms of ADHD. In 1973, Dr Ben Feingold, a paediatric allergist in the United States, claimed that by excluding chemical food additives (e.g. colourings, flavourings and preservatives) from the diet of hyperactive children resulted in marked improvement in their behaviour and health. However, the 'Feingold diet' as it is known, does not work for all children, with only some responding to a very restricted food intake. Parents try changes to their child's diet, increasing essential fatty oils from seeds, nuts and fish oils in the hope of improving concentration. Additional nutritional and mineral supplements have also been used by them. Some find that gluten-free products and restricted dairy produce help their children. Others have eliminated high sugar content from their child's diet including fizzy drinks with good effects.

Medication

Medication is a popular option for ADHD management. Its use over the years has caused considerable controversy but stimulants have been used to treat ADHD symptoms since 1937. They are thought to increase the amount of dopamine and norepinephrine neurotransmitters that relay information to brain areas and this is discussed by Sage (1998) and O'Regan (2007). Stimulants such as methylphenidate

(Ritalin, Concerta, Metadate) or amphetamine (Dexedrine, Adderall), used for antidepressant medication, has a positive effect on ADHD. Ritalin can be used as a short-acting medicine lasting between 3 and 4 hours, depending on the child's body metabolism, or a longer sustained release form of methyphenidate, called Concerta, may be prescribed, lasting 8–12 hours. This longer-lasting version is useful for children who are unable or unwilling to take medicine at school and is more frequently used by adolescents.

All drugs have side effects or undesirable results such as stomach upsets, decreased appetite, weight loss and disruption to sleep patterns. Other medications, such as anti-depressants, are used for those not responding to stimulants or having co-existing conditions such as, ADHD and TS (Clonidine, for example, makes TS worse). Close medical supervision is necessary, as well as collaboration between home and school, to ensure that the child is carefully monitored and the dosage altered if necessary. O'Regan (2007) says that it is also important to remember that when a child is on medication it is the parents who are in charge rather than doctors, teachers or others. For a minority of children with ADHD, behaviour modification or cognitive therapy may be sufficient but the use of medication allows the children to be more receptive to any interventions. The use of this, alongside other treatments, is known as a multi-modal approach and is more successful for the child or adolescent with ADHD than single approaches.

It is important to remember that rather than focusing on what a child cannot do, the emphasis should be building on existing strengths. With this background information in place, we can now consider four case studies, in which the following questions are considered:

- How does the child or young adult perceive themselves?
- What affect is the condition having upon the family?
- What has been put in place to support the sufferer and the family by varying agencies?
- How effective is the management used by the family?

It must be emphasized that not all parents, who have children with ADHD, will experience the same problems as those in the case studies. Each child is unique and every child with ADHD is different in the number of symptoms exhibited and the degree of severity of these. However, these stories exhibit the range of issues that are likely to be involved and give us insight into another perspective of human diversity.

Michael aged 8 years

Michael's mother realized from birth that her son had 'problems'. He cried constantly and had reflux, causing projectile vomiting. At around two years of age, Michael's behaviour worsened and he would scream, head butt and bite himself, with his body becoming rigid when picked up. He was expelled from nursery although efforts were made to support him. The nursery wrote to the family doctor, suggesting that Michael needed help. Mother took him to see a psychiatrist who told her that this was just a stage that Michael was going through and what he required was discipline. His father and mother attended parent classes and were told to physically restrain Michael when he was aggressive. They did this for over two years, sometimes being injured, and continually being stressed because they hated using restraint techniques. Finally, they reached the end of their tether and asked for more help from health services. Michael's mother requested counselling, which was unsuccessful. Aged four years, Michael had a brain scan, which revealed nothing. His mother tried changing his diet following the Feingold principles, avoiding dairy produce etc. but to no avail.

The family endured great hardship and the relationship between Michael's parents deteriorated, resulting in his father leaving home. The parents had no rest as Michael only slept through the night after aged four. He would scream and bang his head and his parents took sleeping tablets, on alternate nights, so one was always available to supervise. His mother was frightened of him because he said that he would murder both parents while they were asleep.

At the age of six years, Michael was on the verge of expulsion from school. He would not sit still, exhibiting poor memory and concentration, and was referred to a psychologist who diagnosed Michael as having ADHD. Michael had low self-esteem, depression and threatened suicide. He has tried to get himself run over by cars and talks about ending his life. Ritalin, a medication given for ADHD, was prescribed. His mother says that within fifteen minutes of taking this, Michael was a totally different child. He was calmer, peaceful, and no longer aggressive. His mother was able to talk to him and discuss his behaviour, which was previously impossible.

Although medication has improved many aspects of Michael's life, as well as that of the whole family, his mother has concerns for the future. She feels that she can protect him at present but when he is a teenager she wonders how he will cope with school and the community. Michael is encouraged by other children in the neighbourhood to behave anti-socially. There is a special lock on the front door of the house to stop him leaving but he regularly climbs out of his bedroom window. Mum says, 'What is he going to be like when he is 15?' She has no concerns about the medication that Michael takes because, in her words, 'it gives him the chance to lead a normal life'. However, he shows signs of improvement for three to four weeks and then suddenly reverts back to not sleeping properly, having night terrors and aggressive behaviours. Every day is a battle with no set pattern to the problem behaviour and no specific incidents that trigger it. This has made his mother ill so other family members have had to step in to look after Michael.

Paul aged 17 years

Paul has been diagnosed with ADHD and dyslexia. His mother suspected that there was a problem when he was younger. She always felt that he was different and put this down to him being a bright, able child as he was very perceptive of things around him. At aged seven, Paul's parents made an appointment to see an educational psychologist who suggested that he was hyperactive with poor concentration. It was difficult for Paul in a classroom situation. His parents were told that he would 'grow out of it' (the ADHD) but of course he didn't and problems just got worse. Horrendous stress was put on the family and his mother was prescribed anti-depressants. The other children in the house were distressed by their brother's outrageous, psychotic and unacceptable behaviour. He was violent and aggressive. Everyone was frightened of him. His brother and sister gave him anything he demanded and were jealous of the fact that he took up so much of their mum's time. She said, 'Paul is a danger to himself and others and this is a constant worry'.

It was far from easy at home and all the near neighbours were put on constant alert. Paul's mother had an arrangement with them so that if Paul had one of his spates she would go to a neighbour's house with the other children and stay until her husband came home to assist and protect them all. They were all frightened to be alone with Paul but understood that he couldn't help what he was doing. He would prowl around the house at night, stealing food and stashing it in his bedroom. When Paul was thirteen, his school peers laughed at his behaviour and bullied him. School staff were not supportive and suggested that Paul courted the bullying because he 'mouthed off' at other children. The school constantly threatened to suspend him, which made Paul's behaviour worse.

Paul's mother says that his self-esteem was fine until he reached the age of eleven at which point it plummeted. He has never been able to play well with younger or older children because of difficulties in forming relationships with others although he can interact reasonably with children of his own age. Paul took medication (Ritalin) when he was fourteen and mother says that: 'It was like a miracle, we had our son back. He was able to concentrate, function in the classroom; he seemed happy, making plans. It was wonderful'. However, the Ritalin had to stop because of other medical conditions that contra-indicated its use. Paul repeats the same things over and over again and has developed no awareness of social graces. Mother feels that if he gets in with the wrong crowd, he would go along with what they wanted him to do, regardless of what might happen. When asked if she has fears for her son's future, she replied that he will probably end up in prison. Paul shows no remorse or fear for the consequences of his actions.

James aged 7 years

James's mother first suspected that her son, James, had problems when he was a tiny baby. He never slept at night and the doctor prescribed medicine to help him rest. The parents were told that he was hyperactive when he started nursery. James was never suspended from nursery but his mother was often asked to pick him up and calm him down. This also happened when James started mainstream school. However, school is more patient with him now that he has a definite diagnosis. As mum stated, 'school now sees that he is not just a naughty boy, but that he has got ADHD'.

James does have friends but not special ones. He gets depressed and very emotional, crying easily and stating that no one loves him. Mood swings are frequent and he gets very angry when provoked. At home, he lashes out at his family. James says that he wishes he was dead and that he had never been born, when he is in one of his despairing periods. Mum says that as soon as James started on medication (Ritalin) she noticed a positive difference and within a week, friends, family and school had all remarked on this. At school, he was calmer and able to concentrate and complete his work. However, his medication does need regulating. James is fine in the mornings but deteriorates in the afternoons. Since taking Ritalin, James has shown an improvement with his reading.

When asked if the ADHD has caused any problems in the class, his mum replied: 'James is James. He's always like this. I can differentiate between him being just naughty and the ADHD behaviour. It is an inconvenience for me because I have to go to the school each afternoon to give him his medication and this is hard work'. Mother does have concerns about the medication. In order to have his health monitored, she has to ensure that his weight, height etc. is regularly checked by medical experts. She feels that doctors and other professionals don't know a great deal about ADHD. His mother worries about the future and wonders if James will make adequate progress in school.

Peter aged 15 years

Peter is a boy, who prior to medication for his ADHD, found it very difficult to make friends. He had low self-esteem, which his parents felt had been caused by school. He was labelled as a 'naughty child'. When he was younger he was not a good sleeper and a boisterous little boy who always ran everywhere. When Peter went to nursery school, they brought in an educational psychologist who said that he was immature. When he went to mainstream school, he was constantly in trouble in the infant section. His mother was called up to school on many occasions and his behaviour was put down to poor parenting. She stated that Peter 'fumbled through' juniors and when he went to the senior school was put on target sheets. He had numerous day exclusions. Mum felt that the school had not helped at all and that they saw her 'Peter' as a 'problem'. She said that he had missed out on so much of his education. The general view was he was too difficult to bother with.

His mother tried to get him a legal statement of his special educational needs, so that he could receive appropriate support in school. She even went to a tribunal but there have been no positive outcomes from this. A great deal of stress has been experienced by the family and his mother says that she is both mentally and physically exhausted by years of anxiety. She never knew from day to day what would happen to Peter and in her words: 'I am on pins the minute he walks out of the door. Some days are great and some are bad'. Peter is not physically aggressive, but he is verbally so, which his mother has great concerns about. She has asked the hospital to re-assess Peter with a view to achieving greater help. The doctors suggested psychiatric therapy, which is not what his mother felt was needed. She wanted assistance with his communication and behaviour problems.

Because things were deteriorating rapidly in school, Peter attended a private clinic that diagnosed him as having ADHD. He has been prescribed medication and after trying one type unsuccessfully was put on Ritalin. There are no other treatments or therapies in place except for this drug. Mother has no worries about Peter taking medication and says that the school have seen a positive change in his attitude and behaviour since this began. There have also been positive changes in school work. Peter will have to stay on medication until he is at least 25 years of age but the prognosis seems good. Mother concludes with the following comment; 'Now that my son is on medication, it means that me and my daughter can also have a reasonable quality of life' .

Review

So often, those with ADHD have low self-esteem, resulting from other people's negative communication with them (Sage, 2000). This in turn manifests itself in socially unacceptable behaviours, which prevent friendships developing. People with ADHD are often criticized for their actions over which they have little or no control. They become trapped in a 'failure' cycle. ADHD is not a socially acceptable 'label' for disruptive individuals, or an excuse for poor parenting but a distressing, chronic, medical condition. O'Regan (2007) suggests that ADHD is in fact, an explanation as to why certain individuals act in a way that other people not only find annoying but also unacceptable.

Early diagnosis and intervention is important, using a multi-dimensional approach to problems. Some parents may be reluctant to seek professional advice because of what they perceive as a stigma attached to the 'label' of ADHD. For others, the diagnosis comes as a welcome relief, as one mother said to me, 'Now he has a label, we can cope!' The situation is explained and can be understood, which is the first step to effective management.

ADHD is not a condition that restricts itself to the child but, as can be seen from the four case studies, impacts upon the whole family in so many different and disturbing ways. Parents may blame each other for their child's condition and criticize each other's approach to management (Cooper and O'Regan, 2001). Marriages or relationships often breakdown. Siblings can feel that they do not get a fair share of their parents' attention because of the demands made by the child with ADHD, so this can lead to resentment. Also, the child with ADHD may be compared unfavourably with their siblings, especially regarding academic performance, which can result in resentment and reduction of an already fragile self-esteem (O'Regan, 2002). Friends and the extended family can be divided and may offer support or reject the child with ADHD, leading to parents feeling isolated.

The Special Educational Needs Code of Practice (2001) clearly states:

> Partnership with parents plays a key role in promoting a culture of co-operation
> Between parents, schools, LEAs (now known as LAs) and others. This is important
> In enabling children and young people with SEN to achieve their potential. (2:1)

The Code of Practice also acknowledges that when parents are involved, what other professionals implement in a specific intervention is made more effective. Emphasis is placed on parents and professionals as partners since communication, cooperation and collaboration are the keys to successful management of problems. Consideration must also be given to involving the child in the process. The child with ADHD will probably feel a failure socially and academically and in order to break this cycle, understanding and support from home and the differing agencies involved is required. Cheminais (2006) suggests that the five goals of the Every Child Matters agenda are fundamental to well-being in childhood and later life (being safe, healthy, making a positive contribution, enjoy and achieve, and achieving economic well-being) and will only be achieved when there is a partnership between everybody involved which is grounded in effective group communication. In a culture where this is less valued than in some others, miscommunication and misunderstanding are common. The case studies illustrate this and point to a need for

1   increased knowledge and understanding of medical and educational problems that affect development by both public and professionals for more enlightened and effective management;
2   improved communication between parents and other agencies, so that damaging assumptions are prevented and the needs of individuals with behaviour difficulties properly addressed; and
3   research focussing on causes and cures that will eventually alleviate family and societal distress.

Suggestions for classroom practice

There has to be a consistent approach to dealing with behaviour problems discussed and agreed with parents, colleagues and pupils. Peers have to understand that we all have problems to surmount, some physical, some emotional, some mental and some social and recognizing these and understanding them is the key to management. Strategies such as time out (working outside the classroom), buddy schemes, rewards and goal charts may be helpful and children need to have these suited to their needs. There is no one panacea and a holistic approach to the situation guarantees the optimum success.

Main points

- Children, whose behaviour deviates from the norm, need early diagnosis and intervention from a multi-discipline team in a multi-dimensional approach.
- Better understanding of this increasing problem in society will only result from improved education and training of both the public and professionals.
- Mainstream schooling for those with diverse, complex behavioural needs may not be beneficial to everyone unless individual, specific requirements can be properly supported on a long-term basis.
- A child problem is a family one so these wider needs must also be addressed.

Discussion point

The three main aspects of ADHD are inattention, hyperactivity and impulsivity. Using a grid, similar to that below, work out the balance of these behaviours in someone you know. Observe over a timed period (preferably more than once) and count the behaviours classified under these headings to ascertain which predominates. Is this behaviour you might prioritize for a management plan?

Name	Age	Date	Time Period
Behaviour:	Inattention	Hyperactivity	Impulsivity
Description:			
e.g. DNA to story			

References

Arnold, L. E. (2000) *Contemporary Diagnosis and Management of Attention-Deficit/Hyperactivity Disorder*, 2nd edn, Pennsylvania: Handbooks in Health Care Co.

Ayers, H. and Prytys, C. (2002) *An A to Z Practical Guide to Emotional and Behavioural Difficulties*, London: David Fulton Publishers.

Cheminais, R. (2006) *Every Child Matters: A Practical Guide for Teachers*, London: David Fulton Publishers.

Cooper, P. (1994) Attention deficit hyperactivity disorder and the strange case of Vincent Van Gough. *Therapeutic Care and Education*, 3(2), 86–95.

Cooper, P. and Ideus, K. (1996) *Attention Deficit / Hyperactivity Disorder: A Practical Guide for Teachers*, London: David Fulton Publishers.

Cooper, P. and O'Regan, F. J. (2001) *Educating Children with ADHD: A Teacher's Manual*, London: Routledge Falmer Publishers.

Dykman, R. A. and Ackerman, P. T. (1991) Attention deficit disorder and specific reading disability: Separate but often overlapping disorders. *Journal of Learning Disability*, 24(2), 96–103.

Gillberg, C. (1990) Autism and pervasive development disorders. *Journal of Child Psychology and Psychiatry*, 32, 99–119.

Hughes, L. and Cooper, P. (2007) *Understanding and Supporting Children with ADHD: Strategies for Teachers, Parents and Other Professionals*, London, Thousand Oaks, CA and New Delhi: Paul Chapman Publishing.

Montague, M. and Castro, M. (2005) *Attention deficit hyperactivity disorder: Concerns and issues*. In P. Clough, P. Garner, J. Pardeck, T. & Yuen, F. (eds). *Handbook of Emotional and Behavioural Difficulties*, London: Sage.

Munden, A. and Arcelus, J. (1999) *The AD/HD Handbook: A Guide for Parents and Professionals on Attention Deficit/Hyperactivity Disorder*, London: Jessica Kingsley Publishers.

O'Regan, F. J. (2002) *How to Teach and Manage Children with ADHD*, London: LDA Publishers.

O'Regan, F. J. (2007) *ADHD*, 2nd edn, London and New York: Continuum International Publishing Group

Pierangelo, R. and Giuliani, G. (2008) *Classroom Management Techniques for Students with ADHD*, Thousand Oaks, CA: Corwin Press.

Pliszka, S. R. (1992) Comorbidity of attention deficit hyperactivity disorder and over anxious disorder. *Journal of the American Academy Of Child And Adolescent Psychiatry*, 31, 145–157.

Richards, I. (1994) ADHD, ADD and dyslexia. *Therapeutic Care and Education*, 3(2), 145–157.

Sage, R. (1998) *An Evaluation of Fluency Courses at the Apple House, Oxford,* Oxford: The Stammer Trust.

Sage, R. (2000) *Class Talk,* London: Network-Continuum.

Sage, R. (2004) *Inclusion in Schools,* London: Network-Continuum.

Singh, I. (2007) ADHD, culture and education. *Early Child Development and Care,* 178(4), 347–361.

Soan, S. (2004) *Additional Educational Needs: Inclusive Approaches to Teaching,* London: David Fulton Publishers.

Travell, C. and Visser, J. (2006) ADHD does bad stuff to you: Young people's and parents' experiences and perceptions of attention deficit hyperactivity disorder (ADHD). *Emotional and Behavioural Difficulties,* 11(3), 205–216.

Working with diversity in a primary school: Experiences of a special needs co-ordinator*

5

Gill Dixon

Overview

This chapter is based upon my experiences as a Special Needs Co-ordinator (SENCO) working to provide appropriate support for children with a great range of diverse special educational needs in a rural, primary school. It examines practice issues considering both the successes and challenges of service provision. The notion of those, who are being supported, having choices and some measure of control of their lives is a central theme. Another topic is the need to rethink educational policies, rebalancing the curriculum to take account of the development of personal skills to support learning. If implemented properly, these strategies would eliminate many of the difficulties and differences that exist in groups.

My background

We are the products of our upbringing and life experiences and I bring these to my role as a teacher. It is, therefore, useful to present a potted version of my own life history, in order for you to understand how culture, attitudes and views influence my actions.

When it was suggested that I write a chapter on working with diversity, it sounded a brilliant idea. However, I soon began to feel very inadequate, as I really do not see

---

* The names used in the case of illustrations are pseudonyms, thus allowing the contributions to be anonymous.

myself as a writer. So, true to form, I have left this account to the very last minute and have spent a number of weeks avoiding putting pen to paper, or fingers to keys. So now there is no time left and here goes with my personal and professional story.

I was born in Dublin, the capital of Southern Ireland. My mother is a Dublin lass and my father came from Ballymena in Northern Ireland. I have three brothers and a sister. We all feel that we had a wonderful upbringing and are often heard describing our early years as an 'Enid Blyton' childhood and we were, indeed, our very own version of the 'famous five'. We did move house frequently, living in England for a short time, where my father was a head teacher, before returning to Ireland. We lived in Limerick, when Dad entered the church, becoming a vicar in a parish in Co Fermanagh, just across the border in the North of Ireland.

I attended secondary school, as a boarder, in Londonderry and at this time life in Northern Ireland was very troubled. There was a great deal of unrest and a huge divide between Catholics and Protestants. I was very fortunate, as my parents raised me to have a very open mind, and to treat people as equal, regardless of their religion, race or nationality. After leaving school in the early 1970s, I trained as a teacher in Bangor, North Wales. My first teaching post was as a PE Mistress in a school in the south of England. After marrying, I had four sons, returning to teaching when my youngest child was at primary school. Now, I work in a village primary school as a class teacher and SENCO. Since returning to teaching, I have undertaken post-graduate training, which has helped me in my role as SENCO. I have gained a diploma in specific learning difficulties and a post-graduate certificate in Asperger syndrome at the university.

Introduction: The situation in our schools

The Department for Families, Education and Schools (DfES) states that: 'All schools must deliver a broad and balanced curriculum for all pupils providing effective opportunities for all children'. In planning and teaching the National Curriculum, teachers have responsibility for

- setting suitable learning challenges;
- responding to pupils' diverse learning needs; and
- overcoming potential barriers to learning and assessment for individuals and groups of pupils.

Today's education system endeavours to be active and reactive in responding to the requirements of all, allowing the needs, ambitions and aspirations of learners to be recognized and met and for them to be fully involved in their own learning.

Coping with diversity in a school is achievable, but only if there is an awareness that there is such a reality. There must be an acceptance that *everyone* is different, with empathy and willingness to look at things from other viewpoints, as well as an intention to implement suitable strategies and change ideas and teaching styles, according to the specific demands of pupils. These goals are more easily achievable in a small, close-knit community, such as a village school. When I talk to colleagues, who teach in vast city schools, where contact and communication is a real problem, because of the number of staff and pupils and the difficulty of getting people together to develop common approaches, I realize the good fortune of my own working environment.

The range of needs that are experienced in a small village school will be different from those in a large inner city because the huge contrasts in these contexts result in very different opportunities. Cities may have easier access to specialist resources but in villages there is the possibility of a stronger network of support. My rural school experiences the full range of learning problems over time, but not in the intensity and quantity that has to be catered for in a large institution. A colleague, in a nearby city establishment of 1,700 pupils, has 800 students on the special needs register and a staff of over 50 to cope with them. I am the only special needs teaching expert in my school with the assistance of two learning support staff who implement the specific programmes of individual children. These pupils' special learning needs must be addressed and supported in order for them to progress, learn and thrive as part of the school and local community. In order to understand what this means in practice, we will consider the issues of the major stakeholders in schools – the professionals, pupils and their parents.

The professionals: teachers and support staff

In my experience, one of the most important factors in coping with pupils having diverse needs is the willingness and attitude of all the staff within a school. Everyone must work together to give children the most positive education possible and to communicate, co-operate and collaborate in a consistent way. Regular review of policies and practices is essential, so that adjustments can be made promptly for any change in circumstances.

Over the years, I have seen an amazing change in staff awareness of diversity and have discovered that one of the most important roles of a SENCO is helping the school staff to understand and deal with this in a positive and productive way. Therefore, this role involves a regular training commitment for all those involved with children, whether they are teachers, support assistants, meal supervisors, administrators, security or care staff. I have had the privilege of working with a number of children with special educational needs. These include specific language disorder, generalized low ability, dyslexia, dyspraxia, autism, Asperger syndrome, attention deficit and hyperactivity disorder and behavioural problems. There is a detailed discussion of the definition and management of these problems in Sage (2004) and a shorter description in Appendix 5 of this text. With such diverse needs, the strategies used are also often equally diverse. Below, we have a story about a child with autism to illustrate some important issues.

Working with autism: A story of William

Some while ago, I worked with a pupil with autism. This disorder results in an inability to make sense of the world. It exhibits a triad of impairments: social interaction, communication, thought and imagination. William came to our school in the reception class with no previous diagnosis. His parents were aware that he had specific needs, but had been told by other professionals that when he started school these would be sorted out, such as communicating properly, sleeping better and conforming to social rules. As William settled into school, we had to help the parents come to terms with his continuing and severe learning needs and find coping strategies to improve matters.

All the standard, formal, procedures, set up by government, were put into place, as detailed in the Code of Practice for children with special educational needs (2000, 2001). As William was a child needing help that was not available within school, a specialist teacher and educational psychologist were brought in to assess his long-term needs. This pupil was awarded a Statement of Educational Needs, as required by law for a child with long-term learning needs, and we took on board all the expert advice given to us.

Implementing a plan of action for William

We began by developing and implementing a whole school approach to meeting William's needs, as he had to be able to cope with everything going on in the building as well as his own, particular class routines. Differentiated planning for teaching inputs and learning outcomes was essential but the most important issue was to give all staff a clear knowledge and understanding of his condition. Proper education and training in complex, developmental disorders is essential if learning needs are to be met and proper progress made. This should be mandatory for those dealing with special needs.

It was at this stage that I undertook the post-graduate certificate in autism/ Asperger syndrome at university. This gave me the confidence as well as the expert knowledge to help staff understand William's needs and assist them in implementing strategies to facilitate his progress. It was essential to ensure that William felt safe and secure in an environment that was predictable and with a high level of structure, as this is an essential factor for children who have difficulty comprehending the world and what happens within it. The school contacted many different organizations for help and advice and sent staff on training courses, so that all were armed with as much information and knowledge as possible to provide maximum support.

William made great progress and remained with us until he had finished KS1. At this stage, we all felt his continuing needs would be better met in a more specialist unit, as with increasing age and the severity of his difficulty with understanding and expression, the distance between him and his peers would grow and become impossible to bridge within a mainstream environment.

The experience of dealing with William was a turning point for the school and enabled us to move forward much more confidently with an agenda for inclusion of pupils with special educational needs. Knowledge is a vital tool. It empowers people and, if used wisely, brings understanding and empathy that enables everyone to learn new skills and deal with diversity in a positive, constructive way. Education and training is essential.

The story of Henry

Many of the children that I have worked with have presented diverse and challenging behaviour. Another particular pupil, called Henry, springs to mind, who was in year 3. He had been at the school since the reception stage and labelled by staff as a 'naughty boy'. Henry seemed to display all those disruptive behaviours that are so very difficult to deal with in a large class of pupils. He shouted out continually and appeared to be in his own world. Henry never knew what to do when the whole class had been given instructions, as he could not bring together this information to produce a coherent message. At the end of a teaching session he would always, without fail, stand directly in front of his teacher and tell her that he did not know what to do! He did not seem able to talk in an appropriate manner and always shouted. Henry found it very difficult to change activities and was very resistant to stopping an activity that he was enjoying and had not managed to complete.

This response demonstrates a fixed mental set, which is characteristic of children with severe thinking and communication problems. In general, Henry caused every teacher that ever taught him much head and heart ache. He endured many trials of different behaviour reward schemes. We gradually began to unpick all his different behaviours by attempting to look at responses from his perspective and finding a reason for these. Staff began to suspect, that far from being a 'naughty boy' he had a range of behaviours that suggested Asperger syndrome. This disorder has the same triad of impairments as autism but these are less profound.

Henry really did not understand that instructions were intended for him, unless you actually made sure that you alerted him to listen, by calling his name. He was, in fact, eager to please and wanted to do the right thing, but required support and, most importantly, understanding of his condition. As he progressed through the school, it became clear that he needed to understand his own actions. Henry had to evolve strategies that he could use to help him work successfully alongside his peers, so that he could achieve success. School staff had to understand and appreciate that he did not always have a choice in the way that he behaved, because of an inability to control thoughts and movements. It was also necessary to make Henry's peers aware of the problems that he encountered, helping them to understand the problems, so that they could assist him if necessary.

It was so rewarding to watch Henry progress and enjoy school, and what a privilege it was to be involved in developing the concept of diversity. Henry has now moved on to secondary school, where he is thriving and taking a full part in most activities. His success, again, was due to a whole school policy on how to tackle the problems that a boy with this syndrome presents. Thorough, regular within-school training is necessary, so that everyone is educated in the disorder and trained to implement a consistent management approach. Effective communication of all stakeholders is the key to successful progress of such pupils. Parents and pupils must be involved in all the decisions made along the way so that they retain ownership and control of what is happening.

Pupils and their participation in decisions

The SEN Code of Practice (2000, 2001) stresses the importance of children and young people participating in all the decisions about their education. It states that schools should seek to ascertain the views of children and young people about their needs and aspirations and how they might like these to be met. Individual Education Plans (IEPs) have been in our schools for many years now, supporting staff in identifying strengths and weaknesses of pupils with diverse needs and enabling them to set realistic goals to make the most of potential. Encouraging pupils to have an input into their IEPs has become good practice, clearly benefiting all involved by giving some control of events. Discussions with pupils, identifying goals, setting targets and suggesting the next step needed to progress in a specific area, allows them to have ownership and a really clear understanding of the reasons for IEPs and their plan for learning.

We encourage discussion and questioning of unwanted behaviour, which is being exhibited in school, to help pupils work out strategies that might be helpful to make improvements. Careful questioning can uncover issues that the pupil may have regarding the triggers to their unacceptable responses, remembering, at each stage, to reinforce what is acceptable and desirable.

One very challenging pupil, Marcus, who joined us in Year 3, with a history of disruption and aggression, made such good progress that the educational psychologist asked to see him each time she came to school, just to check that it was the same pupil and that she wasn't dreaming. Marcus was going through a severe period of unrest in his life. He had experienced aggression at home and his parents had recently separated. Marcus came to us with little respect for anyone whether they were adults, peers or himself. Again the normal, formal procedures had been followed. We had involved the Behaviour and Curriculum Inclusion team, educational psychologist and other outside agencies. Their advice was taken on board and action taken to implement this. Fortunately, we were included in a programme, working alongside a Local Education Authority (LEA) Special School, catering for primary-aged children (5–11 years) with emotional and behavioural problems. This programme insisted upon the participation of parents, and was designed to

- help children form positive relationships with both peers and adults; recognize their success in a school environment and raise confidence;
- encourage positive social interaction, communication and language abilities that result in the development of self-esteem through positive feedback from others;
- promote co-operative activity; and
- promote positive parenting.

We followed these strategies faithfully and any suggestions from the special school. A positive, consistent approach towards his unwanted behaviours was used and Marcus was given choices, but on our terms. We celebrated his improved behaviour and questioned him regarding any negative responses and explained the consequences of his actions. Gradually, Marcus began to take more responsibility for his behaviour and started to see himself as part of the class and a valued member of the school. As he grew in confidence and we began to see him smile and relax, the barriers came down. We submitted a Referral for Statutory Assessment (RSA) for Marcus, as he had missed much of his learning experience. His poor behaviour had prevented this, and I am delighted to say that we were successful and given extra school support by the LEA.

The success and progress, we had been able to show, meant that the LEA was happy to fund further help to enable Marcus to catch up with any lost learning. There were many days when I watched him, in a whole school situation, and he was usually smiling and revelling in every new experience. It was such a joy to see him enjoying school and challenging himself to improve by planning new goals. Marcus was now keen and eager to move on to the next reading book, which was a real achievement for him.

The lessons that we have learnt, as a whole school and a staff group, are immense. Many new strategies to help deal with disruptive behaviour have been acquired. We are really a very positive staff, always looking for 'good' things to say about pupils and this is an important mind-set. Now, we are keen to involve children in taking responsibility for their own behaviour. This is achieved by helping them understand why they are behaving in such a manner and giving them the message that you are on their side. It is vital to listen to a child's opinion and attend to what they are communicating both verbally and non-verbally. Involving the whole school, staff and pupils, in embracing inclusion and understanding diversity is also important. We all need to have an appreciation of diversity in order o feel empowered to accept this phenomenon, as the natural order of things, and an opportunity to acquire the skills to deal with the challenges it presents.

Parents

Parents react to the challenge of supporting their children in many different ways. In our school, we have identified three different types of parents:

Caring parents, who have the best and greatest intentions but life is busy, hey ho!
Concerned parents, who live an orderly life with everything planned and timetabled.
Anxious parents, who are stressed and anxious about everything.

I have worked with all these 'types' of parents, so every time we are in contact, I try to put myself in their shoes and understand where they are 'coming from'. I probably fall into the first category of parents, not always having time to read the book sent home from school or do the extra bit to the homework task. However, our family was generally doing something more interesting and probably just as educational.

We are all part of a very competitive society and, because of this, are seeing far more of the two latter types of parent in schools. The knock-on effect is that there are more and more pupils who are anxious and stressed about life and its constant, relentless demands. The mental health issues of children should be receiving much more attention, as they will escalate with age and place a huge and continuing emotional, social and economic burden on society.

I would like to share with you, as evidence, a very extreme case of *anxious parenting*. This particular child, Matthew, had a number of learning needs and these had been identified and assessed, so that he was diagnosed with dyslexia and dyspraxia (reading and movement planning problems). It was possible to cater for Matthew's diverse needs in school and many strategies were put in place to support him, both inside and outside the classroom. However, the school began to find it very difficult to meet the needs of the *parents,* whose overanxiety brought relentless pressure on everyone. The inclusion of this pupil, in a mainstream school, was becoming more and more difficult, as the parents requested more and more things to be implemented specifically for him. The effect was that the lad was actually becoming less and less included, as parent requests meant that he was being treated completely differently from his peers. On many occasions, against staff wishes, he was not permitted to take part in normal school activities. Is this a case of parents been afforded too much control over school events? They were single-mindedly pursuing their own goals and completely disregarding the needs of others. Is a school supposed to cater for everyone's emotional needs?

The question, that the school had to ask, was whether the majority of the pupils in Matthew's class were actually missing out on opportunities, as activities were being constantly adapted to meet the wishes of his parents. Inclusive principles emphasize the importance of meeting children's individual needs, and of working closely with both parents and pupils, alongside teachers and schools, in the development of suitable approaches. It is right that parents are involved and have input into in their child's education, but equally they need be able to trust the judgment and professional expertise of staff.

This home-school liaison is a tricky partnership that requires understanding from both sides, as parents are focused on just their child, whereas teachers have to take into account the needs of the whole class. Everyone must work together as a unit, regarding all stakeholders as part of a team, so that pupils begin to feel a responsibility towards themselves and their peer group as well as the school as a whole. Parents, from my experience, are often guilty of an insular attitude and do not always see the complete picture or consider the effect of their child's behaviour on others. They continually question the school and its right to discipline their children.

Are we a society that is more interested in ourselves and our immediate families rather than the good of the whole community? Have we fostered a fierce, competitive spirit in and amongst schools at the expense of a more collaborative, cooperative one? We are known abroad as an *individualistic society* in comparison with a nation like Japan that fosters cooperation rather than competition in child-rearing practices, so functioning as a cohesive, collective group. Today, our children live within a circle of constant high expectation from both schools and home, driven by the threats of standard tests and league tables. They have no time to relax and be themselves and therefore fail to develop self-understanding as the basis for the big decisions that have to be made about their lives.

Review

Living in a diverse society certainly brings rewards, as this gives us all a much wider knowledge and understanding of the world and encourages us to question our own attitudes and ways of doing things. Nevertheless, it brings great challenges within an educational context. Catering for a wide variety of backgrounds, abilities and needs requires huge resources, which always seem scare and, at a time when the world has been thrust into recession, such essentials will become more of a problem to provide.

Nevertheless, in a short time we have come a long way and the success of our Paralympians, during 2008, was a superb example of how an inclusive philosophy has enabled them to achieve the previously impossible, competing alongside their peers with huge and humbling success. Nevertheless, there has been disquiet at the way they were overlooked in the 2009 New Year's Honours list. While every Olympic gold medalist, from the Beijing games, was given honours, ranging from an MBE to a knighthood, 17 of the 35 Paralympic champions got nothing at all. Dame Tanni Grey-Thompson, Britain's most celebrated Paralympian, with 11 gold medals, has questioned the 'lack of parity' in the honours system and suggested the government gives equal recognition to the achievements of able-bodied and disabled athletes after the 2012 London games (BBC News, 31 December 2008). We have somewhere yet to go in improving our attitudes to people's differences and are still playing catch up.

Nevertheless, in planning for the future, we need to take account of situations that might hinder this progress and which have been hinted at in this chapter. Our society has become very competitive, which inevitably sets one person against another and increases the sense of fear and failure amongst us. As teachers, we witness the stress and anxiety exhibited by both parents and children, as they seek to survive the instabilities of a global, inter-dependent world. There is little that we, as individuals, can do about this, but we can put greater emphasis on the personal development of children and adults so they are better equipped to cope with what life throws at them.

Those of us, who have taught for many years, have seen this aspect of development eroded by the demands of an academic National Curriculum. We need to take much more notice of countries that have gone through this situation before us. For example, Japan is a country which has had a National Curriculum for about 60 years compared to the 20 years of its existence in the United Kingdom. Until recently this had a very academic focus, but the economic downturn of the 1990s, and the failure of the Japanese population to cope with this, led them to question the balance of their education. Now, the emphasis is on communication and relationships, and these aspects take precedence over subject areas in primary schools. It is surely not just a coincidence that Japanese children are so much more advanced than those in the United Kingdom and have remarkable ability to communicate and cooperate together, operating inter- and independently in a way we rarely see in our society? (Sage et al., 2004, 2006).

Recently, we have seen rapid changes in our educational system, with so many new initiatives that never seem to be give time to be properly tried and tested. Much of what goes on in classrooms is dictated from outside, with the inevitable consequence that educators have become *technicians* rather than *teachers*, so we need to consider the consequences of such a situation. The skill of being able to judge the thinking and linguistic development of pupils, as a guide to their potential success with school tasks, is not being encouraged in our present, prescriptive regime. We must debate this and develop a clear direction for the future that values both academic and practical intelligences and balances the acquisition of knowledge with the pursuit of personal skills such as communication and relationships, self management and problem solving. With such a goal we could eradicate many of our present learning difficulties, as lack of adequate thinking and communication are at the root of most problems. This shift in focus would also lay the foundations of a more caring, concerned society, valuing and appreciating its range of diversity. We would be encouraging people to communicate their thoughts, views and feelings, so leading to a shared understanding.

The future is bright, if we are minded to take account of what is good and what needs more attention in our system of education, in order to provide for many diverse needs.

Suggestions for classroom practice

> Giving children responsibility and control helps their thinking, communication and maturity. In Japan a teacher introduces a topic and then asked how the class wants to learn it. So, in a maths class when averages had been introduced and explained, the pupils decided to use the current European Football Cup the format for this and collect the averages of the competing teams. They discussed how they would find and present this information. (Sage, Rogers and Cwenar, 2004). We need to develop more of this approach in Britain as this builds consensus, cooperation and collaboration.

Main points

> - The inclusion of children from a wide range of background, ability and interest in schools enriches the social mix but is challenging for teachers with scarce resources at their disposal.
>
>   ⇨

- Coping with diversity is possible but more probable in small, close-knit school communities, where communication, cooperation and collaboration for consistent approaches may be easier to obtain and retain.
- If coping with diversity is to be a successful reality, adequate, regular education and training of all staff in schools is a necessity and not a luxury.
- Constant and patient communication between all stakeholders results in sharing information, views and feelings, necessary to develop the rapport for a team approach to learning support.

Discussion points

1. Can you develop a personal plan to enhance your knowledge of diversity and your skill in managing this phenomenon?
2. Are we giving parents too much ownership of something that they actually have no expertise and skills in? Are some children overconfident and so over emphasize their own importance in a social situation such as school?
3. Are we creating a society 'obsessed' about themselves and how they feel? Should we be asking children whether they feel happy/sad/worried etc. Would you find this stressful if every morning you had to analyze how you felt? What would this achieve? When you get to school/work you need to behave in a consistent way, whether you might be feeling happy/sad/worried etc. Is school a place where children should behave in a certain way?

References

Department for Education and Employment (DfEE) (2000) *SEN Code of Practice on the Identification and Assessment of Students with Special Educational Needs and SEN Thresholds: Good Practice Guidelines on Identification and Provision for Students with Special Educational Needs*, London: DfEE.

Department for Education and Skills (DfES) (2001) *Special Educational Needs Code of Practice*, London: DfES.

Sage, R. (2004) *A World of Difference: Tackling Inclusion in Schools*, Stafford: Network Educational Press.

Sage, R., Rogers, J. and Cwenar, S (2004) *The Dialogue, Innovation, Achievement and Learning* (DIAL) Study 1: *A Comparison of English and Japanese Education*, Leicester: University of Leicester.

Sage, R., Rogers, J. and Cwenar, S (2006) *The Dialogue, Innovation, Achievement and Learning* (DIAL) Study 2: *Why do Japanese Children Outperform British Ones?* Leicester: University of Leicester.

The diverse and changing roles of teaching assistants: Supporting diversity in schools

6

Christine Bold

Overview

A major resource for the inclusion of a diverse range of children in the English education system is the teaching assistant (TA). The term 'teaching assistant' describes many people supporting learning, in a variety of ways, with a range of job titles reflecting their role, the school organization and local authority influence. TAs operate at primary, secondary and tertiary levels of the education system, providing both therapeutic and teaching support for learners. Using data, from an analysis of part-time students' TA job experiences, this chapter explores their changing roles and considers future development for meeting the needs of a rapidly changing, diverse society. Names used are pseudonyms, thus allowing the contributions to be anonymous.

Introduction

For many years, schools have employed additional learning support in schools on a paid or voluntary basis. Until legislation required schools to provide specialist support for children, most primaries focused on additional helpers in reception classes. These were qualified nursery nurses, who often worked in partnership with the reception teacher, with major responsibility for the care and education of the younger children. Some primary and secondary establishments provided such support throughout the school, albeit on a limited basis. This supplemented, specialist support for pupils with statements of educational needs was funded by the local authority. Also, there has been a tradition in English primary schools to engage adults, from the local community, to support reading and other school activities, thus creating a collaborative spirit, capitalizing on the skills and knowledge of those in the neighbourhood. For example, at a Wigan primary school in 1992, the children had an opportunity to join a *patchwork sewing club* (popular with the boys!), and create their own video productions, because local parents were able to provide these particular skills and thus develop an important link between home and school.

When the government announced that it was going to make use of the 'Mum's Army' (as dubbed by the press, *The Times*, 24 May 1999), there was dissent among some groups. In particular, a teachers' union thought that this was an unacceptable use of unqualified people taking on the roles of trained teachers. There were concerns that the special needs of an increasingly diverse school community would not be met by employing unqualified staff. This dissent continues, as TAs were required to do things they were not trained for and in some places, this may still be the situation.

Government guidance for TAs

The Department for Education and Employment (DfEE, 2000) produced the first guidance for teachers on how to work effectively with TAs, identifying their role as one that supports pupils, teachers, the curriculum and whole school activities. At the time of publication, the DfEE identified effective TA practice as

- fostering pupil participation;
- enabling pupils to be independent learners; and
- helping raise standards for all pupils.

It was a useful document, but at a time when schools were inundated with guidance about all aspects of their work, it was often shelved rather than used to inform practice. Having a TA was perceived by many teachers as increasing workloads and another government intervention resulting in an unsatisfactory work–life balance. There have been significant changes since the *Workforce Remodelling Agenda*, requiring schools to have a clear plan for improving teacher workloads, by September 2005 (Teacher Development Agency [TDA], 2003). There was initial support by the head teachers' union (who later withdrew this) and *some* teacher unions. However, the '*Raising Standards and Tackling Workload: a National Agreement*' did not include the National Union of Teachers (NUT), who believed that the employment of TAs reduces teacher jobs and lowers the quality of educational provision. Lack of support from NUT members has created difficulties for TA developments in some schools.

The aim of workforce remodelling was to improve teacher workloads, providing guaranteed time for lesson preparation and other responsibilities, as well as covering staff sickness more effectively. The TA was the answer to these problems, but in establishing the plan, during 2005, they began to feel the same pressures that teachers endure. Their responsibilities sometimes spiralled out of proportion to hours worked and payment made. Little attention was given, within the workforce remodelling agenda, to the increasing diversity of school communities and the need for specialist training for *all* education professionals, to address the complex needs of all pupils.

Evidence of change

Most students on the foundation degree 'Supporting Learning and Teaching', at a North West England University, worked full-time as voluntary or paid employees during school terms. Some had other employment, but worked at least one day a week in educational settings, within their course, regarding their studies as an opportunity to change career. Many aspired to become teachers, and have since achieved this goal. From 2002–05, it became clear to tutors that student workplace roles were changing for those in full-time employment. Nevertheless, diversity of roles remained, but plans for workforce remodelling were not necessarily leading to consistency across different local authorities and schools.

Student experiences are unique to their particular settings, regardless of level of pay and status gained from the Higher Level Teaching Assistant (HLTA) standards. As part of the taught programme, students reviewed their role and its changes over a year. Students, from three cohorts, agreed to provide data from assignments in 2005–06, 2006–07 and 2007–08, on condition that only the two course tutors would have access and that the information would be used anonymously for illustrative purposes. Tutors thought that the TA role might be clarified over time, but this is difficult to identify because of the uniqueness of each context and the diverse responsibilities involved. However, there are general trends emerging. The introduction of the HLTA status and TA advisory job profiles (National Joint Council for Local Government Services, 2003) with associated pay guide meant that schools could establish different types of support. An example is class-cover to allow teachers preparation, planning and assessment time (PPA) and the carrying out of general administration functions.

Another university study module required students to reflect on their roles and highlight the tensions, in order to identify a topic for an Action Research Project. The year 2004–05 was a particularly difficult year when many students had the burden of extra duties. Some reported that they were teaching a full timetable, without preparation time or the appropriate level of pay. There was clear TA exploitation, as reported by the BBC News Channel (2005) from a survey of 3,688 UNISON members as detailed below:

- One-third of TAs worked up to four hours unpaid overtime each week.
- 72 per cent believed they were not fairly paid.
- Many were paid in term-time only on an hourly rate.

The government claimed that the workforce agreement expected TA pay to reflect training, skills and responsibilities but contractual arrangements were the responsibility of local agreements. The Unison Survey agreed with our knowledge of TA experience, as related by our students. Their roles were so diverse and within the same local authority standard pay scales, schools interpretation of these was very different. Some TAs are highly respected, valued members of the school workforce. Others are viewed as 'teacher-helpers', with duties such as photo-copying, despite a degree and HLTA status. Some found the workforce reform an opportunity to professionally develop and accept more responsibility, while others found themselves taken away from their classroom role into more administrative functions.

The fact that TAs have no national pay scale or role description means that across-country variation and a lack of parity exists. HLTA status does not guarantee a pay-rise and in 2004–05, several students reported remaining on Level 2 salary for most of their job, while paid Level 3 salary for cover supervision. Opportunities to work at Level 4 should follow HLTA status, but few exist. In some schools, a foundation degree qualification (equivalent to NVQ Level 5) was viewed less than HLTA status, despite its benefits to students' work within the school, in terms of deeper knowledge and understanding and wider skills. Overall, in 2005, there was widespread lack of understanding regarding suitable qualifications and expectations at each level.

Analysis of the TA role

Analysing reviews of student TA roles, in 2005–06, identified many additional responsibilities on job specifications, depending on the school and its needs e.g.

- Attending parents' meetings
- Medical training
- Marking pupils' work
- Training student teachers
- Implementing intervention strategies

- Assisting in the planning and development of IEPs
- Responsibility for keeping and monitoring attendance records
- Putting up displays
- Book-keeping
- Playground duty
- Out-of-school clubs
- Supervising detention
- PPA cover

Several of these emerged directly from the workforce remodelling agenda with emphasis on reducing the administrative burdens of teachers. There has been some specialization of TA roles. For example, some TAs have become the Attendance Officer for the school: telephoning parents, arranging taxis to transport children to school and working closely with the Educational Welfare Officer. Many TAs welcomed such changes as they gave an opportunity to use initiative, to accept responsibility for an aspect of school work, with greater autonomy. However, along with these advantages is greater accountability. TAs have become a valued part of the workforce, in many cases, but report an increase in workload and reduced preparation time, resulting in a loss of work–life balance. During 2005–06, several TAs had to renegotiate roles and although there was minimal change, some were still ill-prepared for their pupil, support function, because they were not invited to staff or team meetings, and were only told what to do as they walked through the classroom door. TAs, therefore, have to be expert at thinking on their feet.

Where there have been no improvements

Through the medium of students' drawings and writings, in October 2006, there were indications of no improvements in TA opportunities. For example, one student from a primary school drew a picture of herself filing documents with a display in the background. She wrote

> My new job requires me to complete a lot of filing, photocopying and laminating. I enjoy putting up displays but would like to introduce some of my own ideas instead of just being told what to do'.

This particular student had just gained her foundation degree, and was completing honours in *inclusive education*. She had previously been the TA, in the ICT base, supporting learners and teachers with her technical skills and her knowledge and understanding of teaching and learning. She was unhappy and unsettled in her new role, which did not take account of her experience and expertise. Another student viewed the change as an opportunity for growth and drew a flower growing taller than some trees. She wrote

> I am the flower growing (learning). The roots are me feeding from others, the children, colleagues and tutors. A flower needing sunlight and water is like me needing encouragement, support and education. At times, I can't see the wood for the tree.

The flower was a metaphor for her professional growth.

From 34 drawings, collected in October 2006, 13 show a clear picture of the diversity of tasks undertaken within TA roles and the tensions arising from these. A common image was a drawing of the TA, with several arms, each one doing a different job. Another popular metaphor was of a TA wearing many hats and having to move to different places. One student wrote that she was a 'Jack of all trades'.

> There are tensions between work, family and social life and I sometimes seem to be going around in circles. I am always very busy supporting a range of learners with different needs, different colleagues and parents. Sometimes the expectations are unclear leading to frustration. There is not enough time in the day and I would like better pay.

A further student likened herself to a Girl Guide, with the motto '*Be prepared*':

> I am very caring, smile all the time and adapt myself to different situations. My work is enjoyable but sometimes I feel myself being pulled in different directions and don't know which way to turn. I work hard, planning, preparing, delivering, assessing and reporting. I communicate with everyone effectively using a range of media. I sometimes provide staff training. The demands of my role can lead to overtiredness and poor eating habits but despite this, I am studying to improve my knowledge and understanding.

It became evident, in the latter part of 2006, that the changes set in place in 2005 were having a negative impact on work–life balance, with TAs feeling more pressured in their work than previously. A common issue raised was lack of time for planning with teachers. The TAs were often given specific responsibilities, perhaps with the aim of reducing the need for joint planning. For example, one TA became responsible for the 'Circle Time' activity to allow the teacher to do other things. Another TA became responsible for organizing and leading 'Golden Time' in school. In these roles, TAs might attend relevant training sessions and cascade this information to other staff.

Changes for the better in the period 2006–07

The greatest change for TAs was that of covering staff absences for illness or PPA time. Many students in 2005–06 had these responsibilities, often taking classes without guidance from teachers. However, students in 2006–07 reported that they usually worked with teachers on planning, and that more posts were advertised as Cover Supervisors, so that TAs were not pressured into undertaking this work. In fact, TAs from this cohort reported mainly positive changes, with more opportunities to plan collaboratively with teachers, and increased status within schools. Many more had contact with parents and other professionals than previously with a reduction in requirements to put up displays. Generally, administrative jobs had lower priority, with specific clerical and display posts now advertised.

More TAs became involved in pupil observation and assessment practices during 2006–07. They completed Foundation Stage profiles, made observations for the class teacher, supported the development of Individual Education Plans (IEPs), marked pupils work, kept records and provided reports to parents. Several became responsible for the health and safety within school. A number ran the intervention programmes within school and recognized the need to be up-to-date with knowledge of the latest legislation and guidance. Out-of-school clubs became popular again, with TAs accepting responsibility for a range of different types of provision, depending on their qualifications and experience. It seemed that once the initial reforms were established in 2005, schools had quickly begun to review and evaluate issues arising, and put into place more robust strategies for ensuring TAs had manageable and effective roles.

Key responsibilities emerging for TAs

The 2007–08 cohort responses show how many TAs now have key responsibilities within schools and that teachers are now working with a broader range of professionals to meet the needs of diverse pupils. Below, is a grid reflecting these responsibilities:

The TA roles and responsibilities for Kath

Roles	Responsibilities
Arrange and deliver effective learning support to students	Liaise with feeder schools Arrange for transition information to be forwarded Assess what support is needed and how this will be delivered effectively to the student. Organize loan of specialized equipment
Take part in interviews	Discuss needs of learner Complete D1 form Discuss previous needs of learner
Organize assessments	Liaise with exams officer Organize reader for tests Arrange dyslexia assessments Arrange exam concessions Arrange educational psychology reports

Kath, a further education TA, appears to have important responsibilities that focus on supporting pupils with specific learning needs. She leads the transition arrangements for pupils entering the college. Such arrangements used to be the responsibility of teaching staff, such as a the Year 12 Head or the Manager of Learning Support. Her job to complete D1 forms (disclosing information about the learner) used to be done by the Inclusion Manager, who also co-ordinated assessments for students with learning difficulties.

Lynn, a primary school TA, supports pupils who present challenging behaviours. This role would previously have been a teacher responsibility, requiring a strong understanding of children and their learning needs, together with the behaviour modification strategies required. She advises all staff, monitors behaviour, works closely with a range of other professionals and provides home tuition for excluded children. Therefore, she needs the skills to work with parents in their own homes. Her role is a specialist one, which can only enhance the provision for all pupils, by providing effectively for those who have difficulty in maintaining acceptable behaviour in school.

Jenny is a Learning Mentor, with specific responsibility for coordinating provision for English as an Additional Language (EAL), Social and Emotional Aspect of Learning (SEAL) and Child Protection. She is the link with the Behaviour Support Education Team and line manager to a range of TA and welfare staff. Jenny also has other roles, which include assisting with the school choir.

In my view, her responsibilities seem excessive for the salary she receives, but her job satisfaction is high and she is clearly valued in school. This acknowledgement of her knowledge and skills can only benefit the pupils concerned. Other students have commented on the demands created by specific initiatives. An example is 'Its Good to be Green', an environmental initiative that is proving time-consuming. It seems common to pass such responsibilities now to support staff.

The Learning environment

Several students have significant responsibilities for learning and the learning environment. For example, one student is responsible for putting up the displays in school. Although such tasks might reduce a teacher's workload, they must also diminish, to some extent, the impact of a display as a teaching resource, unless collaboration takes place. Others plan and deliver specific lessons or interventions. One student implements Art, Design and Technology across Key Stage 2 as part of her role to provide PPA time for teachers. The job goes beyond that expected of her Level (3) and could result in weaker provision in these subject areas. Alternatively, it might strengthen this by developing her specialist role and providing coordination and consistency throughout the Key Stage. There is a sense that lessons are planned and delivered, rather than taught and learned as Helen wrote:

> I have undertaken additional responsibility this year for planning and delivering learning to a group of 11 Year 5. I plan lessons using National Strategy linked material and deliver these to learners, monitoring and recording progress and providing feedback for the class teacher . . .
>
> I have also taken on additional responsibility for implementing and delivering 3 different intervention programmes to groups of children within Year 5 and Year 6 classes, again recording and monitoring pupil progress.

Helen also has a voluntary role, leading the school netball team in lunchtime and after school matches.

There is a view that if one delivers, supervises and monitors a learning plan or initiative that it will be effective. For example, Annie supervises 'Success-maker' lessons, guiding pupils through challenging questions. Since this scheme is designed to monitor individual pupil progression, without adult support, one might question Annie's role. Others teach the most recent phonic programme, introduced into schools to support the literacy. The danger is accepting its introduction without questioning validity and reliability, or modifying teaching approaches to suit requirements. Many new initiatives have little research to support their introduction on a national scale, yet teachers implement them because they believe they have to (and in some cases they do).

With reference to phonic teaching, I assume primary school staff understand the importance of both synthetic and analytic phonics, in enabling the mechanical sounding out of written words, while acknowledging the utility of 'whole word' and 'contextual cue' strategies that focus on building meaning. Readers need a range of ways to analyse and synthesize text. I am not suggesting that bought materials are unsatisfactory. Effectiveness depends on whether they are appropriately *taught* rather than *delivered*, and whether children *understand* beyond *receiving knowledge*. Some mathematics booster resources lead to solid mathematical understanding and prove their worth.

Review

Over the period 2005–08, evidence from students working as TAs suggests a shift from undifferentiated to differentiated roles as schools develop specialist teams to cope with diverse student populations. TAs are achieving a higher status and their self-esteem is boosted by becoming a knowledgeable, skilled workforce. Many TAs now have responsibility for specific aspects of school practice.

However, despite these improvements, which can only enhance pupil learning, there are concerns about the amount and nature of cover supervision now carried out by TAs and the level of subject knowledge this requires. Gibson and Patrick (2008) criticize the implementation of Additional Literacy Support by TAs, when it is delivered as a provided script. The question is whether this raises the quality of primary pedagogy. Boundaries between TA and teacher are now blurred and difficult to identify. The 2006 HLTA standards expect TAs to carry out traditional teacher activities, such as whole class teaching and briefing the supply teacher. An important point, made by Gibson and Patrick, is that TAs may have increased responsibility, but not necessarily the authority to engage in serious professional judgement about their pedagogy. Also, there are clear power imbalances between the teacher and TA workforces. Teachers are perceived as the pedagogical experts and so might respond negatively to TA suggestions for change. Teachers, who mentor TAs in training, have limited time to reflect with them on their experiences (Burgess and Mayes, 2007).

The teacher–TA relationship

Many TAs, in the student cohorts, acted as cover supervisors for PPA time and sickness. A significant number had to plan and prepare teaching materials. This required knowledge, skills and judgement beyond that expected of a cover supervisor at Level 3 on the TA scale. Whatever the situation, cover supervision should be temporary (DfEE, 2003), with pupils' best interested maintained, so that learning is effective. Where a Level 3 TA is planning and teaching lessons, in a subject in which they have received minimal training, one might question whether the school is fulfilling its obligations to pupils and exploiting its TAs. Those intending to become future teachers will generally enjoy the challenge and opportunity to gain whole-class experience. Raising the TA profile as part of the educational professional team should support improvements in pupil learning.

Groom and Rose (2005) highlight the need for involving TAs in whole school development to enhance their ability to provide effective support to primary pupils with social, emotional and behavioural difficulties (SEBP). In their research, conducted before 2005 and the statutory implementation of workforce remodelling, they identified the following key factors:

- Including the TA as a full member of staff
- Involving the TA in target setting, monitoring and rewards and sanctions
- Involving the TA in planning and reviewing
- Creating opportunities for TA training

- Involving the TA in a range of classroom activities
- Involving the TA in developing pupil self-esteem and social skills

(Groom and Rose, 2005, p. 28)

Over the period 2005–08, students suggested these key strategies were in place in many schools, creating an enabling environment, in which they could thrive as part of the professional workforce. Most are working in a situation where they could be described as teacher support and partial substitute or mobile paraprofessional (typified by the HLTA), as defined by Kerry (2005). Roles range from supporting the learning of individual pupils, marking work, cover supervision and supervised class teaching. However, the new HLTA standards (TDA, 2006) use the word *professional* rather than *paraprofessional*. This suggests that those with HLTA status should be considered part of the professional workforce that makes judgements about learning and teaching, rather than technicians that deliver and monitor the materials provided. McVitie (2005) concludes that all adults connected to school should have a professional regard for support staff, thus enabling confidence and self-esteem to develop. In 2008, it is likely that most schools consider their TAs as part of the professional workforce, in particular those working at Level 3 and above.

Clarifying the TA role

The role clarity of a TA is identified as important by McVitie (2005). Over the period of student submissions, 2005–08, there is evidence of a shift from undifferentiated to differentiated roles. In 2008, most students have clear job descriptions, engage in professional reviews and are accepted as a key part of the multi-professional, multi-agency workforce, supporting children and young people. In my experience, TAs have become more knowledgeable and more capable than some of their teaching colleagues, in supporting children with specific cognitive-linguistic conditions, such as Asperger syndrome, or with particular physical needs, like hearing impairment. It is TAs who have the small group and individual pupil time, in which to learn about individuals, and create relationships that are sometimes more difficult to achieve in the larger classroom group.

Groom (2006, p. 201) suggests that schools need to go beyond role definition to ensure effective team management and support through:

- valuing the work of the TA and recognizing their contribution;
- involving TAs as much as possible in planning and review;
- providing good channels of communication through regular meetings;
- providing professional development opportunities;
- providing opportunities for collaborative work and sharing of good practice.

Students from the 2007–08 cohort were involved in planning and review, attended regular meetings, received professional development and worked collaboratively with a range of colleagues. This practice is more evident now than it was in 2005, with students expressing great job satisfaction, despite their demanding roles. In 2006, a survey of HLTAs was conducted by the National Foundation for Educational Research (NFER) and reported by Wilson et al. (2007). This identified that HLTAs having the most job satisfaction were those with greater levels of responsibility, in full-time rather than part-time positions. Lower job satisfaction and increased stress arose through lack of planning time. These latter findings match comments, made by students, in the 2005–07 period when workloads for some TAs were unbalanced and schools were moving through a period of review and reorganization.

Until 2009, there were 50,000 schools in Britain with 300 Special Needs Co-ordinators (SENCOs) without teaching qualifications and this role undertaken by TAs. However, amendments to regulations (SI 2008/2945) set out that by 1 September 2009, the SENCO position must be held by someone having qualified teacher status. Cheminais (2005) described the complex roles of SENCOs as lead professionals with the ability to advocate for different audiences. Such views have led to this tightening of rules (SI 2009/1387), which demand that now all SENCOs must be appropriately qualified to provide a quality seal of approval in their schools.

The evidence, in this chapter, over a period of three academic years, supports the view that TA roles are developing more targeted support for a greater range of pupils. There are indications that this support is now more effective, or has the potential to be so, as TAs become better educated and trained, more highly qualified and respected as professionals. As school communities continue to change and become even more diverse, with the influx of new nationalities of different faiths and cultural norms, the workforce will continue to change. TA roles need to be as diverse and changing as the communities they serve, to meet the needs of all children.

Suggestions for classroom practice

> When there is more than one adult working in a classroom, it is essential that their roles are clarified and the teacher discusses the lesson/day programme with the Teaching Assistant (TA). Those TAs supporting one child need to ensure they are not hindering their contact and relationship with other class peers as this is a major learning opportunity for them. If pupils are too adult protected they lose out socially as well as academically.

Main points

- TAs are becoming an important workforce resource in dealing with the issues of diversity.
- Advanced education and training is leading to a higher status for them in school communities, with more specific responsibility and accountability.
- There is still concern that the TA role in cover supervision could lead to lower standards of pedagogy and this issue needs investigation and clarification.
- Most TAs report an improvement in job satisfaction as they are becoming more accepted within the school team. However, their levels of pay require attention, as they are considerably lower than those of teachers, even when carrying out similar roll.

Discussion point

Talk to a Teaching Assistant and make a note of their many different school responsibilities and evaluate whether they are adequately educated and trained for these.

References

BBC News Channel (2005) *Teaching Assistants 'exploited'*, Friday, 7 October.

Burgess, H. and Mayes, A. (2007) Supporting the professional development of teaching assistants: Classroom teachers' perspectives on their mentoring role. *Curriculum Journal*, 18(3) 389–407.

Cheminais, R. (2005) *Every Child Matters: A Role for SENCOs*, London: David Fulton.

Department for Education and Employment [DfEE] (2000) *Working with Teaching Assistants – A Good Practice Guide*, London: DfEE.

Gibson, H. and Patrick, H. (2008) Putting words in their mouths: The role of teaching assistants and the spectre of scripted pedagogy. *Journal of Early Childhood Literacy*, 8(1) 25–41.

Groom, B. (2006) Building relationships for learning: The developing role of the teaching assistant. *Support for Learning*, 21(4), 199–203.

Groom, B. and Rose, R. (2005) Supporting the inclusion of pupils with social, emotional and behavioural difficulties in the primary school: The role of teaching assistants. *Journal of Research in Special Educational Needs*, 5(1), 20–30.

Kerry, T. (2005) Towards a typology for conceptualising the roles of teaching assistants. *Educational Review*, 57(3), 373–384.

McVitie, E. (2005) The role of the teaching assistant: An investigative study to discover if teaching assistants are being used effectively to support children with special educational needs in mainstream schools. *Education*, 33(3), 26–31.

National Joint Council (2003) *School Support Staff – the Way Forward*, London: Employers Organisation for Local Government; available at http://www.lge.gov.uk/lge/aio/778006 (accessed on 17 December 2008).

National Joint Council (2003) *Guidance on Cover Supervision*, available at http://www.teachernet.gov.uk/_doc/5814/cover%20sup%20PDF.pdf (accessed on 17 December 2008).

Teacher Development Agency [TDA] Workforce Agreement Monitoring Group [WAMG] (2003) *Raising Standards and Tackling Workload: A National Agreement*; available online at http://www.socialpartnership.org/wamg_guidance.aspx (accessed on 17 December 2008).

The Times (1999) Mum's Army to start teaching, Monday, 24 May.

Wilson, R., Sharp, C., Shuayb, M., Kendall, L., Wade, P. and Easton, C. (2007) *Research into the Deployment and Impact of Support Staff Who Have Achieved HLTA Status*; available online at http://www.tda.gov.uk/upload/resources/pdf/n/nfer_hlta_report_07.pdf (accessed on 24 August 2007).

7 My diverse and very modern family

Julie Crofts

Overview

In this chapter I am very pleased to introduce my family to you and discuss some of the issues we have experienced in our life and work. For my husband and myself, this is our second marriage and amalgamating two diverse families has been exciting and exhilarating but also full of challenges. During our life together, we have had to face repeated redundancies at work and the big step of moving to China for work. The reason we have survived is that we have communicated our views and feelings openly to each other and found the support we needed within our family and social networks. Also, we have remained positive when things have been difficult and worked towards a solution that has always kept us moving forwards.

Introduction: Fiction and faction!

Once upon a time there lived a perfect golden haired man who married a perfect golden haired woman. They lived together happily in a picturesque village in the countryside. After a few years of wedded bliss, they had two perfectly formed, golden-haired children, a boy and a girl. The children grew up and went to University where they were surrounded with other perfectly formed, golden-haired children. They each met and fell in love with equally beautiful golden-haired others and both couples produced; yes you've guessed it . . . perfectly formed, golden-haired children who were doted on by their perfectly formed, golden-haired grandparents. Sounds like a fairy tale? That's because it is! Maybe a more realistic tale would be along the lines of . . .

Once upon a time there lived a perfect golden-haired man who married a perfect golden-haired woman. They lived together happily in a picturesque village in the countryside. After a few years of wedded bliss, they had two perfectly formed, golden-haired children, a boy and a girl. As the children were growing up, a stranger arrived in the village. When the children first set eyes on him, they screamed and hid away from the dark stranger. Everyone stared at the man who had long dark hair and piercing sapphire blue eyes that glinted when he smiled. The perfect golden-haired woman could not take her eyes off him and his dark, exotic looks. When he smiled at her, her whole body melted with evil desire and she could not resist him. Falling helplessly in love, she left her family and ran away with him to the city where they bore two exquisite olive-skinned children. Suddenly, her perfect life was no longer.

People openly stared at them in the street and other perfect golden-haired parents refused to let their perfectly formed, golden-haired children play with their dark, exotic children. There was always trouble at school for the children, wicked taunts and bullying. The perfect golden-haired woman became a recluse, as she felt increasingly daunted at the thought of leaving the house and visiting the supermarket only to be met with disapproving looks. Her first two children shunned her and her ex-husband looked at her in sheer disgust whenever she saw him. Her new partner suffered verbal abuse at his place of work. Then one day, desperate for food in the house, she slipped out to the nearby local shop. Upon entering, she gasped as she saw, standing behind the counter, a dark-skinned gentleman who spoke in a strange accent, different to that of her partner and certainly different to the perfect, golden-haired people of the city.

Many years on, she remembered those early days when her new family were so very different and smiled to herself as she thought of those around her now – an amazing numbers of different cultures, creeds, skin colours and accents – and marvelled at the way they had surreptitiously crept into and now become part of everyday life.

Sounds a little more real, doesn't it?

And so, diversity came about and slowly we began to accept other people into our country and our lives. Those considered 'foreigners' now became part of our existence.

The context

When asked to write a chapter for a book on diversity, I was bemused to discover that our immediate family (consisting of myself, my husband and my 19-year-old daughter) is considered to be a 'successful typical twenty-first century' unit! I began to think about that description and was amazed to realize that my family embraced a number of stereotypical modern day phenomena such as a second marriage, step-children, redundancy, racial issues and also living and working in another country.

Second marriage: The importance of effective communication

The first issue, second marriages. They include many facets and presently appears more commonplace than couples who stay married the first time round. These days, divorce is on the increase and the fall-out is broken homes, families and children who, in some cases, do not see both their biological parents on a regular basis. From my experience of working in a hospital psychology department, I know that this can have a major impact on children. Some referrals display a complex range of emotional and behavioural problems with serious communication and social interactional difficulties in their lives.

Speaking from experience again, a second marriage or partnership can be more successful simply because both partners have learned from first time round and try to make more effort with specific issues, the most important being *communication:* Talking – about everything – the greatest partnerships, whether these are business or personal, require good communication on both sides in order to be successful. One cannot stress enough how important it is to talk to one another and to discuss issues within the family, marriage or partnership. Family discussions, that include the children, will teach them that communication is key to any relationships they may have in the future. Partners should talk about the house, financial matters and, hardest of all, the things that annoy us about each other! Key pointers are:

- *Timing* – There is always a right (and wrong) time to bring certain matters up!
- *Arguments:* Try not to go to bed on an argument – one partner should 'give in' and speak or at least kiss the other goodnight as long as it is not always the same person!
- *Negotiation:* There is a definite skill in putting your point forward without losing your temper and without sounding accusing. In negotiation skill training, one is taught to talk about how you feel. If you are talking about your own personal feelings, no one can argue with that and it is more about how the other person made you feel rather than making accusations.
- *Sulking:* Don't sulk – this rarely ever achieves anything.

Obviously, you can only do all this if you consider your second relationship to be better than the first and worth trying harder for! Or maybe, we just work at it because we do not want a second relationship to fail and go through the misery and stress again that a break-up brings. In many cases, a second marriage or partnership can be made even more difficult by other issues running alongside such as your partner's children, ex-wives or husbands and relatives. My step-children are considerably older than my daughter and do not live with us so building a new family network that is scattered takes time and patience.

The new relationship can be hard, especially if the 'ex' is still alone and there are children from this relationship. Depending on the age and sex of the children, there are a number of issues that can arise. Girls can sometimes be jealous of 'Daddy's new wife or partner'. Generally, boys are not as emotional and tend to accept a new regime better. If one partner has not had children before it can certainly be a very different way of life to get used to and embrace, especially if the previous one lays down hard and fast rules such as access to the children, time limits and sometimes unreasonable dictates to follow. It can take compromise and sensitivity to make things work with minimum hardship and in a way that least affects the children. When a couple split, friends and relatives will sometimes take sides and many women report that some 'so-called friends' stop inviting them to social occasions, simply because they do not want a single female around.

It takes an enormous amount of patience and give and take when dealing with children who have experienced mum and dad going their separate ways. In second marriages, there may be step-children who need to be handled with 'kid gloves' in order to show there is no favouritism or bias compared with one's own offspring. In my experience I was quite fortunate as my daughter's real father had decided he wanted no more involvement with her, which, at the time, was extremely hard to cope with. Luckily I had a great family who supported me through the hard years but when I met my second husband it made things much less complicated. My daughter was four years old when I met my new husband, so he is the only father figure she has ever really known. From my point of view, although it was tough in the early years without financial support, it also meant that I did not have to share my daughter with anyone every other weekend or at holiday time, something I would have found extremely upsetting and difficult. Obviously, when a child has been used to seeing his or her father, then arrangements have to be made so that both parties have regular contact. Later on, when my second husband was offered a contract in China, we needed no one's permission to go as all we had to do was to make our own decisions.

Mixed marriages and bi-cultural children

Another issue that requires great skill in managing is the growing number of mixed marriages or relationships. My daughter is a beautiful, dark-skinned girl of mixed race. I grew up with children from a range of races and backgrounds as my parents fostered them for the Dr Barnado's charity and they stayed with us on a short- or long-term basis. My parents instilled into us that we were all the same, despite different skin colours, and they taught us to be positive about life and whatever it threw at us. It is unsurprising that I grew up to have no racial prejudices and have many friends from all walks of life and backgrounds.

I was determined to bring up my daughter with the same values and ethics and she has grown up to be a friendly and personable human being of whom I am very proud. When she was five years old, I moved to the village where we still live. On visiting the local primary school, I was somewhat dismayed to find that there were no children with coloured skin attending. The headmistress was a lovely lady and she promised me that there would be no problems for my daughter. I have to say that I did not share her confidence at the time, but I am very happy and relieved to say that she was right. Fifteen years ago, the local school was just beginning to embrace all cultures and creeds and taught the pupils about different races and their varying ways. When I speak to people who have seen my daughter grow up, they tell me that it was mainly due to her that no one saw her as being different, because she did not feel any different to them and signal this to others. She was one of the most popular children at school with a lovely, caring attitude about most things.

Facing redundancy

Redundancy is another issue that my husband and I have faced. We have both been made redundant twice but, thankfully, found work again fairly quickly. Again, the situation requires flexibility and a range of skills at one's disposal. I have had to diversify and adapt to different work situations. My husband has worked in logistics for most of his life and found it particularly difficult to adapt when he took a job in the computer industry. He noted on one occasion, after a board meeting, that 'it was almost like having to learn a foreign language', getting used to all the technical jargon. In my role as a personal assistant/secretary, I have worked as a 'temp' for a few years now and constantly must adapt to whatever industry I am asked to work in. The job is mainly the same but the language (or jargon) is very different, which hampers communication and relationships.

When hit by redundancy, one has to draw on personal strengths and, whilst 'tightening the belt', try to remain positive and upbeat about the situation. A very real danger is to feel alienated and unwanted. My father suffered a major stroke not long after he was made redundant at 62 years of age. One of his regular comments was that he had been 'thrown on the tip, of no use to anyone'. Sadly, his usual cheery and positive outlook on life deserted him and he went into a decline and suffered an early death. When you have seen a person you love dearly, deteriorate so rapidly, partly because of the cards that life has dealt them, it makes you more determined to be strong and not go the same way. When you are knocked down by circumstance it is whether you can pick yourself up and go forward again that really matters.

It can be very difficult to be optimistic in a situation where you have been crushed as your confidence takes a large knock and the very thought of starting to look for another job can be quite daunting. It takes courage to go through the rigmarole of applying for jobs, attending interviews and being turned down time after time. Fortunately these days, there is more help available with updating CVs, interview skills and all the issues that are involved in finding a new position.

Coping with life in another culture

As a family, our greatest challenge to date has been, without a doubt, our move to China. Following my husband's redundancy a second time, he took the wise move of registering with an executive agency that trained people in the best ways to find a new job. One of the main issues they concentrated on was communicating and networking. This entailed making a list of all the people from your past working and social life and then contacting them all. This was not to specifically ask for a job but just to let them know of your situation and to stay in touch. We all find it quite difficult actually admitting to people that we do not have work, so our first reaction is to hide away to avoid others knowing that we are struggling. Sometimes the great British 'stiff upper lip' can work against us. In some situations, it can be a case of 'right time, right place'. If your CV lands on someone's desk or you happen to contact them just as they are looking for a person with your skills, then the process is made easier, but it can be simply a numbers game and about putting yourself forward to others confidently while communicating your assets effectively. Bizarrely, the one person who offered my husband the opportunity of a life-time was the one he had least wanted to contact.

I can still remember the feelings of trepidation, mixed with excitement that I had when my husband telephoned me at work to tell me he had been offered a one-month consultancy contract in China.

'China?' I asked, surprised and horrified at the same time. 'It couldn't be any farther away! Couldn't you be offered a job somewhere civilized like Spain or France?'

That conversation took place on the Monday and, much to my amazement, the following Saturday, I found myself driving Robert to Heathrow Airport for him to board the Virgin flight (business class of course) to Shanghai. The next few weeks were a whirlwind as this very different and exciting way of life was thrust upon us.

The one-month contract turned into seven weeks and before long it became apparent that the temporary assignment was about to turn into much more.

Robert would phone me with exciting tales about this amazing city and how much he was enjoying the whole experience. He went to banquets and ate strange and exotic foods such as eel, turtle and chicken feet. I had to get used to him phoning me around three o' clock in the afternoon to say goodnight, because of the eight-hour time difference. He was living in luxury on the 28th floor of the Hilton Hotel and at weekends, he spent the little spare time he had, walking around this very busy and exhilarating city, which is home to around 20 million people. Just a little different to the tiny village in Northamptonshire where we lived.

In January 2004, my husband was offered a two-year contract in Shanghai. He accepted the job in March and in July of that year, my daughter Georgie and I joined him out there. Georgie was 14 at the time and was none too pleased at the prospect of living in China and leaving behind all her friends. Despite her protests and after much soul-searching and many lists of 'for and against', we decided that this was such an exciting opportunity and we would regret it forever if we turned the offer down. Of course, financially it was one of the best things we ever did too.

A new life in China

It took us just a matter of weeks to settle into our fascinating new life. We lived in a fabulous, American-style villa situated on a large housing complex called 'The Emerald'. This was complete with guards on the gates, who saluted every time you drove in or out, making you feel a little like royalty. The complex was on the south side of the Huang Pu river, in Pudong, and about thirty-minute drive from the centre of Shanghai. We chose the complex for its location near the British International School that Georgie would attend. It was a little like living at 'Centre Parcs', the famous British holiday camps. There were indoor and outdoor swimming pools, a gym, tennis courts, football field, driving range and restaurant that were all set in beautifully designed gardens. We had a lovely chauffer called Michael, who spoke quite good English and whom we often took shopping with us to negotiate much better prices than we would ever get. I had a part-time maid who did all the cleaning, washing and ironing. She was known as the Ayi. This word, literally translated, means Aunty as an Ayi would traditionally look after the children and do all the cooking for the family.

Once Georgie had started school, she made many friends and was soon speaking in an American accent. She loved visiting 'The Mall' and going to her friends' houses for sleepovers and movie nights after eating out at restaurants or diners.

Initially, I was a little worried about how I would fill my days once Robert had left for work and Georgie had gone to school, so in the first week I joined an Ex-Pat association called 'Brits Abroad'. Soon, my days began to fill up with lunches, coffee mornings and social get-togethers as I met more and more ladies in the same situation. Suddenly, I had many friends and before long was a woman who lunches.

I learned to play Mah Jong (a Chinese tile game) and every Monday I would meet with a group of women and play this game from around 11 am to 4 pm (breaking for lunch of course!) Our group consisted of two from Brazil and Singapore, one from Malaysia, South Africa and Japan and me, the only 'Brit' abroad! We had amazing days and the memories will last forever. We chatted throughout the games and learned about each other's cultures and traditions. I can remember getting together on the 5th of November and telling them about our 'Bonfire Night'. They were somewhat bemused by this event and I have to admit that, trying to explain it did lose a little in translation and made it sound very strange. Another time, we were talking about our children growing up and starting work. The Eastern ladies were horrified to hear that we took money off our children for 'board and lodgings'.

I was very soon a devoted member of 'Brits Abroad' and decided to join the committee, helping to arrange lunches, outings, cultural visits and social evenings. One day, we organized an outing to a traditional Chinese tearoom. Upon arrival, it was evident that things were not going according to our plan as the tea was not ready. This is a long and intense process and the Chinese would not serve the tea until they were entirely happy that it was perfect. We chatted amongst ourselves for a while but soon became bored with the very long wait. Also, the staff, realizing that they were losing money as the tea was taking so long, suddenly tried to put the price up. A few of us then decided that we had been in the tearoom long enough and started to prepare to leave, only to find the entrance blocked and two Chinese girls demanding that we still pay. The majority of us initially refused, until we discovered that the girls had phoned the police. We were all aghast at this but the thought of spending the afternoon in a Chinese police station did not appeal so we paid and left. We laughed afterwards at the thought of our husbands asking what we had done that day and our reply: 'Oh, not much really, I just got arrested and thrown into jail!'

Learning to communicate and cope in another language and culture

I also started to learn Mandarin and had weekly lessons at home with a very young, sweet Chinese girl called Amy. Most of the Chinese people you meet have an English name as well as their Chinese one. I found the language quite easy to learn as there does not seem to be any tenses or male and female gender words as in French or Spanish. The difficult thing to get the hang of is the voice tone, which according to its pitch level indicates different meanings. These tones were difficult to master, but before long, I was able to order food and barter for better prices at the markets. The Chinese loved it when you tried to speak the language and giggled at the 'Waiguorens' (Westerners – literally translated as 'big noses'!) and their strange pronunciations.

At the gym on the complex, I took yoga lessons with a delightful young girl named Cherry who also taught Georgie, Kung Fu. Georgie was very busy too, not only with her new friends who were Canadian, Dutch and Belgian, but also learning to play the piano. Before long, she was part of 'The Emerald' football team, which mainly consisted of 'lads and dads'. Georgie, who has always been a bit of a tomboy, was allowed to play because she was so good. She also captained the girl's football team at school, leading it to victory for two consecutive years. Georgie was allowed to play in the boy's team, too, possibly because she was better than most of the boys that played. Luckily for them, the rules that apply in England about girls and boys not playing together, once they are over a certain age, did not pass muster in Shanghai.

Georgie took her GCSE exams in Shanghai and her time there was rather a roller coaster with many ups and downs over the two years. This was mainly due to the senior part of the school being in its first year when she joined. There were three headmasters in the time and many of the teachers were on world travels and only signed up for short contracts, resulting in many changes. Towards the end, we paid for Georgie to have extra private lessons in Maths and English and fortunately, she did really well and left with 6 GCSE's meeting the requirements for her to enrol at Moulton College, Northampton, on a two-year Sports Diploma course when we returned to England.

My husband's job, communication and relationships

Robert's job was extremely busy and took him all over China so he was often away. He worked long hours but found the role extremely challenging and interesting. When he was home, which thankfully was most weekends, we met with other ex-pat couples and often ate out, with 3,000 restaurants to pick from. Weekends were a complete break with no D-I-Y or gardening – as it was all done for us by the army of Chinese staff who smilingly swarmed around 'The Emerald', keeping everything in good working order and the place spotless. Robert obviously mixed with the Chinese more than I did as the majority of his staff were Chinese and he dealt with Asian business people on a day-to-day basis. This is what he has said about his experiences:

My only experience of Asia had been a stop over in Singapore airport on the way to Sydney. I had spent my working life in the UK and mainland Europe in logistics' businesses, mainly with TNT. I arrived in Shanghai, the world's fastest growing economy in early November 2003, into a very different world from the one I had left. It was warm for a start, very impressive, busy, well kept and graffiti free. Numerous expressways, intersections and elevated roads passed through hundreds of skyscrapers gleaming in the dim midday sunshine. A very modern city in every way and one we would come to know and love over the next 3 years.

Relationships are important in any walk of life and they count even more in China. The Chinese concept of 'Guanxi' is about networking connections. It is a sort of tit-for-tat arrangement where they or you can be counted on to do favours and bend the rules, etc. It is a reciprocal obligation with foreigners expected to understand Guanxi and behave according to its rules. The currency of Guanxi is normally favours, not cash. It is surprising just how strong and deep these life-long relationships are so they should never be underestimated. I once had a business meeting with a Managing Director who was accompanied by the City Mayor.

In business, you are always greeted warmly, particularly when you are from an internationally renowned Fortune 500 company. In my experience of meeting Chinese business people in 30 cities all over China, very few speak or understand English so having an interpreter you know and trust is vital. Having one from your own business, who has an understanding of your activity and any technical terms, is preferable. In meetings, body language and expressions change very little as the Chinese never seem to hesitate or be under pressure when answering questions. Completing the deal and getting to know your Chinese customer or supplier is always important. Over dinner, relaxing in a pleasant restaurant is the expected and best way.

In China 'face' (self-respect, prestige, reputation and honour) is everything. I will always remember one of my first meetings in Shanghai. My Chinese colleague and I were met by the Chairman and the board of directors. During the meeting I picked up a bottle of water and attempted unsuccessfully to remove the cap. I tried to be very casual about it but to my alarm a young lady walked round to me and picked up the bottle. She attempted to unscrew the cap without success at which point all those present chuckled. I have to say I would have been somewhat embarrassed if she had succeeded. Thinking back, perhaps she only did it to save my face. I have also experienced situations where my staff did not inform me about certain issues to save their face. They do not want to give you bad news as they feel they have failed and let you down. This does not mean they had done nothing to put things right. In fact it was very much the opposite as they always tried to solve the problem.

It took me a while to realize that the word 'no' does not exist in Chinese. Conversely, 'yes' does not always mean there is an agreement to do what has been discussed or that it is even understood. This may just be acknowledging they have heard. So you soon learn to avoid asking *closed* questions. I always took detailed notes of all conversations and followed through to check everything was understood or what had been agreed actually happened. Note-taking is a good habit and the Chinese are very expert at it.

China is a complex and challenging environment from all business points of view. This particularly goes for the legal system and local regulations. Central laws are adopted in all the 34 Chinese provinces, administered by Beijing, but how they are interpreted by local officials can be very different. There is always a solution to the problems that arise but it can take time. You may well get varying views from different professional people and these have to be worked through carefully.

Working and living in China surpassed our expectations and fundamentally changed our perceptions of this vast place. You can literally see the environment changing before you and feel the energy of a country rapidly developing in the twenty-first century. In China a city is built in the time it takes to approve a simple road project in England. You have to admire the ability to change and the plans in place to support the future. A substantial amount has already been invested in the infrastructure, be it air, road or rail and much more is planned. China has had a modern-day industrial revolution, benefiting from all the latest technology while having the advantage of a large and low-cost labour force. Being an 'Expat', you can argue that you only see the best parts and hear through the media only the good things. I have been lucky enough to get a more balanced view and have seen many extremes and conditions. One thing that did surprise me was the absolute faith Chinese people have in their local and central government. We are rather more cynical about our rulers in the UK. The Chinese are fascinated by westerners so make the first move and you could find it very rewarding.

Moving back to England

Sadly, our two-year contract was almost at an end. In September 2005, Robert was told that his assignment was not going to be extended: it made financial sense to put in a local manager to run the operation that he had set up.

Meantime, I continued with my hectic life, possibly cramming in even more and hoping against hope that something would change and we could stay. In March 2006, I joined a Writers' group. To cut a long story short, we decided to produce a fictional book based on Ex-pat life. When the family returned to England in August 2006, I continued to send in my bits of the tale by e-mail and in November returned to meet up with the group again. We each put in £400 and found a Chinese company to publish our book. The result is *Shanghai Cocktail* (Bonell et al., 2007) of which we are all extremely proud. The launch was tremendous fun and the reaction to the book has been exciting. To date, we have sold over half of the 1,000 books published and have made our money back, with the profits going to two Chinese charities. The book proceeds have paid for life-saving operations for at least two Chinese children. This is lovely legacy for my time in China and a big 'thank-you' for such a wonderful experience there.

Many 'ex-pat' friends warned us that it was not the going out to China that we would find difficult, but the coming back and they were certainly right. Settling back into English life after such an amazing experience proved hard but now, two years on, we are enjoying different things, such as seeing friends and family again with trips to Europe, green fields and the joy of good English food. We often reminisce and recall brilliant times and I still shed the occasional tear but the memories stay strong with us forever. I think we can safely say that we have fully embraced diversity with gusto within the tangled web that our rich and blessed lives have woven.

Suggestions for classroom practice

All the pupils in a class will have complex backgrounds because of the nature of today's life with both parents working often away from home. Children can have a very unsettled upbringing and this makes them less able to concentrate on their learning. Again, valuing personal development with groups such as the Communication Opportunity Group Strategy (Sage, 2000) will help children to work through their difficulties and realize that they are not the only ones in the class facing problems in their lives.

Main points

- Today, the straightforward, traditional family of 2 parents and their children has been supplanted by many, different, complex, living formats.
- Coping with today's diverse family situations demands effective communication and relationships to survive the challenges.
- In a global society, families may have to move for short spells to countries on the other side of the world and although there are logistic difficulties the insights and experiences that this presents is life enriching.
- Being a good communicator develops the confidence to survive redundancy, relationship and family break-ups and make new contacts.
- Flexibility, a wide skill-base, a willingness to learn and a positive attitude to life are the tools for survival.

Discussion point

Can you come up with a list of necessities for surviving life within a diverse society?

References

Bonell, C., Clarke, T., Crofts, J., Hinde, L., Jones, A., Stanbridge, L. and Thomson, D. (2007) *Shanghai Cocktail*, Shanghai: Lucinda Lee Austin.

Sage, R. (2000) *The Communication Opportunity Group Scheme*, Leicester: The University of Leicester.

Issues for living and learning in another culture: Discussions with Miki Nishimori from Japan

8

Rosemary Sage

Overview

To most Westerners, Japan is an exotic and mysterious land of geisha girls, tea ceremonies, temple gardens, sumo wrestlers and martial arts. It is a world where antiquity sits comfortably with modernity. This is curious to Britons as we have been busy tossing out tradition and replacing formality with informality. Why is this? For a start, there is a vast difference regarding history, geography, religion and culture that influences how we think and live. It is obvious that when people from different national backgrounds meet there are going to be all kinds of communication and relationship problems. With the help of Miki Nishimori, from Japan, who has studied and worked in Britain, we examine some of these cross-cultural issues.

Culture

What is culture and how do we define it? Culture is the bundle of beliefs, values and modes of operating which typify a community and is exposed, expressed and extended in various codes and practices. Such a community may be a nation, such as Britain and Japan, or a bigger grouping as in Western versus Eastern culture. Since religion has been important in determining our beliefs and behaviour, it is also possible to refer to Christian, Jewish, Muslim, Hindu and Buddhist cultures amongst others. The appendices 1–4 gives further detail of some of these major religions.

In Britain, we apply the word 'culture' in other ways, to define 'popular culture', referring to art and entertainment such as pop and rock music, television soap operas, paperback novels, tabloid newspapers and fashion etc. There is also 'high culture', prized by the educated, which since Victorian times has involved the pursuit of 'spiritual perfection' through serious music, art and literature.

Today, resulting from post-war Commonwealth immigration, we are truly a multicultural society. However, one intriguing but painful social process has been the way settler groups, with their own cultures, have struggled to relate to the dominant British one. Early attempts by black people to be integrated into British culture received a hostile reaction from the white majority, although the Notting Hill Caribbean Carnival, marking the last Bank holiday of the year, is now a valued UK tradition. Nevertheless, Jews, Sikhs, Muslims, Hindus, Buddhists, Greek Orthodox Christians and others maintain their respective religions, because they are central to their communities, identities and preservation of customs and ceremonies. Even if these various groups can all speak English, difficulties occur as a result of the different cultural assumptions that speakers make. An example of cross-cultural comparisons between British and Japanese cultural features is shown below:

Cultural feature	British	Japanese
Greeting	Shake hands and kiss cheeks if on familiar terms	Bow from the waist – the degree depending on relationship, role and context. It is customary to take a present on a visit and in a work context to present your card.
Entering a house	Wipe shoes on a door mat	Remove shoes and don slippers
Taking a bath	Fill body-length bath with hot water and wash *in* the bath	Fill a waist-high tub. Soap and rinse *beside* the bath and soak in a clean tub
Gardens	Flower-beds, shrubs, trees and lawns, many in formal geometric design	Trees (the flowering cherry is famous) shrubs, rocks and pools that imitate natural landscapes. Few coloured flowers.
Religion	Christianity	Shintoism and/or Buddhism
Writing	26 characters of the Roman alphabet	50,000 ideograms *(kanji)* adopted from China
Diet	Bread, meat, cheese, cooked fish and vegetables	Rice, noodles, raw fish, cooked meat and sushi

Try this grid with other cultures to start an interesting discussion at school, college or work regarding cultural differences and their influences on us.

Discussions with Miki Nishimori from Japan

Miki Nishimori is a lecturer in Early Education, initially at the Women's University, Nara and now at Otani University, Kyoto. She is the research co-ordinator, in Japan, of the Dialogue, Innovation, Achievement and Learning Project (DIAL), a UK–Japan initiative to prepare citizens for the twenty-first century. I have been visiting Japan since 2004, with colleagues, Professor Jennifer Rogers and Research Associate, Stasia Cwenar, in order to learn about their system of education. This has been consistently successful in producing well-educated citizens, as rated by international league tables, such as TIMMS (Gonzales et al., 2008).

Miki, as the overseas co-ordinator at her University, has visited many parts of the world and can be regarded as truly international. She studied for her Masters in Education at the University of Cambridge and has had close contacts with the Shetland Isles, off the coast of Scotland, organizing Japanese student projects, in connection with the Learning School on the Global Classroom Partnership. She is particularly interested in motivation and has completed qualitative and quantitative studies, by following students over a school day. Miki has observed that the Japanese system of education, which values both personal and academic development, closely mirrors that of the Czech Republic as both value personal development and freedom to explore and express. The Japanese are taking links with Britain seriously now that their Ministry of Education has decreed that English studies are to be given prominence in the curriculum, as the recognized international language. Student teachers, therefore, are encouraged to take part of their education and training in English speaking countries, such as the United Kingdom or United States.

Language and culture

One of my great surprises, when visiting Japan, is that although their speech has fewer sounds than most languages, it has a system of writing than is more complex than anywhere else on earth. This is surprising, in a nation with almost 100 percent literacy. Miki has said that historically the Japanese lacked their own script, but waves of Korean and Chinese monks, carrying Buddhist philosophy to Japan during the 4–7th centuries, brought with them ideograms (*Kanjii*). These were adopted and adapted by the Japanese, to indicate grammatical inflections that were needed for their own language (*Kana*). Chinese is a monosyllabic language, relying on word order rather than inflections, to convey meaning. Japanese is exactly opposite, highly inflected with numerous endings and grammatical particles, to indicate the relationship between words and make meaning possible. It is similar to Korean and Mongolian.

Japan's post-war Ministry of Education selected 1,850 Kanjii (from the 50,000 available) for general use. This list has been revised several times, but the average college graduate has to be able to read over 3,000 characters. St Francis Xavier, a sixteenth century Jesuit missionary, regarded the Japanese language as invented by the devil to frustrate, although he rated the people as the best race yet discovered, because they are sociable, communicate well, value honour and are usually good to themselves and others. It is a culture that many have admired.

Consider how pronunciation has to change to say the English word 'two' according to context: 2, 12, 20, 1/2 and 2nd. Multiply this by 2,000, adding the complexity necessary to differentiate many times that number and you have some idea of what Japanese children are required to learn between first and ninth grade (length of time in statutory schooling). Nevertheless, they are enthusiastic readers and each household takes, on average, two daily newspapers. Miki has suggested that academics have expressed the view that the adoption of Chinese written symbols has been unfortunate in the country's history. However, researchers at Nara told us that children grasp meanings through Kanjii with greater speed and comprehension than they do through a system of phonetics. Some of the university staff, such as Professor Hidenori Sugimine, have had links with UK schools for over 40 years and so able to make such direct comparisons. The following information illuminates this assertion. Take a look at these Japanese words and their English equivalents:

Buu- buu – oink-oink; Wan-wan – bow-wow; guu-guu – snoring; pika-pika – flashing

Japanese is full of similar words and they make descriptions memorable and real. They fall into more or less two word groups: *giseigo*, describing sounds and *gitaigo*, expressing quality or manner. Unlike English counterparts such as verbs, nouns or adverbs, Japanese onomatopoeic words function as adverbs. Insofar as language is a direct indicator of cultural traits, Japanese's large glossary of onomatopoeic expressions for sounds of birds, insects, animals and phenomena like falling rain or snow show people's particular interest and sensitivity to natural things. For example, 'rain' can be described in Japanese as *potsun-potsun* (a drop here, a drop there), a *potsu-potsu* (a few drops here, a few drops there), a *shito-shito* (a steady, gentle drizzle) or *zaa-zaa* (raining cats and dogs) to mention just a few possibilities.

Words of this sort, relating to the sense of *touch*, are more numerous than those of *taste* and *smell*. This brings to mind a comment, by Miki, that the Japanese are a very tactile race (*Shokkaku minzoku*) in connection with a discussion on the difference between English and Japanese teachers, on one of the DIAL studies: Why do Japanese Children perform better than British ones? (Sage et al., 2006). The communication and emotional styles of teachers, in both countries, are very different as observed in this study. The Japanese referred to these as 'dry' or 'wet' ways of interacting (*dorai* and *uetto*). A 'dry' manner is rational, logical and unemotional whereas a *'wet'* one is personal, emotional and interpersonally complex, with much tactile communication. For example, in the number tasks completed by 130 four-year-olds, when children had to represent the number of different sets of cubes, all Japanese children did this with both word and action (two fingers held up) whereas none of the English cohort used any sort of gesture to accompany words.

Much of what we saw, in Japan, was of the 'wet' variety, with school activities sparking the interest of children, gripping them emotionally and involving them intimately with others. We loved the perfume-making factory, created by a group of three-year-olds, demonstrating effective communication, cooperation and problem solving in a fun way. By comparison UK practice appeared 'drier'. Teachers showed greater reserve and control, with children inclined to more lonely and isolated pursuits, toiling away at abstract tasks and worksheets. In Japan, learning was essentially an emotional enterprise in which all children were regularly encouraged to tell personal stories about things and events in their lives. By narrating their activities to others thinking, communication and judgment are developed. Communication and relationships precede the study of traditional subjects, as Japanese understand that speaking and sharing ideas in a formal way with others, is the necessary step into literacy and numeracy and the way in which to learn effectively.

Another task, in the DIAL study, referred to above, was to retell a story in order to evaluate *narrative thinking and structure* across the two cultures. Japanese children completed this with more awareness of the organization of ideas than did those from the UK. This is because they are taught a succinct three-part scheme, resembling the Japanese poetry form *haiku*, as the way to organize ideas. In this structure, the narrative omits information that the audience is judged to be able to infer, consistent with the Japanese value for empathy and collaboration (Minami and McCabe, 1995, 1996). Mothers and teachers support children to narrate everyday events, in this format, and encourage them to think what is in other peoples' minds, in order to 'read' what the meaning is behind words. The English, in contrast, produce narratives that are more descriptive of settings and emotions. Such different formats may contribute to habits of thought and how one examines evidence to support a claim or specifies ideas to oneself and others. An example is the research report format, encompassing the structure of thought and communication known as 'the scientific method'. Information is cast in ways that fit with a culturally recognized and valued structure so others can grasp it.

These examples provide some of the reasons for Japan's success. The Japanese are keen on tradition and formality, which is reflected in their speaking and writing. They value talk in a different way to us, promoting it continually in schools as fundamental to learning in contrast to our view that it is important but not essential. We pursue literacy and numeracy with children who do not have the thinking and articulacy to support secondary modes of expression and this would be unthinkable to Japanese teachers.

Miki feels her studies in England were not a problem to her. Having wrestled to gain command of the Japanese language, English did not seem intimidating or daunting and although she only had a 'school-girl' level when she started her postgraduate studies in Cambridge, she soon acquired the necessary formal literacy for completing assignments. Although language was not an issue, lifestyle provided more of a problem as explained below.

Lifestyle and culture

For those living, studying or working abroad there is a mixture of the frustrations and stimulations of a different environment. The Japanese live in a privileged world. By all the usual indices – infant mortality, malnutrition, child abuse, family stability, drug abuse, poverty – the people of Japan are very fortunate, even compared with other advanced, industrialized nations (Shwalb, 1993). Miki was surprised by some of the students, encountered in cities like Leicester, where there is a strong under-class of the indigenous white population, with a history of unemployment going back four or more generations. In a country, such as Japan, with consistent high employment, this situation is unsettling. Japan is a very disciplined society and the liberal and often loose behaviour of the English, both at work and play, is sometimes quite shocking, such as students sleeping and having sex together and going out to pubs with the goal of 'getting plastered'. This is neither decent nor desirable to the Japanese, who prize moral perfectionism beyond the limitations that are posed by general conceptions of moral or religious education.

The Japanese value for communication and relationships

The Japanese devote great attention to social, ethical and personal development of people and have escaped the pendulum swing between this and academic rigour that has blighted our system. Their practices build personal commitment to responsible behaviour, rather than reliance on rewards and punishments. In schools, elected monitors take responsibility for class leadership and group behaviour, with pupils taking care of their environment, cleaning their school and serving meals etc. Therefore, they enter higher education from a system that has focused on long-term internalization of values and the creation of committed, responsible learners, rather than on immediate compliance for the next test scores as we do in Britain. Close, communicative, supportive human relationships are not just useful but essential to ethical and social development and to the onerous task of rigorous learning in Japan.

Miki and her colleagues speak frequently of the influence of John Dewey on their child rearing practices. Dewey is an American philosopher, emphasizing moral perfectionism and education. His idea of the art of communication is a good starting point in considering how to create an environment for mutual perfection. In *Democracy and Education* (1916, p. 7), he presents the view that communication is the condition of growth and says that:

> Communication insures participation in common understanding.

He goes on to suggest that consensus demands effective communication, which is not simply a matter of skill or means, but the art of creating a democratic community. Friendship and relationships are the condition for this and conversation involves more than the understanding of the other as an object of knowledge or framing the other in one's own perspective. Rather it is a matter of mutual learning, by being attentive to the other. Openness to the difference of others means the reception of their lives as a part of one's own structure of thought.

While Dewey's art of communication and conversation can provide teachers and students with a key to achieving education for global understanding within the classroom, a challenge remains. Dewey identifies a need for breaking down barriers of class, race and national territory, which keeps man from perceiving the impact of their activity. How is it possible to break down inflexible thinking and open one's eyes and ears to the faces and voices of different others? This involves the art of translation, the art of word and world making and the transformation of the self and its relationship with the world (Emerson, 1990).

Emerson's perfectionist education requires translation more broadly than the experience of self-transcendence. As a mediator between two parties, whose worlds are mutually alien, the 'translator' needs to 'travel' from one place to another and then back again. In search of shared areas of language and culture, Emerson redefines the indefinite boundary of one language in the light of another. The 'translator' must have the courage to persevere in the face of uncertainty, searching for a common focus through which both parties in the dialogue can transform their mutual identities. It is, therefore, through the mode of sharing and learning that common ground may be found within diversity. This is exactly our experience of the DIAL projects, where students and teachers have come together from two very different cultures, in order to find a common focus in education, so narrowing the initial differences that exist between us in the way we think and conduct our learning and living.

Different voices invite us to start again from a lack of common ground by reminding us of the impossibility of full articulation, understanding and translation between us. Those, like Miki, who experience studying and living abroad, undergo this sense of imperfect translation between two cultures: of crossing distances and sometimes falling into a big, black hole. We must shake ourselves out of our normal rut and leave home to then find it again. A little of the experience of leaving home is created in the foreign language classroom without travelling abroad. Creating an awareness of distance and difference is a precondition for the teaching of another language as the art of translation. If students study a foreign language with the impossibility of full translation and perfect comprehension, they will be encouraged to perfect their understanding of others. The assumption that a foreign language is another code for saying the same thing will be cast aside and respect for those who have a different language, culture and lifestyle, experienced.

Education for global understanding gains important insights from Dewey and Emerson. When facing the gap in an encounter with another person, there is no opportunity for mutual learning if we stay within our own space. We cannot imagine a global community, as if the difference created by distance were just a temporal source of insecurity or evil to be eradicated. Both of these bring a danger of obliviousness and perhaps violence in regard to the lives of different others.

In a world in which 'the tragic' inevitably and regularly occurs, this educative perspective copes with this circumstance beyond what is considered good or evil, right or wrong. It neutralizes negativity, retaliation and revenge and represents a search for a better world through constant, patient dialogue with different others. By preparing for such dialogue, among many conflicting values and religions, the standpoint of mutual perfection serves the conversation, cooperation and collaboration of everyone. Sir Sigmund Sternberg, from the Three Faiths Forum, has suggested an A-level in the art of dialogue to promote harmony. He talks not just about the ability to converse with one another but to do so in order to listen and learn and break down the barriers between religion and races that comprise the population of Britain today and prevent the cultural isolation that leads to fear and hatred (Sternberg, 2009).

Contacts with Japanese people and their culture illuminate issues of equality and the politics of mutual recognition and understanding. The Japanese ethic of care and 'otherness', self-reliance and self-transcendence is not built on the perspective of the 'I' of the self, isolated from the world, but what Dewey envisages in the 'I Believe' ,with the individual self as the centre in the field. With emphasis on the 'pain of individuation', as much as the 'joy of communion', the Japanese education system encourages the cultivation of self-knowledge amongst teachers and students in order to acquire the standpoint of 'otherness' within and without of one's self. This demands openness to possibilities and a desire to perfect oneself, not in terms of self-aggrandizement but in the challenges that confrontations with others present: facing up to their demands and the difficulties of the experience for us. In this encounter one becomes aware of one's limitations, but energy for life is released through mutual understanding.

Review

One does not have to be long in Japan to appreciate how keen people are on formality and ceremony. It is quite a culture shock to see a stationmaster draw himself up to attention, square his shoulders, raise his white-gloved hand to his cap and send you off with a salute similar to that given to the prime minister himself. Since Japan started its drive towards democratization in the late nineteenth century, the culture of the high warrior class has been extended to everyone. As a result, white-gloved service, symbolizing the shift to Western chic elegance, was no longer confined to the great and the good.

Similarly, the low sweeping bows of the school staff as they greeted us on our visits, showed the deep respect the Japanese have for themselves and others. This is further demonstrated in the *senpai* relationship. This is a senior, at school or work, who acts as one's guide and mentor. The relationship is based on seniority and status and is the structure for welcoming new people into the community and teaching them the ropes. Since Japan opened up to the West in the nineteenth century, their people have eagerly accepted capitalism. But as with so many Western imports, they have made additions to reduce tensions and protect their social structures. The *senpai* relationship is an example, softening an atmosphere that might otherwise be intolerably competitive. Although hierarchical, the relationship is one in which superiority brings obligations and where friendship humanizes the distinctions between people.

In the United Kingdom, we have lost many of these organizational structures. Since the last world war in the 1940s, we have tried to iron out class differences, but it is generally recognized that Britain is divided on class lines more than ever before with a 'us' and 'them' outlook on every question, whether it is the way individuals are taxed or the hiring or firing of BBC presenters. A free society and a class-based one both go hand-in-hand. If you allow wealth creation, you enable people to buy privilege and satisfy their hopes and desires.

Somehow, Japan has coped rather better than most with differentiation and diversity in their society, by teaching that everyone is born to make an important contribution to life. Preserving traditional values for living and learning has respect for others at the top of the agenda. I shall never forget a moment when waiting in the queue for a visit to a Shogun palace in Kyoto. A small boy in another line caught my eye, smiled broadly and bowed low. This unspoken message of respect and welcome for a foreigner is one that is etched in my mind forever.

Japanese society is much more homogeneous and stable when compared with Britain, so that it is easier to preserve traditional values and adapt them to modern living. We can reflect on their collegiate culture that promotes communication, cooperation and collaboration in a way our more individualistic one cannot. Yet in an increasingly diverse British society such communication and community is essential if we are to bridge the barriers of difference and seek common ground. This will enable us to build a society that is more at ease with itself and appreciative of what each other has to offer. It is a Utopian vision, but one which philosophers, such as Dewey, have strongly advocated and nations such as Japan have warmly embraced.

Suggestions for classroom practice

> The collegiate, communicative culture underpins Japanese educational and economic success and can be cultivated in schools in the way we group students for tasks and promote relationships between them.

Main points

- Living with diversity and difference demands a patient and continual dialogue amongst us all to bridge the gaps between people and work for common purposes.
- Japanese society provides us with a model of living that has coped with globalization rather better than most. Its value for tradition and respect for everyone, symbolized in common courtesies to all citizens, is something we can cultivate more strongly in our homes, schools and workplaces.
- Learning and living another language introduces us to the art of translation, opening our eyes and ears to the faces and voices of different others.
- Communication is the condition of growth within our selves and our communities as well as the art of creating a democratic society.

Discussion point

> Dewey, Emerson and Sternberg are all strong advocates of dialogue. What are some of the barriers about promoting this in schools and how can they be overcome?

References

Dewey, J. (1916) *Democracy and Education*. Middle Works 9 (1980), Boydston, J. A. (ed.), Southern Illinois University Press.

Emerson, R.W. (1990) *The American Scholar, Ralph Waldo Emerson,* Poirier, Richard (ed.), Oxford: Oxford University Press.

Gonzales, J., Williams, Jocelyn, L., Roey, S., Kaotberg, D. & Brenwall, S. (2008) *The Trends in International Mathematics and Science Study (TIMSS): 4th and 8th Grade Students in the International Context.* U.S. Dept. of Education, Institute of Educational Sciences, pub. NCES 2009001

Minami, M. and McCabe, A. (1995) Rice balls and bear hunts: Japanese and North American family narrative patterns. *Journal of Child Language,* 22, 423–445.

Minami, M. and McCabe, A. (1996) Compressed collections of experiences: Some Asian American traditions. In A. McCabe (ed.) *Chameleon Readers: Some Problem Cultural Differences in Narrative Structure Pose for Multi-Cultural Literacy Programs* (pp. 72–97), New York: McGraw-Hill.

Sage, R., Rogers, J. and Cwenar, S. (2006) *Why do Japanese children perform better than British ones?* 2nd Report of the Dialogue, Innovation, Achievement and Learning (DIAL) projects, Leicester: University of Leicester.

Shwalb, D. (1993) The source of Japanese school readiness: Preschool or family? *Cross-Cultural Psychological Bulletin,* 27, 25–28.

Sternberg, S. (2009) *An A-Level in the art of dialogue would promote harmony.* Letter to the *Daily Telegraph,* 26 August.

A call to arms: Developing diverse students through service learning

9

John Patterson and Alison Patterson

Overview

This chapter explores diversity within the context of student volunteerism. It describes a cross-curricular arts and citizenship project in a city primary school, managed by teacher students and evaluated by those involved. This service learning model helps educators gain insight into local communities surrounding schools and develops teacher and learner practical skills of communicating and relating to people with different backgrounds and abilities. It is considered a value-added tool for the new Professional Standards Framework for Teaching and Learning in Higher Education, whilst balancing the present academic National Curriculum (NC) with opportunities for personal and academic teacher and learner development.

Myriad policies and ongoing change

New and enthusiastic trainee teachers, embarking on their classroom practice, must surely feel somewhat crest fallen as they come to terms with mountainous documentation, expected outcomes, strict targets and numerous statutory requirements interwoven with professional 'hidden curricula' and demands for a 24/7 commitment. This is on top of the challenge of teaching the greatest diversity of culture, ability and background, amongst students, that we have experienced in the history of education. How are they, as learners themselves, making sense of successive directives entering education? How are individual strengths nurtured beyond that of 'exam technicians' (implementing a prescriptive NC) to prepare students for independent lives? Before looking at 'service-learning' as an opportunity for this development to flourish, let us set our questions in the context of current educational policy and practice.

Current educational policy and practice

The 'Every Child Matters' Government agenda (2003) calls for all those involved in child education to synchronize their approaches. It expects a joined-up effort across five areas that young people informed government they most wanted to see: to be healthy, stay safe, enjoy and achieve, make a positive contribution and reach economic well-being. To secure these outcomes, the government targets four areas: supporting parents and teachers, early intervention and effective protection, account-ability and integration (locally, regionally and nationally) and workforce reform. A sigh of relief must have echoed around primary schools, driven by Standard Assessment Tasks (SATs) and League Tables, as the Government acknowledged that:

> Children learn better when they are excited and engaged . . . Different schools go about this in different ways. There will be different sparks that make learning vivid and real for different children. (Every Child Matters, 2003: Foreword)

The introduction of 'Excellence and Enjoyment: A Strategy for Primary Schools' (DfES, 2003) appeared to offer opportunity to generate these 'sparks', by employ-ing cross-curricular activity within creative fields of music, art, dance, drama, sport and Information Communication Technology (ICT). It called for schools to take 'ownership' of the curriculum and be creative and innovative in developing a dis-tinct character. It was a departure from the prescriptive 'one-size-fits-all' National Curriculum (NC) (1989), which promised to be 'broad and balanced', but has proved the reverse, as schools focus on academic pursuits to increase ranking on league tables.

The detrimental effect of schools concentrating on NC basic literacy and numer-acy skills, for SATs results, has been reported regularly in the media. Research by Black and William (2001), called 'Inside the Black Box, Raising Standards through Classroom Assessment', may have informed government thinking regarding the 'Excellence and Enjoyment' strategy. In promoting formative assessment across subjects, Black commented on the torrent of initiatives facing educationalists, stat-ing: 'the sum of all these reforms has not added up to an effective policy because something is missing.' (Black et al., 2001) More recently, Lewis (2005) suggests that 'risk-aversion' exists in classrooms, resulting in 'side-lining' communication, collab-oration and creativity within the curriculum. Black sees the lack of foundation sub-jects and the pushing of SATs 'outcomes' as stifling creativity. He promotes a vision where 'learning is driven by what teachers and pupils do in the classroom . . . where pupils are given . . . opportunity to think and to explain their ideas', as communication organizes and extends ideas (Black et al., 2001).

This is very much the focus of Sage (2000, 2003, 2004, 2007) in a range of studies across age and ability, showing the relationship between articulacy and attainment. It is, therefore, a confusing time for teacher students as products of the NC and now SATs drivers themselves. Where and how are they learning to ignite the 'sparks' of education and take 'ownership' of the curriculum? The developing position of 'Citizenship Education' (CE) may offer guidance, as we seek what is 'missing', especially in establishing links between communication, community, curriculum, the voluntary sector and the training of educators.

'Cross-cutting themes': The case for Citizenship Education

The *National Curriculum Handbook* (1999) for primary teachers linked Citizenship Education (CE) with Personal, Social and Health Education (PSHE), as a non-statutory subject for primary schools in England. It was influenced by the Report of the Advisory Group on Citizenship, led by Professor Bernard Crick (QCA, 1998: Crick Report). This underpinned the Department for Education and Employment's *National Curriculum Citizenship Order* (DfEE, 1999) with three strands: moral and social responsibility, community involvement and political literacy. Although non-statutory, teachers are expected to record and report on children's learning in the subject, remaining part of the framework for PSHE in primary schools (QCA, 2000). Indeed, the Office for Standards in Education (OFSTED) investigates CE in schools, as a requirement of the 1992 Education Act, reporting on good practices regarding children's spiritual, moral, social and cultural development, whilst identifying areas for improvement. Furthermore, OFSTED inspectors are now looking at how CE is being taught across courses in the primary sector.

Although not constituting 'research', such inspections are providing 'a developing picture of the delivery of the subject in schools' (Gearon, 2003, p. 3). Indeed, the NC has now been modified to include a specific focus on CE content. 'Active Citizenship' has been included with six clear components (1) awareness and knowledge; (2) interests and motivation; (3) decision-making ability and skills; (4) peaceful action; (5) collaborative action and community building; and (6) refection (Qualification and Curriculum Authority, 2004). It comes at a time where The Evidence for Policy and Practice Information and Coordinating Centre (EPPI) and the Organization for Economic Co-operation and Development (OECD) have both mentioned the development of Citizenship Education (CE) as a place to engage 'higher order critical and creative skills within the process of learning itself ' (EPPI, 2004). The need to include 'values', within a formula to 'reconcile economic success with social cohesion' (OECD, 1998), is an attempt to generate a partnership approach. This drive to create a 'values' formula brings a raft of personal, training, timing and funding issues:

> The pace of change is having a significant influence on the nature of relationships in modern society at a number of levels, including within, between and across individuals, community groups, states, nations, regions and economic and political blocs. This period of unprecedented and seemingly relentless change has succeeded in shifting and straining the traditional, stable boundaries of citizenship in many societies. (Kerr et al., 2003, cited in Gearon, 2003, p. 7)

Heater (2001) adds: 'the absence of any specialist professional training for teachers and teachers' nervousness about handling subject-matter that might provoke accusations of bias or indoctrination'. (Heater, 2001, p. 104)

Cross and Price (1996) report that 'teachers express very real concern about the expression of personal opinion'. (Cross and Price, 1996 cited in Oulton et al., 2004, p. 492). What can be put into place to allay such fears? How can we establish what 'works' as we consider action towards establishing value, seen by Kushner et al. (2003) as

> compromised in all sorts of ways by educational researchers and teacher educators having to share their fortunes and funding streams. In departments, which are reliant on the Department for Education and Skills and the Teacher Training Agency for their survival, the stresses of conducting politically independent, critical research sponsored by them is a challenge for departmental and university managers. (Kushner et al., 2003, p. 24)

Working towards answers, the EPPI recommendations, within initial and continuous professional development (CPD), recommended that there is a real need for: '. . . teachers to be supported to develop a richer, deeper, broader process oriented pedagogy. This involves having an understanding and vision of learning and achievement, seen from a more holistic perspective, where different kinds or categories of learning are viewed as complementary, not separate' (EPPI, 2005, p. 5).

Listing families, churches and voluntary associations as supportive groups, Gray called for

> a strong commitment to the intermediary institutions in which individuals are formed and in which for the most part their lives find meaning. (Gray, 1994, p. 52)

Teacher students, therefore, have much to gain by volunteering to work alongside local 'intermediary institutions' (churches, clubs, voluntary organizations etc.) as part of their training experience. Volunteering in education across diverse communities is an under-researched area. There is a real need to understand the nature of individual community settings (Butcher et al., 2003; Berry and Chisholm, 1999), and much to consider in light of Gearon's (2003) *Professional User Review of UK Research* for the British Educational Research Association, which noted:

> . . . a major area for future research will be those sectors external to the school that aid and assist the delivery of citizenship through active participation and wider community involvement. (Gearon, 2003, p. 3)

Although there is immediate value in gaining additional Curriculum Vitae evidence for teacher students, there are wider implications for their academic and pedagogical understanding. Let us look at some of the benefits brought to students through volunteering, in advance of investigating 'service learning' as a specific tool of engagement.

The role of volunteering has gained pace since The Crick Report (1998), which stated:

> We firmly believe that volunteering and community involvement are necessary conditions of civil society and democracy. Preparation for these, at the very least, should be an explicit part of education. (Crick, 1998, p. 10)

Its importance was echoed in the new National Framework for *Youth Action and Engagement* (The Russell Commission, 2005), which encouraged volunteering of worth and quality, recommending a series of campaigns to promote its benefit, stating that:

> . . . it should be common place for young people to volunteer whilst they are at school, college or in higher education. All education institutions should have a volunteering ethos . .' requiring '. . a stronger emphasis on volunteering within the citizenship curriculum and training for citizenship teachers. (Russell, 2005, p. 14)

Volunteering would seem to offer teacher students the opportunity to try out and analyse what constitutes 'good practice', within the 'holistic perspective', suggested by the EPPI. Furthermore, it provides the type of atmosphere Wragg (2005) suggested as essential for teacher motivation and creativity. In considering teacher training, he underlined the need for freedom from fear and for encouragement but stressed the need for 'structure' (Wragg, 2005, cited in Wilson, 2005, p. 186).

How can this 'structure' develop in synergy with current thinking? This calls for teachers to consider 'preferred learning styles' of pupils, as Visual Auditory and Kinaesthetic (VAK) (Reinhart, 1976; Dunn & Dunn, 1978; O'Connor, 2001). Cognitive theories rooted in the work of Lewin (1952), advanced by Kolb (1983) and Myers (1993), suggest learning comes through experience. Accelerated learning models from work on 'multiple intelligences' (Gardner, 1999); 'emotional intelligence' (Salovey and

Mayer, 1990 popularized by Goleman, 1996); 'brain-based learning' (Dennison and Dennison, 1986; MacLean, 1990) and 'reciprocal learning' (Clarke, 1997) are popular ideas that need evaluating within a deeper knowledge of how we develop our thinking and communicate this (Sage, 2007). Could volunteering provide a safe, encouraging environment for teacher students to investigate, learn, evaluate and understand the fundamental communicative learning processes that are marginalized in the curriculum? If primary-age children, as Black suggests, are to be given 'the opportunity to think and to explain their ideas', it would surely make sense to incorporate this activity into the education and training of teachers. As researchers, in essence, they would have the opportunity to see what works in the school settings in which they find themselves. The work of Lewin (1948) and Stenhouse (1975) has long upheld the vision of teacher researchers. There is still debate regarding professional development research as to whether this counts as 'real research in the academic arena' (Campbell, 2004, p. 381), but it acts as a starting point for teacher students to experience and comment upon the 'higher order critical thinking' called for by the EPPI.

Excellent examples exist of structured volunteering, such as Harvard Business School's (HBS) Public Education Leadership Project (PELP, 2005), in the United States, and initiatives at The Centre for Community Engagement, at Bradford University. 'Knowledge generation' is seen as a driving force behind these models. Research suggests raised achievement in pupils and higher quality teaching resources. This is positive, but students need to understand what this means for them in terms of addressing the statutory requirements of the new National Professional Standards Framework (HEA, 2006). Following the white paper 'The Future of Education' (2003), institutions must design professional development programmes to improve student learning, by enabling them to meet the required standards. A descriptor-based approach, in which higher education institutions determine their own criteria, consists of six areas of activity, core knowledge and professional values (www.heacademy.ac.uk). In studying the framework, it appears that volunteering 'ticks the boxes' for many of the descriptors, not least of which is a 'commitment to the development of learning communities'. What shape should this volunteering take if it is to add value to teacher experience and be of educational worth to the recipients?

Review of a case study of service learning

The developing landscape of 'service learning' (SL) offers some form of structure in answer to the issues raised. It embraces different ways of learning and allows for students to formulate and articulate their thinking and experiences into a practical set of values, relevant to their setting and future employment. It offers a 'bridge' between academic information and the application of knowledge, skills and understanding. When considering the National Professional Standards Framework, it offers outcomes across each of the descriptors, opening a debate on personal development and areas for future research.

Definitions of SL, models for its delivery and forms of assessment vary greatly. There is commonality in the primary aim to balance service with learning. However, the focus 'on a balance between service and learning is relatively new' (Patterson and Loomis, 2007, p. 122). There is a growing interest and recognition of opportunities and possibilities presented by SL. Writing to advance knowledge and transform the field, McKnight et al. (2005) describes SL as:

> not simply a pedagogy. Rather, SL is a means to empower students and educational institutions to become more aware of the needs of the communities of which they are a part and to become engaged and civically active in mutually beneficial ways.

The National Service-Learning and Assessment Study Group (USA, 1999) offers the most comprehensive definition of SL in stating:

> SL is a teaching and learning strategy that combines the principals of experiential learning with service to the community. Through SL, Students develop as citizens, learn problem-solving skills, and experience a sense of social responsibility by engaging in thoughtful action to help their communities. Students involved in SL deepen and reinforce their newly acquired content knowledge and skills by using them to address real community needs. They experience themselves and are perceived by others as competent contributing members of the community.

A local Service Learning Art Project

A recent Art Project, delivered by volunteer teacher students in a city primary school, has taken into account the need to provide wider learning experiences for teachers and pupils, embracing the vision of SL. The project developed from an ongoing initiative called SIGNAL (Schools Intergenerational Nurturing and Learning Project). In this model, the local football club community officers deliver citizenship assemblies in schools, supported by the police. Messages range from anti-bullying, drug awareness to gun crime and teamwork, and made directly relevant to each community's issues at the time. Teacher students are encouraged, in teams, to follow these key messages into school, designing the curriculum and running projects within the 'Excellence and Enjoyment' subject areas (music, art, dance, drama, sport, ICT), trialling current educational theories (Accelerated Learning, VAK etc.) in a supportive atmosphere. Parents, community police officers and volunteer organizations such as Rotary (www.rotary.org), the Dark Horse Venture (www.darkhorse.rapid.co.uk) and local faith groups are invited to assist by providing helpers and mentors.

A celebration of children's work ends the project, when parents, pupils, teachers and volunteers come together to share experiences. The framework provides scope for individuals to participate at a number of levels. Each project, however, is very different; according to the dynamics in the teacher teams, the intermediary agency volunteers and the creativity of the whole partnership. Once underway, each teacher student 'specializes' in an educational practice within their project, and shares experiences with peers in informal seminars. At this point, engagement is nurtured by tutors and students are encouraged to read up on findings, record and reflect on them as 'action researchers', within relevant literature. Evidence suggests this approach increases academic study, manifested in more reflective assignments, with this outcome supported by existing research (Simons and Cleary, 2005). Tutors, engaged in projects, offer ideas from their own school experiences and academic subject knowledge.

The school, in which the Art Project was delivered, began by defining their relationships with the local community. As there were over 20 languages spoken in school, the staff wanted to achieve an outcome that represented this diversity. The football team, therefore, focused their assembly on the benefits of teamwork and the school and teacher students decided to introduce the concept of non-verbal forms of communication, via music, art and dance, as the curriculum topic follow-on. Over 10 weeks, children and teacher students, supported by intermediary agents, drafted pictures in teams, with the brief to represent themselves and their families within the city of Liverpool. A number of collective drafts were generated, using ICT, and once approved by all participants the artwork was painted as an interior wall mural.

Two local graffiti artists volunteered to paint the mural with the children, so ensuring a professional finish. Simultaneously, a dance routine was developed, employing a mix of musical genres, with dance moves suggested by children from their own cultural traditions. These moves were researched on the Internet with children sharing their cultural backgrounds with peers through oral presentations. The dance routine was then used in a celebration assembly, revealing the mural to parents and emphasizing the communication, collaboration and cooperation of the children and volunteer helpers.

Something magical happened during the process, in which children, teacher students and intermediary agencies shared ideas and learnt from each other in a creative atmosphere. This was the development of a democratic team, sharing a vision, realized in a marvellous artistic representation of their families, within a vibrant multi-racial community. Is there something in this project for this particular school community, within the vision of SL that may help us find what Black felt was 'missing'? The process should be repeated and measures of different levels of performance, produced to record added value and provide a valid and reliable evidence base, as used in the Communication Opportunity Group Scheme (Sage, 2000).

What emerged in this project was teacher student engagement beyond the call of duty, catalysing the community into collaborative action. Individuals embedded their own interests and strengths within an academic framework to increase student knowledge, skill and understanding, as measured by assignment criteria. Against the new Professional Standards Framework for Teaching and Learning in Higher Education, interviews with participating students suggested they were making links between the six areas of activity, core knowledge and professional values, within the context of their own experience and learning. It is important to develop the role of teacher students as volunteer community project leaders, organizing similar projects and reporting back on their value to peers and intermediary agency partners. It is here where we believe SL has real potential. It builds a bridge between a school and its increasingly diverse community. Rather than just 'parachuting in' a SATs driven curriculum, here is a tried and tested opportunity to explore what value a small army of creative teacher students could bring to the present battlefield of those fighting for the educational process, versus others waging war for the products of learning.

Suggestions for classroom practice

Community links are essential to provide the resources now needed to cope with learning within a diverse population. It enables the school to promote its philosophy and practice and brings in support and expertise from outside. Develop networks that can bring sustained community interest starting with the parents association and friends of the school.

Main points

- The service learning model encourages student teachers to look at issues of personal development that underpin National Curriculum tasks and allows them to focus on communication, collaboration and cooperation for successful learning.

⇨

- Service learning is a model that is developing worldwide, which brings the local community into the learning process, enabling a diversity of culture, background and ability to be harnessed for maximizing learning potential and bridging divides amongst people.
- Improved educational standards was seen in teacher students' assignments, which demonstrated greater knowledge and understanding of pupil diversity.
- Improved pupil learning was shown in their increased engagement in work and higher levels of communication, cooperation and collaboration between them.
- Involving local communities provides learners with a circle of support, both within and outside school, allowing them to choose topics that have meaning for them.
- The challenge is to create assessments that provide clear baseline performance measures, to be compared with those after this learning opportunity. Those researched within the Communication Opportunity Group model (Sage, 2000) produce a tried and tested approach that could facilitate student teachers' assessment skills and give objective, evidence-based measures.

Discussion point

Community involvement is an untapped resource in supporting inclusion and diversity in schools? How can this be achieved in your own context?

References

Berry, H. and Chisholm, L. (1999) *Service Learning in Higher Education around the World: An Initial Look*, New York: The International Partnership for Service Learning.

Black, P., William, D. (2001) *Inside The Black Box. Raising Standards through Classroom Assessment*, King's College London School of Education; available online at (http://www.ngfl.northumberland.gov.uk/keystage3ictstrategy/Assessment/blackbox.pd (accessed on 23 September 2007).

Butcher, J., Howard, P., Labone, E., Bailey, M., Groundwater Smith, S., McFadden, M., McMeniman, M., Malone, K, Martinez, K. (2003) *Asia Pacific Journal of Teacher Education.* 31(2), 109–124.

Campbell, A. (2004) Teacher's research and professional development in England: Some questions, issues and concerns. *Journal of In-Service Education*, 29(3), 375–405.

Clarke, E. (1997) *Designing and Implementing an Integrated Curriculum*, Brandon, UT: Holistic Education Press.

Cross-and Price (1996) *Teaching Citizenship* (cited in Oulton, C., Day, V., Dillon, J., Grace, M. Controversial issues – teachers' attitudes and practices in the context of citizenship education (2004). *Oxford Review of Education*, 30(4), 492).

Davies, H. (2002) *A Review of Enterprise and the Economy in Education*, London: Her Majesty's Stationary Office (HMSO).

Dennison, P. and Dennison, G. (1986) *Brain Gym*. Edu-Kinesthetics: Body Balance Books.

Department for Education and Employment (DfEE) Qualifications and Curriculum Authority (QCA) (1999) *The National Curriculum for England: Citizenship*, London: QCA.

Department for Education and Employment (DfEE) (2000) *Curriculum Guidance for the Foundation Stage*. London: QCA.

Dunn, R. and Dunn, K. (1978) *Teaching Students through Their Individual Learning Styles*, Reston, VA: Reston Publishers.

Every Child Matters Green Paper (2003), London: Her Majesty's Stationary Office.

The Evidence for Policy and Practice Information and Coordinating Centre (EPPI) (August 2004) *An International Review of Citizenship Education Research*. The Evidence for Policy and Practice Information and Coordinating Centre. A Systematic Review of Citizenship Education on Student Learning and Achievement. London: EPPI.

The Evidence for Policy and Practice Information and Coordinating Centre (EPPI) (March 2005) *An International Review of Citizenship Education Research*. The Evidence for Policy and Practice Information and Coordinating Centre. A Systematic Review of the Impact of Citizenship Education on the Provision of Schooling. London: EPPI.

Excellence and Enjoyment (2003) Department for Education and Skills (DfES) *A Strategy for Primary Schools*. London: DfES.

The Future of Education. White Paper (2003), London: DfES.

Gardner, H. (1993). *Frames of Mind. The Theory of Multiple Intelligences*, New York: Basic Books.

Gardner, H. (1999) *Intelligence Reframed-Multiple Intelligences for the 21st Century*, New York: Basic Books.

Gearon, L. (2003) *How Do We Learn To Become Good Citizens?* A professional user review of UK research undertaken for the British Educational Research Association. BERA.

Goleman, D. (1996) *Emotional Intelligence. Why It Can Matter More than IQ?* London: Bloomsbury.

Gray, J. (1994) *Beyond the New Right: Markets, Government, and the Common Environment*, London, UK and New York: Routledge.

Heater, D. (2001) The history of citizenship education in England. *The Curriculum Journal*, 12(1), 104–120.

Kerr, D., Cleaver, E., Ireland, E., and Blenkinsop, S. (2003) *Citizenship Education Longitudinal Study First Cross-Sectional Survey 2001–2002* (DfES Research Report 416), London: DfEs (cited in Gearon, L. (2003) *How Do We Learn to Become Good Citizens*. A professional user review of UK research undertaken for the British Educational Research Association. BERA: 8.

Kolb, D. A. (1983) *Experiential Learning: Experience as the Source of Learning and Development*, Englewood Cliffs, NJ: Prentice-Hall.

Kushner, S., Simons, H., Jones, K., James, D., BERA Symposium. *Transforming Learning Cultures in Further Education;* available online at http://www.tlrp.org?dspace/retrieve/410/BERA+Paper04james+final-logos.doc-supplemental (accessed on 12 October 2005).

Lewin, K. (1948) *Resolving Social Conflicts*, London: Harper and Row.

Lewin, K. (1952) *Field Theory in Social Science*, in selected Theoretical Papers. D Cartwright, London: Tavistock.

Lewis, N. (2005) *Innovation in an Era of Caution*; available online at http://www.innovationtools.org (accessed on 25 September 2007).

MacLean, P. D. (1990) *The Triune Brain in Evolution*, New York: Plenum Press.

McKnight Casey, K., Springer, N., Billig, S., Davidson, G. (2005) *Advancing Knowledge in Service Learning. Research to Transform the Field*. RMC Research Corporation, Greenwich, CT: IAP Publishing.

Myers D. G. (1993) *Social Psychology*, New York: McGraw-Hill.

National Curriculum Citizenship Order of 1999 (DfEE, 1999).

National Framework for Youth Action and Engagement (2005 The Russell Commission) cabinetoffice.gov.uk/russellcommission/publications/press.html

National Service-Learning and Assessment Study Group (USA 1999).

New National Framework for Professional Standards in Teaching and supporting Learning, the Standing Conference of Principals (SCOP) Universities UK (UUK) and the Higher Education Academy, 23 February 2006.

O'Connor, J. (2001) *NLP Workbook*. Element Publishing.

Organization for Economic Co-operation and Development (OECD) (1998) *Fostering Entrepreneurship*. The OECD Jobs Strategy: OECD.

Patterson, J. and Loomis, C. (2007) *Combining service learning and social enterprise in higher education to achieve academic learning, business skills development, citizenship education and volunteerism*. Learning Teaching and Assessing in Higher Education. Developing Reflective Practice. Learning Matters.

Qualifications and Curriculum Authority (QCA) (1998) *Education for Citizenship and the Teaching of Democracy in Schools* (Crick Report), London: QCA.

Qualifications and Curriculum Authority (QCA) (1999, 2000) *The National Curriculum Handbook for Primary Teachers in England.* London: QCA.

Sage, R. (2000) *The Communication Opportunity Group Scheme,* Leicester: University of Leicester.

Sage, R. (2003) *Lend Us You Ear,* Stafford: Network Press.

Sage, R. (2004) *A World of Difference,* London: Network Press.

Sage, R. (2005) *Inclusion in a Midland City,* Leicester: University of Leicester.

Sage, R. (2007) *Inclusion: Making it work,* London: Network-Continuum.

Salovey, P. and Mayer, J. (1990) Emotional intelligence. *Imagination, Cognition, and Personality,* 9, 185–211.

Simons, L. and Cleary, B. (2005) *An Evaluation of Academic Service Learning: Student and Community Perspectives on Lessons Learned in Advancing Knowledge in Service-Learning. Research to Transform the Field.* RMC Research Corporation. IAP Publishing.

Stenhouse, L. (1975) *An Introduction to Curriculum Research and Development,* London: Heinemann Educational Books.

Wragg, A. (2005) cited in Wilson, A. (2005) *Creativity in Primary Education.* Learning Matters: 4.

Useful websites

www.heacademy.ac.uk
www.rotary.org
www.darkhorse.rapid.co
www.hbs.edu/socialenterprise/whatis.html
www.schoolsinteractive.co.uk
www.participationworks.org.uk
www.volunteering.org.uk

The role of charities in supporting diversity and inclusion: The Selective Mutism Information and Research Association (SMIRA)

10

Alice Sluckin and Lindsay Whittingham

Overview

Children and adults, who suffer from communication difficulties, have particular problems in being included in everyday activities and integrating into a diverse, complex society. This chapter presents the work of a charity in providing support for such a group, demonstrating that such organizations 'can reach the parts that government services fail to do so'. The definition and difficulties of selective mutism (SM) are discussed and the facilities developed by the Selective Mutism Information and Research Association (SMIRA) described, to help sufferers cope with their lives. This charity has been overwhelmed with requests for help all over the world, so demonstrating the tremendous needs of those who struggle with their differences and the lack of statutory provision to support them on a long-term basis.

Introduction

In Britain, there is a long tradition of charities supporting parents, child and professionals with diverse problems as well as influencing health and education policy in line with family needs. In this connection it is relevant to mention the National Autistic Society. This was set up some 40 years ago by parents who were often given very conflicting advice by a range of professionals, becoming both confused and disillusioned with inadequate statutory provision. Dr Kanner (1973), a highly respected child psychiatrist, had been the first person to describe the symptoms that these children displayed. Ill-informed professionals, lacking appropriate education and training, coined the term 'refrigerator mother', asserting that maternal rejection early in life was causing autism. The parents, rebelling against being blamed, joined together with sympathetic professionals in tune with their views forming the Autistic Society, to support each other and encourage useful studies into its condition. Over the years, this has been a most successful charity, becoming an important centre for research into all the many aspects of this condition, as well as providing information, advice and support for families for as long as it is needed.

Like autism, selective mutism has not been given the attention it deserves until recently. Children, with this condition, do not talk in unfamiliar contexts and pose no trouble to others. Even now, after a good deal of media attention paid to the disability, some psychologists view the child as having a speech problem. In contrast, some speech and language therapists consider the cause is anxiety, with responsibility for action lying with psychiatrists and psychologists. Therefore, parents tend to be passed from one lengthy waiting list to another with no one willing to take responsibility for managing the presenting problems. Out of the desperation of not being understood and catered for, the parents support group, SMIRA was founded in 1992 with the help of sympathetic professionals. Forming an agenda based on family needs, the organization has gone from strength to strength. It provides a telephone advice line, information pamphlets for parents and professionals, regular news letters, workshops and conferences to share experiences and facilitate better awareness. Members include both parents and interested professionals.

This chapter describes the development of the SMIRA charity and its work nationally and internationally. A focus on voluntary organizations is timely at this point in our national history. We are in a period of looming state insolvency. The United Kingdom will no longer be able to afford the full range of state-funded amenities and benefits that contribute to quality of life such as libraries, leisure centres, parks and perks for pensioners as well as extra opportunities for those who need them. It is possible that public services may become means tested and much of our cultural infrastructure has to be taken out of the state budget and left to survive by charity and commercial effort. Such reductions in state provision can be met by an invigorated voluntary sector to which jobless and retired citizens might profitably turn their energies. In this new austerity period, community activity of all kinds could replace our present individualistic goals. This gives us an opportunity for neighbourliness and mutual respect to improve our quality of life in a less materialistic way and provide greater support to those who need it. In the next section, the condition of selective mutism is discussed as a prelude to considering the role of a charity in supporting their needs.

What is selective mutism?

Selective mutism is a rare childhood disorder, with only 2–5 youngsters per 10,000 population exhibiting this problem at the age of 6–7 years old (Goodman and Scott, 1997). Those affected communicate informally and appropriately with people they know well, but remain silent when confronted with strangers in an unfamiliar environment, such as school, where discourse patterns are formal and very different. In contexts outside home, communication is explicit rather than implicit, with meaning in words, arranged in a narrative form, rather than available largely from the context. This represents a huge jump in communicative ability for children, and for those with less competence and confidence, a fearful, forbidding experience.

Children with SM may also have problems talking to peers and are often sensitive to noise or touch and may avoid eye contact. The problem behaviour is usually noticed as soon as the child enters play group, around three years of age, with girls more likely to be affected than boys. This is a reverse pattern to that found with other developmental difficulties. Children, with learning problems, can be selectively mute, but also very intelligent and appear frightened of making a mistake in case they face disapproval. Unlike shy children, those with SM do not improve their behaviour with time. When starting school, they do not speak to the teacher and as they also fail to communicate with peers they fall behind in both social and academic learning.

The condition was once known as elective mutism (Tramer, 1934), a term still occasionally used to define children thought to be 'stubborn or contrary'. Tanner and Klein (1992), two eminent American child psychiatrists, recommended a reclassification for the Diagnostic and Statistical Manual (DSM 1V, 1994) of the American Psychiatric Association of Selective Mutism, stressing that: 'evidence is lacking to assume that these children have a deliberate preference not to speak'.

With regard to causation, recent research findings point to excessive fearfulness as a likely cause, possibly related to paralysing social anxiety in adults. Environmental factors may contribute, such as isolated living, frequent moves, family or postoperative stresses and a bi-lingual upbringing. Research into childhood anxiety, by Kagan and Snidman (2004), points to genetic factors influencing temperament. Thus, children with SM may have a predisposition to withdraw in the face of the unfamiliar. It is known that as a result of anxiety, a temporary paralysis of the larynx can occur so making communication impossible. Interestingly, 90 per cent of parents answering a SMIRA questionnaire in 2008 reported a history of shyness in their families, although this might be the result of an innate problem of shifting from informal to formal communication (Sage, 2000b). Below, we have a mother's account of how she was left to cope with her child with SM in the early 1990s:

A parental account of a child with Selective Mutism

When our daughter was about three years old and starting play-group we became aware that she would only talk at home, where she was very vocal and spoke with an excellent vocabulary. However, at play-group she was completely silent and would not talk to the staff or other children. We were worried and grew more and more concerned as her silence continued. We took her to professionals for help and asked for an explanation or causation but no-one could offer us any information or advice. We were told that having a quiet child must be a blessing!! In desperation we wrote to a women's magazine and through their helpline were put in touch with SMIRA, a recently started charity giving support to parents of children with problems like our daughter's.

Alice Sluckin, the chairperson, had written some papers about elective mutism (1977), as the condition was then called. We were given literature by her on the problem and it was suggested that fearfulness might be the cause of our daughter's non-speaking habit. We gathered that a step-by-step approach might help (breaking done events into small units of behaviour to be worked through). We passed the information back to school and with the condition now having a name and an explanation, which was 'fear' we found the teacher was more than willing to support a step-by-step programme to help our daughter gain confidence. Having SMIRA's support over the telephone and now understanding the way our child behaved stopped us from blaming ourselves and this took pressure off us and, therefore, off our daughter. Within a few weeks she agreed to try talking to her teacher. She succeeded with support and the school then built on what we had achieved. Within three months of having spoken a few words in school, she stood up and led the school assembly for her class!! This gave her great confidence.

Rachel has fully recovered, as her problem was tackled early in her development with the help of parents, professionals and support from SMIRA. When children with SM grow older they become more resistant to change because non-speaking becomes a habit as well as part of their personality and self-image. This is regularly reinforced by their peers who do not expect them to talk and develop strategies to circumvent the issue. There is now general agreement that early intervention, preferably at the toddler stage, has the best prognosis (Cline and Baldwin, 2004).

The Selective Mutism Information and Research Association (SMIRA)

SMIRA came into existence as a result of a chance meeting with a mother of a daughter with SM, Lindsay Whittington, and Alice Sluckin, a retired senior psychiatric social worker, who had in the course of her clinical work successfully treated children with SM (Sluckin et al., 1991). Lindsay had been referred to Alice by the headmaster of her daughter's primary school which she attended. Both home and school had found it exceedingly difficult to get help for this eight-year-old girl with SM. Lindsay and Alice, with the support and assistance of school, worked successfully on the SM problem. As they had formed a strong relationship and had taken a liking to each other, they both started a support group for local, Leicester families of children with SM. This group met monthly and was supported by professionals in the area.

From very small beginnings, SMIRA developed in 1992 and the driving force was Lindsay Whittington and her desire to use her experience to help other families. As SMIRA became nationally known, it became clear that there was a tremendous need for information and guidance over a larger area. Requests for hand-outs and the regular Newsletter came from all parts of the country, from parents, teachers, speech and language therapists and mental health clinics. This has led to members of the organization being invited into schools to talk to teachers and others, giving advice and ongoing support. These professionals have joined in our conferences and contributed to our newsletters helping to expose the problems that are experienced by all stakeholders and tackling these in a team approach.

In 2004, SMIRA, jointly with Dr Rosemary Sage (then a Senior Lecturer at the University of Leicester and now Professor of Communication in Liverpool and London), obtained a grant form the DFES to record and evaluate the situation for children and families coping with SM. Many people co-operated in the production of a video/DVD and accompanying book. Some of the participants in the film were teenagers who had recovered from SM. There were also parents, teachers, speech and language therapists and psychologists involved, who presented the problems, a wide spectrum of views and a range of successful management strategies. The outcomes of this research and development project have found great recognition from abroad and translations have been made of the book into Japanese and French, using sub titles in both languages for the accompanying DVD/video. As a result, parent support groups have now been started in both these countries, as well as in Norway, which all link up with the UK group and participate in annual conferences. Lecture tours and presentations, by Alice Sluckin and Professor Rosemary Sage, have been made in several countries to disseminate the research and share effective policies and practice.

Thanks to a grant in 2007, it was possible to appoint Lindsay Whittington as a part-time paid co-ordinator. Another step forward was the launching of a website in 2008. Registrations to this are running at 100 new members a month, with SMIRA having 307 registered parent members, 35 professional members and 75 website registrations, with many more general visitors to the site.

In the spring of 2008, on the suggestion of parents, an awareness campaign was launched, as there was still a widespread view amongst them that many teachers and professionals were unaware of the condition. The DVD and book were sent to all teacher-training establishments and speech and language therapy faculties in universities as well as educational psychology training departments. The awareness week featured several television programmes on the BBC and its local channels. In addition, there was a most compelling account by a teacher, Alyson Hall, of how she helped a child, in school, published in the *Times Educational Supplement* (October 2008). Part of the awareness week involved a SMIRA conference in Cardiff, organized by a Welsh parent-member and attended by the Minister for Children, Education and Life-long Learning, from the Welsh Assembly. These events have helped to air the problems and share effective practice that is leading to more successful school experiences for those with SM as shown in feed-back by the SMIRA membership.

SMIRA does not charge a membership fee, in order not to exclude parents who might not be able to afford this. As a charity, running on a shoe string, its income and expenditure is annually inspected by the Charity Commission. SMIRA is a partner in the Communication Trust, which incorporates and links all charities, helping children with speech and language disabilities. It partakes in joint activities and promotes the fact that communication is a central ability for life. The Department for Children, Schools and Families (DCSF) is the major funder of the Communication Trust.

Comment

There is no doubt, that over the last few years the status of charities has risen, as a result of the huge contribution they are making to society at a time when government services and institutions are set a specific agenda that necessarily exclude some interests. This input by charities is increasingly valued in a world where coping with the vast differences between people and their particular needs has become an ever-pressing, complex challenge. As a result, charities are now being administered by the Office of the Third Sector, occupying a place in the Cabinet Office, in recognition of the fact that: 'charities have always been good at getting at the parts of society that the state fails to reach'. (*The Times*, 4 March 2008). This recognizes their freedom to set their own agenda and develop resources in a more holistic way than is possible in separate health, education and social services. During a recent government sponsored enquiry, headed by John Bercow, Member of Parliament, into improving provision for children with communication problems, charities were asked to act as advisers and SMIRA was included in this list and asked to give evidence.

SMIRA has, right from its beginning, been a charity comprised of parents and interested professionals, working harmoniously together and speaking up for children, who have a rare and misunderstood problem with formal communication. While we as an organization favour a step-by-step approach to management of the problem, as advocated by Maggie Johnson et al. (2001), we are open to other methods, provided they are ethical and acceptable to parents and schools. Regarding the formal communication development of pupils with SM in schools, the Communication Opportunity Group Scheme (COGS, Sage, 2000a) has been successful in developing and supporting their needs to understand and respond to others in formal settings, for both personal and academic success. This group of children, with specific requirements, must be taught group communication abilities if they are to have the optimum chance of competing with their peers in the world of work, as they do not acquire these naturally. Formal communication underpins all school learning and its literate, explicit structure forms the important step between oracy and literacy (Sage, 2000b).

SMIRA's main function is giving and receiving information amassed on this particular disorder, as well as initiating and contributing to research that some of our professional members are engaged in. Thanks to our website and the helpline functions, parents of children with SM, as well as their teachers, need no longer have the agony of suffering alone. There is always someone available to lend a listening ear and a helping hand when ever they need. This level of help is just not possible from statutory services.

Charities support people who have difficulties and differences that often go unrecognized in both professional and public circles so that policy and practice is slow to develop. They now operate in a business model and employ experts in finance and law to plan and regulate their activities. One of their major strengths is that they are not subject to the same bureaucratic constraints as statutory services and can respond more quickly and appropriately to their members' needs. Most charities work closely with existing services and enact a complementary role to what is provided through these channels. Because they rely on public donations and time-limited funding sources they are suffering with the recession. However, those involved in charities are developing innovative partnerships with similar bodies in order to survive.

Although the Code of Practice (2001, 2003 plus revisions) outlines the duties of professionals to appraise parents of children with special needs of the range of services available to help them there are many who are unaware about what is on offer because they have limited knowledge. Most experts have no education or experience regarding the full range of special educational needs and service provision in their training period. The European Union, through a project begun in 2001, is attempting to build information resources that can assist those planning and implementing specific programmes and initiatives. These are now being used by researchers and service providers to enable more judicious decisions. It is likely that charities will play an increasing role in supporting diverse needs of populations and the UK organizations now are a powerful force for change. The fact that a small charity like SMIRA can have such an international impact speaks for itself and the role it plays in creating a better level of awareness reinforces the importance of strongly communicating the issues of diversity and difference.

Review

Charities are a necessary support for families who need not just equal but extra opportunities if they are to make the most of their potential and learn to manage problem areas in their lives. Such organizations, supporting developmental conditions, are led by parents so the agenda is not politically motivated and able to offer help when needed rather than when professionals can provide it. Parents offer a rich resource of practical expertise, which is shared through web chat rooms, seminars and conferences, which give everyone a chance to hear a range of experiences and swap ideas. This is especially important in an era that is increasingly disenchanted with professional knowledge and expertise. Randall (2009) discusses this in relation to employers who believe that some degrees and training programmes are worthless. He was shown a list by a global organization that divided the top 24 British Universities into three groups – gold, silver and bronze, which were not looked beyond for graduate recruitment as 'trawling all 125 UK universities for talent is sadly a waste of time'.

This was the view of an Education Authority with which Leicester University had a contract for continuing professional development for teachers. The Authority preferred to employ staff from the Russell Group (the top twenty universities) as they were well educated and trained. The Policy Exchange (2009) think-tank has pointed out in their report 'More Good Teachers', that two-fifths of post-graduate trainee teachers received a 2.2 or lower in their first degree and in one year 2,000 were accepted with a third class or a pass. The report found that applicants for teaching degrees had an average A level score of a B and two Cs, compared with other degree applicants of an A and two Bs. As only 2.5 per cent of teachers failed their course the report suggested the standard was far too low.

Burghes' (2008) study comparing the ability of primary teachers in England during their final year of training with counterparts in seven other countries (China, the Czech Republic, Finland, Hungary, Japan, Russia and Singapore) found that only 20 per cent could correctly answer a question requiring logic and reasoning compared with 97 per cent of Russians. Professor Burghes said he was alarmed that so many teachers in England got 'very basic questions wrong' in contrast to the other seven nations who all performed much better. The Government Committee for Innovation, Universities and Skills has been considering degree grade inflation with the conclusion that there are 'dud institutions giving dud degrees to dud students'. (McDonagh, 2009). This obviously has a negative impact on knowledge and expertise that applies to any professional group.

Of course high entry qualifications do not mean good teachers, therapists, social workers or doctors etc. as personal abilities are equally important. However, professions must attract graduates who can attain the right level of knowledge with ability to understand and apply it effectively. Universities were once places of learning, teaching and research but are now about earning the country billions of pounds a year (Government Report: Higher Ambitions, 2009). Professor Kealey (2009), Vice Chancellor of the University of Buckingham, has pointed out that once universities directed research according to their own goals but *Higher Ambition* says they should contribute to economic growth through the commercial application of the knowledge they generate. To ensure that universities do what is wanted business people play an important role on governing bodies. This ties universities to specific agendas and areas that can make most money. As a result, charities dealing with minority issues are forced to amass their own expertise and commission appropriate research, selecting reputable professionals to assist them, as with SMIRA's 'Silent Children' project at the University of Leicester (Sage and Sluckin, 2004).

Charities, therefore, can develop policies and practice that meet client needs in preference to the political, professional and institutional ones of statutory services. They are able to adopt a holistic approach, offering a very supportive and recognizing experience for their members. The interaction with others of like minds provides the vital process of someone sympathizing with them who knows what they are going through in their personal lives. Members of SMIRA value the feeling that something is being done and that they are more in control of their situation and destiny. They also appreciate being able to contribute to the process of helping others with similar problems as this recognizes their expertise and gives them confidence and satisfaction. The opportunity to chat in a relaxing context with perhaps a drink and snack, at SMIRA events, provides great support. Statutory services have a duty to provide the most cost-effective care/education for those using them whilst charities have the potential to offer a greater range of help for the time it is needed. Those who are members do not work for economic gain and are involved because they have a passion and an interest in developing something worthwhile. They provide the human touch and the tea and sympathy that is lacking in our prescriptive health, education and social services.

Suggestions for classroom practice

Find out what charities operate locally to support the diverse needs of learners and attempt to involve them in school activities. Students can be encouraged to think up schemes that might provide financial support for these organizations, which in turn will assist families who have specific requirements for their resources.

Main points

- Charities can reach the parts that state institutions fail to do so. They are often run by those who directly benefit from their activities, such as parents and professionals, and so target practical needs very quickly.
- Charities also function as strong lobby groups and now that they are working as partners with government departments they have an influence over future policy. They are able to give rapid feedback on the implementation of policy to those charged with further developing this at government level.
- Charities are not tied to the agendas and performance targets of the statutory services and have the freedom to respond more directly and speedily to changing circumstances that are affecting the population they serve.
- Charities, as community-based organizations, develop local expertise, which means their advisory roles are essential to effective development of service provision.

Discussion point

Have a look at the selective mutism website (www.selectivemutism.co.uk) and consider how you could use the information supplied to enhance your own knowledge and practice.

References

American Psychiatric Association (1994) *Diagnostic and Statistical Manual of Mental Disorder,* Washington, DC: American Psychology Association.

Burghes, D. (2008) *A Comparison of abilities of primary school teachers in their final year of training in England, China, the Czech republic, Finland, Hungary, Japan, Russia and Singapore.* Study funded by the CfBT Education Trust.

Cline, T. and Baldwin, S. (2004) *Selective Mutism in Children,* 2nd edn, London: Whurr Publishers.

Culture change will take time (2008). *The Times,* ,2 March, p. 5.

Goodman, R. and Scott, S. (1997) *Child Psychiatry,* London: Blackwell Science.

Government Report (2009) *Higher Ambitions: The Future of Universities in a Knowledge Economy.* London: HMSO.

Hall, A. (2008) *Ready to talk, The Times Educational Supplement,* 3 October 2008, pp. 6–9.

Johnson M. and Wintgens, A. (2001) *The Selective Mutism Resource Manual,* Bicester: Speechmarks.

Kagan, S. and Snidman, N. (2004) *The Long Shadow of Temperament,* London and Cambridge, MA: Harvard University Press.

Kanner, (1973) Reflections on communication, *Journal of the National Autistic Society,* V11.

Kaplan Taneer, N. and Klein, R. (1992) *Elective Mutism: A review prepared for the DSM 1V Source Book,* New York: Columbia University, 4 March 1994.

Kealey, T. (2009) *Beware of selling your soul to the knowledge economy.* London: *The Independent Education Opinion,* 19. November 2009.

McDonagh, M. (2009) *Our universities are in a first-class mess. Daily Telegraph,* 30 January 2009.

Randall, J. (2009) *How the class war backfired and put social mobility into retreat.* Telegraph.co.uk/jeffrandall (accessed on 21 November 2009).

Sage, R. (2000a) *The Communication Opportunity Group Scheme,* Leicester: The University of Leicester.

Sage, R. (2000b) *Class Talk,* Stafford: Network Educational Press.

Sage, R. and Sluckin, A. (2004) *Silent Children: Approaches to Selective Mutism* (plus video/DVD), Leicester: University of Leicester (obtainable from SMIRA).

Sluckin, A. (1977) Children who do not talk at school. *Childcare, Health and Development,* 3, 69–79.

Sluckin, A., Foreman, N. and Herbert, M. (1991) Behavioural treatment programmes in selectivity of speaking in a sample of twenty five Selective Mutes, *Australian Psychologist,* 26(2), 132–137.

Tanner, N. and Klein R. (1992) *A Review for DSM1V Sourcebook,* New York: Columbia University College of Physicians & Surgeons, Psychiatric Institute.

Tramer, M. (1934) Elektiver Mutismus bei kindera, *Zeit Schorsift fur Kinderpsychiatric,* 1, 30–35.

International perspectives regarding inclusion: Comparing Cyprus and the United Kingdom

11

Panayiota Christodoulidou

Overview

Recently, I completed an MA in Education at the University of Leicester specializing in diversity and inclusion. As a teacher from Cyprus, I found the course fascinating, as it included participants from China, Japan, Africa, Italy and Eastern Europe. Philosophy regarding child education differs across east and west. For example, Japan has traditionally included all children in mainstream schools, supported with specialist unit facilities for those needing them. In their system equal emphasis to personal and academic development is given in a flexible curriculum without public tests. This contrasts with the United Kingdom's recent inclusion programme and a fixed, one-size-for-all curriculum, with standard assessments emphasizing products of education rather than the process of learning.

The chapter compares Cypriot and UK mainstream practice regarding inclusion of children with special educational needs (SEN). These result from physical, mental, emotional and social problems preventing learning in line with their peers. It considers teacher perceptions, with regard to inclusion, suggesting changes to make this reality rather than just rhetoric. Similarities and differences between the two nations reflect the range of practices across the world. Ways forward for policymakers and practitioners are suggested.

The history of special needs education in Cyprus

Until 1960, Cyprus was an English colony with administration, legislation and education reflecting UK models. The history of Cypriot SEN education sets the context for recent changes that have occurred in three phases. The first phase (1929–79), called the 'Gradual Establishment of Special Schools', witnesses their growth over the island, with some institutes specializing in particular problems, such as hearing or visual disturbances. SEN establishments accommodated a variety of individual needs and provided medical care, training and education. The second phase (1979–88) called 'Unified Legislation', required special schools to follow the same policies and practices for a consistent approach. The third period, from 1988 until now, has seen children with SEN integrated into mainstream, with a fundamental change occurring after legislation in 2000, when they have attended their neighbourhood schools (Phtiaka, 2000, p. 2). Special units, in mainstream, have been established in schools, in order to meet the needs of children requiring expert support (Official Newspaper of Cypriot Democracy, 2001, p. 11).

Inclusive practices in Cypriot mainstream schools

Inclusive education has only fully been adopted in Cypriot schools for eight years. Special units became practice for the first time in 2001, as a result of the 1999 legislative reforms (Official Newspaper of Cypriot Democracy, 1999, pp. 338–339). These were experimental until 2006, with only 19 on the island. Now 50 per cent of public secondary schools have specialized teaching units (MOEC: online). This has enabled children with SEN to be included in mainstream with support to achieve this.

The number of children who attend special units in school varies according to local needs and regulations (Official Newspaper of Cypriot Democracy, 2001, online, p. 11). Those with SEN must have an individual education plan (IEP) and attend some lessons with their peers participating in whole-school activities and celebrations. The time children spend in special units depends on their level of learning difficulty, with a curriculum differing from mainstream in line with their development. In some cases they may be exempt from normal curriculum subjects, such as ancient Greek and Latin. At public secondary school, called the 'Gymnasium' for 12- to 15-year-olds, the programme in special units focuses mainly on additional language and numeric tuition (European Agency, 2007, pp. 1–2).

Teachers in special units provide social and emotional as well as educational support for children. They give training for their future lives, such as communication, social, self-help and vocational abilities (Official Newspaper of Cypriot Democracy, 2001, online, p. 8). Special educators, psychologists and therapists support school educators (Official Newspaper of Cypriot Democracy, 1999, p. 347). For children with SEN in special units there is an entitlement to transition services for moving them into mainstream. Pupils with sensory disabilities are supported by specialist establishments (European Agency, 2007, p. 2). Also, the Ministry of Education in

Cyprus organizes seminars, conferences and training programmes to help teachers and support staff who work in mainstream special units (Official Newspaper of Cypriot Democracy, 1999, p. 346). A coordinator of special education (SENCO or special needs advisor) visits special units to assist teachers, parents and support staff in the implementation and organization of individual programmes for children (European Agency, 2007, p. 1).

The barriers to inclusive practices

My research (2007), conducted in 9 public secondary schools with special units over Cyprus, involved 33 teachers and suggests that the real situation may differ from legislative demands. Teachers participating in the survey said they targeted social and emotional development of children with SEN. They were less successful in preparing them to cope with the mainstream curriculum. Children with SEN were welcome in mainstream classes and their peers generally accepted them and were willing to give assistance. A third of teachers in the study have introduced inclusive practices into mainstream, using grouping, differentiated tasks and extra explanation as their main strategies. They felt these had improved self-esteem of students with SEN but not equal participation in the curriculum. Reasons acting as barriers to inclusion are as follows:

1. Cypriot schools are not yet ready to support full inclusion of children with SEN in the classroom. A third of teachers felt schools do not have enough facilities.
2. Teachers spend limited time with children in special units with 49 per cent working in them for 3–5 hours per week. Sometimes they deal with over ambitious parents and 6 per cent reported problems working with them.
3. Insufficient training of mainstream teachers working in special units with 2/3 of the cohort having no SEN certification and 1/4 saying training was 'adequate', but did not tackle the use of technological equipment, inclusive strategies or organization of special unit experiences in preparation for mainstream.

Teachers' perceptions about inclusive education

Teacher attitudes are a barrier implementing inclusive practices in Cypriot secondary public schools. According to my research (2007), teachers were uncertain about inclusion and what the concept meant. Two-third of teachers supported integration of children with SEN into mainstream, but only one-third wanted inclusion. When asked to explain the terms integration and inclusion, one-third of teachers believed that participation in all school activities defined the latter. Children with SEN spend time in the ordinary classroom with peers, but are not fully involved in the general curriculum. Two-third of teachers believed that children are integrated into mainstream if they are in special units, with some opportunities to mix with peers. Teachers focus on meeting basic communication, social and emotional needs of children, in special units, rather than encouraging participation in mainstream learning. They emphasized the primacy of interactive development of children and how this enhanced acceptance of them in school. No one believed the academic development of these children was helped in mainstream.

School head teachers felt that inclusive practice in mainstream did not work, due to the lack of training of ordinary teachers. Children with severe difficulties had already left mainstream units and returned to special schools. The ideal model suggested is 'Double inclusion', meaning that children with SEN are included part-time in mainstream but attend units or specialist schools for expert help which is not available to the same extent in regular classrooms. Teachers, however, felt that inclusion of children with SEN in mainstream benefits everybody. Links between mainstream and special schools must be made, however, in order for them to develop the academic abilities of these children more successfully.

Inclusive policy in the United Kingdom

Special needs education in England began in 1870 and for the next 100 years was largely segregated from mainstream provision in special schools with the emphasis on care rather than education (Wearmouth, 2001, pp. 5–7). Educational provision and policies for children with special needs changed after 1944, with a gradual understanding that these children could benefit from relevant teaching. Important legislation followed the Warnock report of 1978 (Des, 1978 quoted in Cigman, 2007, p. 103). It recommended that children with SEN should be integrated into mainstream schools with a legal statement, outlining resources required, for those wanting long-term support. The 1997 statement 'Excellence for all Children' and the 1999 document 'From Exclusion to Inclusion' identified the need for children, with SEN, to participate in the mainstream curriculum and other educational activities. The Code of Practice (2001) acknowledged the right of parents to decide their child's education and the importance of networks between school and home, as well as the cooperation and coordination of health, education and social services (Alcott, 2002, p. 15).

Special needs education started in Cyprus almost 60 years later than the United Kingdom. However, the move to full pupil inclusion in mainstream, rather than just integration, for both countries, has been in the last decade. This was supported by the Salamanca Statement in 1994, promoting Human Rights and education.

Table 11.1 Similarities and differences of SEN education in England and Cyprus

	England	Cyprus
Differences		
Start of special needs education	1870	1929
Integration	After Warnock Report (1978) and 1981 Education Act	With 1988 legislation
Inclusion	From 1994	From 2000
Context	Special classes/centres in some mainstream Schools	Special units in all mainstream (presently 50 per cent)
Similarities		
First period of special needs education	Special schools focus on vocational and life-skill training	
The role of special schools and categories of SEN	England: 1945 Regulations	Cyprus: 1979 Legislation

A significant difference, however, is in the implementation and interpretation of this philosophy. In the United Kingdom, focus has been on academic achievement, in line with National Curriculum requirements to enhance school league tables. This has resulted in children forced into literacy and numeracy before achieving competency in thinking and articulacy, so that their understanding is limited. In Cyprus, this academic push has not been as strong and the emphasis has been on the communication, social and emotional development of children with SEN, to enable contact with their peers and group acceptance. Practice in England and Cyprus was similar for students, before the UK National Curriculum came into place in 1989. Special schools then focused mainly on vocational and life-skill training. Policies were introduced in England in 1945 and in Cyprus in 1979, acknowledging the academic role of special schools and the categories of children to be educated (Table 11.1).

Inclusive practices in UK schools

In the United Kingdom, mainstream teachers have adopted Individual Educational Plans (IEPs) to focus on the basic skills that each child should achieve in reading, spelling, writing and numeracy. Educational activities are designed to build on what a child has achieved. Children and parents are expected to be involved in learning (Ofsted, 1999, pp. 6–7). Specialists, such as psychologists and therapists, provide

Table 11. 2 A simple model for an IEP (quoted in Ofsted, 1999, p. 9)

The first side includes:

Name:	Start date:
Date of birth:	Review date:
Year group:	
Class/tutor group:	Teacher's initials:

Nature of special need (this varies in length and detail, but need not be repeated on subsequent sheets if no change has taken place).

WHAT　　HOW　　WHO　　WHEN

(Specific targets)　　(Method and materials)

The second side to include: - Outcomes/targets:

　　　　Review of IEP:

　　　　List of names of people·

---

additional support to achieve goals in line with National Curriculum requirements (Ofsted, 1999, p. 7). Learning support assistants help children with SEN across a variety of subjects. Groups of schools are encouraged to develop a 'bank of IEP goals and strategies' to be used for students (Table 11.2) (Ofsted, 1999, p. 19).

The Ofsted research suggested this framework was effective, as targets were based on student skills and interest and the local resources available (Ofsted, 1999, p. 12). However, anecdotal evidence of teachers would suggest that this is a stressful bureaucratic demand that takes them away from the business of teaching and learning. In the technical learning model that now predominates in education, teacher focus is on how they present information to the whole group and individual needs have to be sublimated to this requirement.

Research by Sage and Sommefeldt (2003–05), discovered a situation similar to Cyprus, with teachers supporting inclusion in theory but not in practice. In a survey of over 300 teachers and support staff in Midland city primary, secondary and special schools, there was a strong feeling that 'training is an important issue but there has always been the view in education that teachers can cope with anything and everything regardless and that further education for them is a luxury rather than a necessity' (Sage, 2005, p. 8). This survey came up with the following issues to be addressed if inclusion was to be reality rather than rhetoric:

- Staff need accredited courses with detailed knowledge of SEN and supporting issues to make more informed decisions about pupil assessment and teaching
- A curriculum that values personal as well as academic skills
- A thought-through approach to SEN management with less ad hoc initiatives
- Appropriate resources so that pupils can access learning alongside peers

The heads of schools also identified their ideas for inclusion to be successful (Sage, 2005, p. 7).

- Human resources that matched pupil needs for support
- Dual registration of pupils with SEN (mainstream/specialist provision)
- Links with other providers for more joined-up approaches
- Pre-admission risk assessments for more effective planning
- Clearer guidelines on violence from authorities
- Therapy services for psychiatric/psychological problems
- Team-building opportunities for students outside school
- More flexible transport arrangements
- Integrated ICT support across schools to enable better networking

They felt there was insufficient national and local support for the inclusion agenda:

> The local authority should be addressing SEN issues properly – not through the back door. There is ad hoc provision in the City. The current systems thwart progress.

Sage (2005) suggests this throws up important questions regarding appropriate training and resources for educators implementing inclusive education. The emphasis on school academic attainment devalues the personal and social achievements of those who have more practical intelligences. The fact that significant numbers of staff cannot articulate what inclusion means, in terms of accepted definitions (mean total for Teachers = 89 per cent and non-teachers = 86 per cent) and feel they do not have the knowledge and skills to cope with a range of special needs (mean total for Teachers = 56 per cent and non-teachers = 66 per cent), questions their adequacy for dealing with diverse needs. This is a serious professional issue, based on the false premise that educators, trained largely to implement the content of the National Curriculum, are capable without further education of dealing with the complex issues of children who learn differently from the norm.

The data reflects Jordan and Goodey's (1996) study of Newham Education Authority, in London, which noted parents' common concern that school staff did not have sufficient knowledge, experience and confidence to meet their children's special needs. Sage (2005) says that talks with parents suggest the situation has not improved, due to a view that teachers, once trained, can play the teaching game competently even when the rules change. Although there is inconclusive evidence for the success of *inclusion* as measured by pupil performance, Baker et al. (1994–95) have reviewed three studies and reported a small, social and academic benefit of inclusion for the limited sample considered. However, for every reported success there is reported failure, with rising numbers of families consulting the Independent panel for Special Educational Advice (IPSEA) because of dissatisfaction with their children's progress (Sage, 2004, 2007). Parents feel their children's problems have not been clearly identified and appropriately managed. 'In a devastating attack on the way the Government's inclusion policy is being implemented, parents of the Special School Protection League (www.gsspl.org.uk) are campaigning for extra rather than equal opportunities in education. Inclusion of their children in mainstream schools has been a failure and they would be better prepared for inclusion in the outside world in small classes where teachers have specific expertise to target key skill development before concentrating on subject knowledge. Human Scale Education, an educational charity, was set up to promote such values – a holistic approach to learning in a democratic structure and partnership with parents in achieving initially the personal skills of pupils and then academic abilities'.

In its widest sense, education is about acquiring and using knowledge, developing brain abilities to understand, reflect and evaluate, as well as gaining personal competences of communication, cooperation and collaboration. The latter abilities are vital in making an inclusive school philosophy work as students must be able to participate with others to be involved equally in what goes on in school. There is also an expectation that schools can cure social ills and compensate for poverty, abuse and any other personal difficulties that a child might bring into school. Clearly this is nonsense when teachers have so much curriculum content to cope with in a strict time-scale.

In summarizing the implications of Sage's and Sommefeldt's study (2005), it would appear we need to identify more clearly the tasks faced by schools and society in periods of rapid, large-scale, cultural change and specify the knowledge and skills needed. These are not only academic abilities but most importantly personal competences that allow people to communicate and cooperate successfully in their social, learning and work contexts. The present drive for academic success for all pupils ignores the value of practical and social intelligences and provides little opportunity for their teaching and assessment in the present curriculum. We are aiming for more school leavers to enter higher education but what about those for whom this is clearly not appropriate? They are often intelligent in ways that are less valued in the education system and therefore do not receive a curriculum suited to their needs.

Main points in the report by Sage (2005)

- Inclusion is not fully supported by respondents in this review and many educators feel they do not have the knowledge and skills to help all children achieve their potential.
- Education has evolved from an elitist to an inclusive system aiming to provide equal opportunities but not necessarily extra opportunities for those who need them.
- Anxieties are expressed regarding a National Curriculum for everyone, as it ranks children in a public way to an extent that it has never done before and devalues non-academic abilities, so affecting the life chances of a significant number of children, particularly those with SEN.

- Our multi-cultural society ensures that children not only have diverse abilities and interests but very different backgrounds and values, which education has to merge and manage without proper mandatory, accredited training to support inclusion.
- Support staff play a major role in developing inclusive schools and coping with diversity by providing support for a large range of needs. The curriculum could be balanced by training them to deliver key skills to underpin learning.

Comparing inclusive practices in the United Kingdom and Cyprus

A comparison across countries is helpful if we are to make inclusion a reality rather than rhetoric in order to reflect more deeply on the range of practices. From my experience of studying on a UK inclusion course, with participants from east and west traditions, this comparison reflects world-wide issues. Nations are working towards a programme of both social and educational inclusion, but are on different stages of the journey, which is the case with Cyprus and the UK. Schools, in the UK have adopted 'full inclusion' of children with SEN, who are involved in the same academic curriculum as mainstream peers, with tasks differentiated according to need. However, there is indication that educators do not feel fully confident about this model, due to lack of appropriate education and training themselves. In Cyprus, my research (2007) indicates schools have been mainly applying a model of 'functional' or 'social inclusion' (Alcott, 2002, pp. 8–11). Children with SEN participate in social classroom activities but specialist tuition is given outside mainstream classes focusing on literacy and numeracy relevant to needs. Many professionals support this 'double inclusion' model.

This review has found that many issues regarding the implementation of inclusion across nation are similar. Until recently, segregation of pupils according to ability was regarded as the most effective teaching method for pupils. Teachers, in schools worldwide, who were educated in this philosophy, find it difficult to change their view. There has been insufficient input into teacher training on special needs and disability in both the United Kingdom and Cyprus as well as elsewhere. However, all Cypriot teachers in charge of special units must have post-graduate training in special needs to work in mainstream, but in the United Kingdom this is not mandatory. The Sage study (2005) found that less than 1 per cent of teachers had received accredited training and this was regarded by them as a real barrier to making the system work. Both countries feel resources are a major issue and although there are schools where the policy is working well for all children, there are many examples that suggest that a great deal more needs to be done for everyone to reach their potential. Sage (2004), in the *World of Difference*, suggests that inclusion policies

Table 11.3 The UK–Cypriot situation

	England	Cyprus
Model of inclusion	Full academic inclusion	Functional-social inclusion
Learning process	Educational support inside class, sen forum, bank of ieps	Meeting individual needs in special units, 1/3 teachers adopt inclusive practices
Teachers'perceptions	Inadequate For range of culture, ability and background of students	Adequate Confused over inclusion and integration
School policy	Teachers, teacher assistants , parents, school = collaboration	Schools do not always provide facilities to students with sen
Teachers' support	Social, emotional, personal development of SEN children seen by both as primary	
Training	More specialist training required in both nations	
External provision	both developing networks between special and mainstream schools	

do not sit comfortably with a rigid one-size-fits-all curriculum. Flexible assessment methods and a re-think of league tables that discourage schools from taking children with special needs would create a more facilitative environment. Table 11.3 below summarizes the UK–Cypriot situation.

Guidance for the future

According to the previous analysis, the educational systems, in Cyprus and the United Kingdom as well as the rest of the world, are largely under-resourced to meet the diverse needs of all pupils in mainstream. The situation must be changed to make inclusive education effective. The following suggestions are advocated:

(a) Ministries of Education need to
   o appoint more special educators, therapists and teacher assistants in schools;
   o fund specialist equipment so teachers can support the participation of children with SEN in the mainstream curriculum;
   o develop teacher pre-service and in-service SEN education and training, with a continuous programme of both practical and academic opportunities; and
   o fund studies to provide clearer evidence regarding inclusive practice

(b) School communities should
   o support the teacher with appropriate resources for a diverse range of pupils;
   o motivate teachers to be involved in special needs educational provision;
   o increase special educational facilities by involving local communities;
   o organize public events to increase awareness of diverse needs in society;

○ promote collaboration between teachers, students and parents within and across nations to improve knowledge, understanding and support; and
○ develop collaborative networks between mainstream and special schools

(c) Teachers should
   ○ develop greater awareness of child needs through education, training and experience;
   ○ examine attitudes towards inclusion through discussion with stakeholders; and
   ○ seek new ways to support all children using community resources.

According to the theory of 'multiple intelligence' (Gardner, 1993), children have different profiles of abilities and interests and learn in various ways. This suggests teachers should develop practices that not only encourage socialization and acceptance of children with SEN in mainstream but also ones that involve them in learning. Teachers should

- develop trusting relations in classroom by fostering effective communication;
- produce individual educational plans (IEPs) to meet a child's personal and academic needs that supports thinking, speaking and then recording (literacy/numeracy) and manage additional support for this if required;
- plan with support staff, specialist teachers, therapists, psychologists and parents for a consistent approach to management; and
- allow students to be more actively involved in their learning.

Review

Today, the aims of education have changed to prepare learners for their life and work in a technical, global society. Education now involves everyone in the same learning process regardless of abilities and background. Declarations of Jomtien in Thailand (1990) and the Salamanca statement in Spain (1994) have had worldwide influence, advocating equal opportunity for all, resulting in the education of children with SEN alongside peers in mainstream schools.

Specialist resources are necessary for an inclusive policy to work, with some children requiring not only equal but extra opportunities to fulfil society's demands. This has enormous economic implications for all nations and some are in a better position to provide required resources than others. In a global world, we need to work together towards better educational standards for all citizens, through international research and relationships. Regarding the United Kingdom and Cyprus, a 'one-size for-all' philosophy, which has dominated curriculum development, must be changed to encompass more flexible formats that meet the needs of diverse populations to learn at their own pace and in various ways according to interest and ability.

Suggestions for classroom practice

Comparing practices across the world is like looking in a mirror as it makes your views clearer. Help children achieve this through Internet links with schools abroad. Look into school visits and exchanges that can be funded for teachers and pupils under the British Council and European Commission schemes. Take on board everyone's needs to be better educated in special needs matters and use the expertise of those around school to develop knowledge and skills in this area.

Main points

- Education and training for diversity and inclusion, within a framework of human development in a multi-cultural society, must be strengthened to give educators more confidence.
- A flexible rather than a fixed curriculum is compatible with an inclusive philosophy.
- Nations are on the road to social and educational inclusion with some further ahead than others. Across country links accelerate world progress.
- There is no clear evidence about the overall benefits of inclusion in practice and this needs to be prioritized for future educational planning.
- Communication and relationships are the basis for successful participation in learning and valued by high achieving countries, so this needs emphasis in training and practice.

Discussion point

What are your views regarding inclusion of children with special needs in mainstream schools? Do you support the single inclusion policy of the United Kingdom or the double inclusion model that appears the compromise in Cyprus?

- Organizations such as The College of Teachers, based at the Institute of Education in London, have courses in many countries and are a major resource for understanding inclusion in world terms. Use Google to access their several websites.

References

Alcott, M. (2002) *An Introduction to Children with Special Educational Needs*, 2nd edn, London: Hodder and Stoughton.

Baker, E., Wang M. and Walberg, H. (1994–95) The effects of inclusion on learning. *Educational Leadership*, 52(4), 33–35.

European Agency (2007) *Special needs education within the education system;* available online at www.european-agency.org/nat_ovs/Cyprus/4.html (accessed on 5 March 2008).

Gardner, H. (1993) *Frames of Mind: The Theory of Multiple Intelligences,* 2nd edn, London: Fontana Press.

Jordon, L. and Goodey, C. (1996) *Human Rights and School Change: The Newham Story,* Bristol: CISE.

MOEC (2007) *Ediki Ekpaidevsi;* available online at www.moec.gov.cy/eidiki/pdf/statistika_stoixeia.pdf (accessed on 15 August 2008).

Official Newspaper of Cypriot Democracy (1999) *o peri agogis kai ekpaideusis paidion me eidikes anagkes nomos.* In my translation: *The legislation of support and education of children with special need;* available online at http://www.moec.gov.cy/eidiki/nomothesia/Kanonismoi_KDP_186_%202001.pdf (accessed on 16 July 2008).

Official Newspaper of Cypriot Democracy (2001) *o peri agogis kai ekpaideusis paidion me eidikes anagkes nomos,* in my translation: *The legislation of support and education of children with special needs;* available online at http://www.moec.gov.cy/eidiki/nomothesia/Kanonismoi_KDP_186_%202001.pdf (accessed on 5 March 2008).

Ofsted (1999) *The SEN Code of Practice: three years on: The contribution of individual educational plans to the raising of standards for pupils with special educational needs;* available online at www.ofsted.gov.uk/assets/833.pdf (accessed on 15 August 2008).

Ofsted (2003) *Special educational needs in the mainstream;* available online at www.ofsted.gov.uk/assets/3408.doc (accessed on 15 August 2008).

Phtiaka, H. (2000) *Special Education in Cyprus: A critical historical account;* available online at http://www.isec2000.org.uk/abstracts/papers_p/phtiaka_1.htm (accessed on 5 March 2009).

Sage, R. (2004) *A World of Difference,* Stafford: Network Educational Press.

Sage, R. (2005) *Inclusion in a Midland City,* Leicester: University of Leicester.

Sage, R. (2007) *Inclusion in Schools: Making a Difference,* London: Network-Continuum.

Wearmouth, J. (2001) *Special Educational Provision in the Context of Inclusion: Policy and Practice in Schools,* London: David Fulton Publishers.

12 Succeeding in diversity

Rosemary Sage

Overview

This chapter brings together some of the main issues revealed in the book and reflects on these for future planning and practice. A strong message to emerge is the importance of being able to communicate, collaborate and cooperate across cultures whether these are national or indigenous groups with differences or disabilities that affect the way they interact. Conversation with others, who are different from us, helps us to become more critical watchers and listeners so that we can interact more effectively. Through talk we develop awareness of the ways in which verbal and non-verbal language is valuable for understanding and explaining the world together with the people who live in it. However, language can be a dangerous tool as we noted in chapter one. If its power is not recognized, it can become a weapon to attack the weak and powerless. Nevertheless, it is the effectiveness of our verbal and non-verbal communication as well as an understanding of the rules of situations, the relationships we make, our social abilities and the ideas, concepts and attitudes we form which makes us successful in coping with diverse people and cultures.

Language for succeeding in diversity

The role of talk for successful living and learning should not be underestimated. There is a great deal of research, which shows that collaborative talk for all, especially for those who are bilingual or have learning problems, is the secret of success. Initiatives such as the Government National Oracy Project (Norman, 1992) following the National Curriculum in 1989, showed how talk contributes to effective socializing and learning in a huge number of ways. One of the important aspects of this communication is the way in which it supports thinking and problem solving because of the opportunities it gives to construct knowledge and understanding together. Wells and Chang-Wells (1992) provide examples of talk from multilingual contexts which offer chances for collaborative meaning-making with others. They argue that talk is the very essence of social and learning activity and develops 'literate thinking' which exploits the symbolism of language to enable thought processes themselves to become the 'objects of thought' so helping to construct inner meaning. This is essential to understanding others and the world as well as living together harmoniously.

In a multi-cultural society, multilingualism is just part of everyone's lives. Even if people's first and only language is English, the varieties encountered outside home may be very different in content and form to what is familiar. Do you know what 'mashing' or 'going on the gas' means? This is 'making tea' and 'walking on the pavement' in Nottinghamshire where I was born. These differences all add to the context – in either positive or negative ways, depending on how participants can deal with the situation and their competence to communicate across language and culture. An ability to 'read a situation', relate to others and appreciate the non-verbal components of messages (such as voice, gestures and movements conveying affective meaning) are necessary for effective interaction.

Despite overwhelming evidence for the positive effects of speaking more than one language (Cummins, 1996), it is still perceived as a problem in many mainstream classrooms. This attitude reflects the power relationships that exist between bilingual communities and the wider society. In communities with a good socio-economic level, additive bilingualism is valued if the languages are viewed as having high status such as English and French, which are both spoken in Canada. However, in groups with low economic levels, whose community languages have no cultural capital in the society at large, attitudes are reversed. The outcome is generally subtractive bilingualism with negative cognitive effects. Thus, some groups suffer from assumptions that lead to low expectations of them and these include those with language and learning difficulties.

This dual language situation does not just involve those who speak different national languages. In all cultures, there is a 'high language', spoken in formal contexts, and in the United Kingdom referred to as 'standard English', the version spoken in London and the home counties. The language spoken at home and with familiar contacts is known as 'low language' and includes local dialects which have quite different words and pronunciation to the standard form, as we have seen above in an example of Nottinghamshire dialect. In order to communicate effectively, speakers require competence in both forms. However, due to the fact that 'standard English' has been considered elitist it has not been promoted in state schools so lessening some children's chance of social and work mobility. Who ever heard of a High Court Judge or Chief of the Army, Air Force and Navy speaking in anything other than standard English? This contrasts greatly with our French neighbours, who all learn Parisian French as the 'high language' and, therefore, can more readily communicate with people from other regions or countries. A similar experience is encountered with those who have learning problems, as they frequently communicate in a different way to others with a high proportion having differences which hinder learning as well as socializing (Sage, 2000).

Cultural differences

Differences in language, reveal a variety of beliefs, rules and general ways of living so that those who deviate from what is the majority norm are often rejected as accounts in the preceding chapters have indicated. Dijker (1987) reports a study of the effects of physical proximity in Amsterdam. He found that proximity led the Dutch population to like the Indonesians but not the Turks, suggesting that cultural differences were at the root of this rejection. One reason why people can not tolerate others is that they hold different beliefs and values, thinking differently and being incomprehensible and not quite human in their terms. Rokeach et al. (1960) found that similarity of belief was more important than that of race.

Conflict between groups

Bad relations between people are often based on conflicts between them. We have seen this between management and workers, as revealed by Yaasmin Mubarak in Chapter 2. There has been a long history of animosity between Blacks and Whites, Israelis and Arabs, Protestants and Catholics, heterosexuals and homosexuals, people who work and those who do not etc. Brown (1986) found that hostility at work was the result of perceived conflict and not of in-group identification, suggesting that the solution was 'super-ordinate goals' that were acceptable to everyone (Sherif et al., 1961). He studied the resolution of conflict, giving an example of a boys' camp, where the water supply was interfered with so that everyone had to cooperate in pulling a water cart with a rope that previously had been used in opposite directions in a tug-of-war. This was successful in resolving hostilities between the boys.

However, Brown enquired what workers would do if the management declared a 10 per cent redundancy but only 20 per cent favoured a cooperative strategy as they were primarily concerned with defending their own particular group. Nevertheless, political leaders have succeeded in integrating their nation's actions by directing aggression against another group, as demonstrated in the recent Iraq war. This is a clear case of a 'super-ordinate goal'. It maybe that positive, shared goals only work readily on a small scale, while aggressive ones do so on a larger, national/international scale.

The 'contact hypothesis' suggests that close and frequent interaction between people is all that is needed for positive attitudes to develop between them. However, Argyle (1992) cites evidence to suggest that education and training are necessary for this to happen. The Japanese place great importance on training people to work abroad in other cultures, so it should be possible to use their strategy more widely. Small group education has proved more successful with a prestigious speaker to lend weight to information. It is necessary to provide knowledge and understanding of both similarities and differences between people and active methods, such as role play, are important to effecting a real change in attitude. When I was training to be a speech and language therapist, we had to be taken out in the street in a wheelchair and be blindfolded in order to understand the feelings and experiences of those who had disabilities. A specialized form of teaching was used, known as the 'culture assimilator'. Students were required to survey a large sample (50–100 incidents) of difficulties within a group they were studying (e.g. disability), which were then embodied in a workbook text which was discussed in small groups. Each incident presented a problem as below:

> One day, a middle ranking administrator for housing kept a man in a wheelchair waiting for nearly an hour for an appointment regarding his move to a new apartment. This was to give him more facilities, such as room for a motor vehicle, so that he could become more independent. When the administrator walked in, he acted as though he was not late, making no apology or explanation to the man who had been waiting to see him.

The contents convey a great deal about the rules, ideas and social relationships involved. Such activities allow trainees to consider issues in depth so that they become much more conscious of their behaviour with others. The next section focuses on non-verbal communication as an important but often ignored area of making and maintaining relationships. In Japan, they directly teach these competences to children in a way never seen in this country. There is no doubt of their importance in making and maintaining relationships and they play an enhanced role when verbal language ability is weak.

Non-verbal communication (NVC)

This aspect of communication is crucial in interaction with others, adding to and completing the meaning of utterances, giving feedback from listeners and providing synchrony and coordination. There are several aspects of NVC to be considered.

NVC from the speaker

The tone of voice frames speaking with a melody or pitch pattern. A question, for example, has a rising tune, whilst a statement a falling one. Stress is placed on a word to emphasize its importance, indicating which of several possible meanings are intended as in 'Luke's ball', signalling that it is *his* possession and not that of someone else. Voice conveys manner – suspicion, sarcasm, amusement, hostility, dominance, submissiveness etc. It also indicates an emotional state as depressed people speak in a low, slow voice with falling pitch and excited ones in a reverse pattern. Accent shows social class and regional origins and people will react to these signals in varying ways depending on their views, attitudes and experiences.

Pauses in speech are longer if the topic is difficult or the talk is amongst strangers who might with unfamiliar with one's speech patterns (Markel, 1990). Speakers spend 30–40 per cent of the time in silence. This device helps 'thinking time' and is important for listeners as they are less in command of the topic content like the speaker.

Gestures, particularly with the hands, illustrate what is being said, as in copying shapes, objects and movements or signifying close relationships through touch. They are also used as batons to mark new points. Gestures act simultaneously with words, or just before them, and without them understanding is impaired (Argyle, 1992). Studies show that gestures develop alongside speech and are controlled by the same brain area in joint production, but babies use them in preference to words initially (e.g. bye-bye sign) because they are easier to make. 'Emblems' are quite different and are symbolic gestures replacing words in some contexts, such as a hitch-hike or V sign.

Gaze is used by speakers for around 40 per cent of the time at a distance of two metres and more than this if they are farther apart. Glances are of about three seconds, which include mutual gaze of around one second in duration. Gaze coordinates with speech with speakers looking just before finishing an utterance as well as at grammatical brakes in order to collect listener reactions. They look away when starting to speak and during hesitancies in order to avoid cognitive overload. If people gaze continually more speech errors occur.

NVC by the listener

Listeners send many NVCs without being aware and these are detailed below:

Vocalizations include '*uh-huhs*' and other grunts, which are maintenance moves to signal that the listener wants the conversation to continue. Words, such as 'good' and 'really', help out the speaker if he/she needs extra reassurance.

Gestures such as head nods show attention to what is being said, with large ones signalling agreement. Head shakes are much rarer.

Facial expressions are important feedback information for speakers. Mouth and eyebrow movements show whether a listener understands, is pleased, puzzled, disbelieving, annoyed and angry or perhaps agrees or disagrees with the speaker.

Posture indicates degrees of alertness or sleepiness as well as more specific actions such as disgust. If listeners are bored they prop their heads up and if interested they lean forwards. Disagreement is shown by folding the arms and is a defensive movement.

Gaze is used more by listeners than speakers, usually for 75 per cent of the time. They are looking intently to pick up the vital non-verbal signals that accompany speech and if they are deaf, the lip movement sequence of utterances. The reason that this is less than 100 per cent is to reduce cognitive overload or arousal.

Body synchrony between movements of a speaker and listener/s is an important part of establishing rapport between them. As the person begins to speak they look away and start to gesture but when they stop the opposite occurs. People, in conversation, adopt congruent postures, usually mirror images, adding to feelings of comfort and signifying positive feeling. Argyle (1988) suggests that if a listener copies the other's bodily movements they are liked more and he describes this as a 'gestural dance'.

Conversational sequences

Talk between people consists of sequences of utterances and those who are socially inept have problems with these. They do not know what to say or they make an inappropriate remark. They can, however, be trained and Grice (1975) came up with conversational rules:

1. Provide no more or less information than is required by the situation.
2. Say only relevant things.
3. Speak the truth.
4. Speak clearly and concisely.

Grice has not offered empirical evidence for these rules but everyday experience supports them and they have stood the test of time in communication training circles. There are, however, plenty of examples of times when rules are not adhered to. Take the evasive answers to questions by politicians or teenagers. Furthermore, rules are often broken in the interests of politeness and it is often the irrelevancies of talk, such as the odd joke or amusing story that keeps us interested and alert during an exchange.

Politeness

We would all agree that politeness is important to establishing good relationships and although it is often defined as 'good manners' (courteous, refined behaviour etc.) there are probably many different ideas of what this constitutes. Politeness has been seen as comprising a number of social abilities (Leech, 1983):

(a) *Friendliness*: responding warmly to others both in words and actions
(b) *Consideration of other's self-esteem*: praising the successes of others should be maximized
(c) *Indirect requests*: leaving the other to choose. E.g. 'Would you like a drink?' rather than: 'Here's a drink'.
(d) *Expressing points of agreement rather than disagreement*: disagreement should be wrapped up in utterances with positive verbal and non-verbal elements. In Japan it is rude to say 'no' and questions are avoided where this might be the answer.
(e) *Making repairs*: When offence has occurred this is usually done by expressing regret as in being late for an appointment. Often this is accompanied by an explanation as an excuse. *Concessions* (most mitigating), *excuses* and *justifications* (most aggravating) are the three major types of repairs used.
(f) *Avoidance of rule breaking*: Such as interruptions, talking too much, telling dirty jokes etc. However, rules of politeness vary between situations. For example, in university seminars it is acceptable to disagree in a friendly way but this would not be appropriate for a party occasion or perhaps in a job interview.

Accommodation

Speakers usually accommodate to each other and change their speech styles to be more similar to help form a positive dynamic between them. This can be in respect of the *language* spoken (*as in English and Scottish encounters*), of *accent* (*as between those of different social classes*), or *loudness* or *length of utterance*. They do this to be accepted as well as better understood. An example of this was demonstrated when I visited Japan. The Japanese give many more back-channel responses, such as grunts and head-nods, because they speak in shorter sentences than we do, so there are more pauses. When speaking with Japanese colleagues, I found myself giving more of these signals and noticed that they used less than they did with their own fraternity when talking with English counterparts.

Beginning and sustaining relationships

Research by Trower (1980) found that friendly non-verbal communication (in face, voice tone and gesture etc.) was more important than words in creating a favourable impression. People who find it difficult to make and retain friends are always deficient in their use of non-verbal cues. The following are found to be effective when communicating with others in a face-to-face situation:

Proximity – move closer and lean forward if seated
Orientation – face-to-face or side-by-side positioning dependent on situation
Gaze – more of this as well as mutual gaze
Facial expression – more smiling
Gestures – head nods and lively, positive movements
Posture – open arms rather than folding or putting them on the hips
Touch – more touch if appropriate
Voice tone – higher, upward pitch with pure tone
Verbal content - more self-disclosure so that people can judge one better

Verbal behaviour: contributing to reward

Paying compliments – maximizing praise without overdoing this
Pleasure talk – keeping to cheerful topics so enhancing joy and reducing depression
Agreeing - to avoid antagonizing
Using names – making the listener feel *valued* as a person
Being helpful – offering information, sympathy or practical help
Humour – breaking down barriers and relaxing everyone to produce shared feelings

Verbal behaviour: contributing to relations

Finding commonality – in the topics discussed to develop shared interests
Questions – taking personal interest without being too intimate to assist self-disclosure
Self-disclosure – giving information that helps others to know and trust you

Talk has five main areas which are relevant for different situations

Sociability – casual chat, jokes etc. for enjoyment
Gossip – news about friends and acquaintances
Common interests – disclosing feelings and thoughts about shared topics
Problem solving – the social network is the best source of advice/information
Social support – demonstrates empathy and sympathy when required

Being critical, intolerant, negative, nagging or jealous, as well as revealing confidences and not showing support, loses friends and these unspoken rules should never be broken. There are, however, other factors that also are influential when considering relationships between diverse populations. These are the following.

Social class

In Britain there is much more blurring between people of different classes than there used to be. However, middle class people (defined by economic and educational criteria) choose friends more cautiously, mainly from work or organizations to which they belong, inviting them home to occasions such as parties. Those from a working class background see more of their neighbours and give mutual help – lending sugar, bread, tea etc. They socialize at the pub and do not entertain their friends at home in a formal way. On average, they marry and have babies sooner and women make close relationships with other females as they find men poor confidants.

Age

For young people friendships with their peers are their most important relationships and they spend up to three hours a day talking with them on phones (Argyle, 1992), which is probably longer now 18 years later. After marriage there is less time for these relationships until middle age when people are retired and friendships assume great importance again.

Gender

Women have close bonds with other women, providing much social support. They hold families together by keeping in regular contact. For men, work relationships are important and develop into a world-wide network in many professions which are vital for career success. For women who work, the social contacts are often more important than the job itself. Those in senior positions generally handle those under them in a more caring, democratic way than corresponding men.

Culture

Friendship is part of all cultural traditions but is more formal in some than others. Matey relations, amongst males, are important in professions such as mining, where people work in isolation. The famous Welsh Male Voice Choirs arose from this situation. 'Blood brothers', developed in the ancient world is still practised in parts of Africa by cutting the skin and rubbing in each other's blood or even drinking it. The idea is to create an alliance between individuals or groups based on trust and mutual support.

Marriage varies greatly between cultures and this is expanded on in the appendices. Muslim marriages may include four wives with divorce very easy to achieve. Chinese men, traditionally have a wife and a concubine with less rules regarding faithfulness. Recently, with smaller families and greater numbers of working wives, there is more emphasis on love and fulfilment and equality. In all cultures, an increasing number of dual-career couples are finding life very stressful and demanding. Kinship networks are important in Africa, India and in the less developed parts of the world are relied upon for jobs and help of any kind. In these networks, there is respect for the elderly.

Work relationships are more hierarchical in Japan and countries outside Western Europe and North America. In Japan, people train to be obedient on management courses and conformity is important. Although globalization has made work patterns more mobile, working groups often keep intact for many years. I found, in the central Japanese regions, that wives frequently assisted their husbands with work tasks. In Japan, as well as Hong Kong and China, there are stronger rules for avoiding face, such as not criticizing in public, obedience to hierarchies and concealing emotions and feelings (Argyle, 1987). Because of the fundamental differences amongst groups due to their histories, traditions, languages and ways of living, there have been serious social problems faced by the world. These have been revealed in detail in the previous chapters and it is appropriate in the closing sections to review problems and possible solutions.

Review

This book has aired differences between people with the purpose of reviewing how these might be bridged in order to avoid misunderstanding and conflicts between groups. In a global world in which we are so interdependent, living together in peace and harmony has become increasingly important. Today, as we are all immersed in a period of world recession, the way we communicate, collaborate and cooperate with one another is how we can survive.

However, aggressive conflict between groups is widespread as media reports constantly demonstrate. Political commentators such as Ruth Dudley Edwards (2010) have suggested that our universities are breeding grounds for extremist views, described as 'seats of learning and loathing'. She attributes this to greed and pusillanimity as 'starved of funds and bullied by the government into dropping standards in the name of social and ethnic diversity, universities court more foreign students than they can cope with and do nothing to upset them'. The 'festering ideological cesspits' within universities corrupt confused young people and their aggressive acts are partly defensive, with a physiological response that is stronger in males. However, it is also the product of our socialization and cultural differences.

These produce various social stresses that can be restrained by the social norms we create and the encouragement of empathy for others. Assumptions are often made of one group by another because they do not communicate and disclose issues of concern. Negative stereotypes easily develop as they seek superior in-group identity. Much aggression has roots in racial prejudice, competition for jobs and resources as well as socialization factors and personality differences. How groups behave will depend on their traditions and the grievances or otherwise of their leaders. Economic and political causes, such as seeking independence or the integration of traditions, such as Islamic, Sharia rules into the British legal system, are inspired by leaders with a convincing ideology.

Attempts to prevent or resolve differences between groups include the presentation of super-ordinate goals, which appear to work on a small-scale. Contact and communication between groups, in the right conditions, is the most effective strategy. Education and inter-cultural training at all levels of learning make good use of research into differences and we all need to develop the rules of negotiation so that we can work together for good solutions to problems.

Our society does not need a uniform ideology or religion but requires binding norms, values, ideals and goals based on the importance of everyone. This will only be acquired by patient, continuous dialogue and shared understandings. From face-to-face communication evolves an ability to imagine and a capacity for compassion. Let us make time to talk. Indeed it is good to talk but even better to listen. But listening requires legitimizing other point of views, with an enhanced understanding of the communicative process which now must be taught in all our educational institutions.

Suggestions for classroom practice

> Make communication a curriculum topic. In high-achieving countries communication, rhetoric and philosophy figure prominently on time-tables. Our public schools give high value to communicative activities and view an educated person as one who talks well.

Main points

> - Coping with diversity involves good contact, communication, collaboration and cooperation to be successful.
> - Research shows that people, at all learning levels, need to be trained in issues regarding culture and communication.
>
>

- Training is best carried out in small groups with an expert contributing to give credibility to the message.
- Conflict between groups has been present throughout history but in a global world with everyone interdependent on each other good relationships between people is of paramount importance.
- Greater available knowledge about the world and its peoples gives us an opportunity to develop peace and harmony amongst us more successfully.

Discussion point

Ask colleagues and students to identify the issues they have experienced in dealing with those who are different to them. Lead them to consider solutions to their problems.

References

Argyle, M. (1988) *Bodily Communication*, 2nd edn, London: Methuen.

Argyle, M. (1992) *The Social Psychology of Everyday Life*, London and New York: Routledge.

Brown, R. (1988) *Group Processes*, Oxford: Blackwell.

Cummins, J. (1996) *Negotiating Identities: Education for Empowerment in a Diverse Society*, Ontario, CA: California Association for Bilingual Education.

Dijker, A. (1987) Emotional reactions to ethnic minorities. *European Journal of Social Psychology*, 17, 305–325.

Edwards, R. D. (2010) *Seats of learning and loathing*. News Review and Comment, p. 23. *The Daily Telegraph*, 2 January 2010.

Grice, H. (1975) Logic and conversation. In P. Cole and J. Morgan (eds), *Syntax and Semantics*. Vol. 3. *Speech Acts*. New York: Academic Press.

Leech, G. (1983) *Principles of Pragmatics*. London: Longman.

Markel, N. (1990) Speaking style as an expression of solidarity: words per pause. *Language in Society*, 19, 81–88.

Norman, K. (1992) (ed.) *Thinking Voices: The Work of the National Oracy Project*. London: Hodder and Stoughton.

Rokeach, M., Smith, P. and Evans, R. (1960) Two kinds of prejudice or one? In M. Rokeach (ed.) *The Open and Closed Mind*. New York: Basic Books.

Sage, R. (2000) *Class Talk*, London and New York: Network Continuum.

Sherif, M., Harvey, O., White, B., Hood, W. and Sherif, C. (1961) *Intergroup Cooperation and Competition: The Robert cave Study,* Norman, OK: University Book Exchange.

Trower, P. (1980) Situational analysis of the components and processes of socially skilled and unskilled patients. *Journal of Consulting and Clinical Psychology,* 48, 329–339.

Wells, G. and Chang-Wells, G. (1992) *Constructing Knowledge Together: Classrooms as Centers of Inquiry and Literacy,* Portsmouth, NH: Heinemann.

Appendix 1: Religious diversity

Overview

The United Kingdom is a diverse, multi-faith society. Until recently religion has been mostly missing from discussions on equality because of a focus in public policies on race and minority ethnic communities. Now we recognize that religion, along with ethnicity, gender and sexuality matter to people as a source of positive identity. Equality is about not having to hide origins or apologize for one's family or community and being respected by others. Attitudes, arrangements and facilities in society must adapt so people's heritage is supported and accommodated.

Ethnicity and religion

The interrelationship between ethnicity and religion is complex:

- Ethnic groups are often multi-religious. For example, Indians may be Hindus, Muslims, Sikhs, Christians or members of other belief systems.
- Religious practices can cut across ethnic groups. For example, Muslims can be Albanian, Bangladeshi, Bosnian, Chinese, Indian, Indonesian, Iraqi, Malaysian, Nigerian, Pakistani, Somali, Turkish, English, Irish, Scottish or Welsh.
- Ethnic and religious identities can coincide. Both Jews and Sikhs are recognized as ethnic groups under the Race Relations Act (RRA), 1976.

Internal diversity

Each religion has an internal diversity of traditions, movements, cultures and languages. For example, Black-led churches have joined traditional Christian groups in the United Kingdom. The religious practices of members of minority ethnic communities may emphasize characteristics of their place of origin, combining belief and practice along with cultural and religious allegiances. Many Africans may be Muslim or Christian but live in a distinctly African cultural manner. The same goes for people from South Asia. Cultural differences, within any group, may involve distinctions according to age, gender and social status. Individuals differ in their adherence to and practice of religion. There is no typical Hindu, Muslim or Sikh and we make assumptions to convey an idea of the basic principles of various religious traditions.

Main belief systems in the United Kingdom

The 2001 Census showed that 71.6 per cent of respondents (37 million) stated their religion as Christian, while 15.5 per cent (9.1 million) said they had no religion and a further 7.3 per cent (4.2 million) failed to respond to the question. Some 3.1 per cent of England's population and 0.7 per cent of the Welsh gave religion as Muslim, making this the most common religion after Christianity. Some 8.5 per cent of London's population stated their religion as Muslim; 4.1 per cent as Hindus and 2.1 per cent as Jewish.

Discrimination arises when attitudes and actions are based on assumptions and stereotypes about members of a specific faith. For example, a Muslim woman with a hijab may be seen as oppressed and forced to wear it, whereas a Sikh man with a turban, is rarely viewed in this way. Many attitudes evolve from the time when British society was less diverse and multi-faith than it is today. Doing things as they have always been done disadvantages those who are different, instead of appreciating the 'dignity of difference' discussed by Rabbi Jonathan Sachs (2002).

The Baha'i faith

Key points

- Based on the teachings of Baha'u'llah born in Iran (1817–92).
- Members spread throughout the world with the largest groups in South Asia, Africa, Latin America and the Pacific Islands.
- Community established in the United Kingdom, Europe and the United States in the 1890s.

Beliefs

- Uphold the unity of God and his prophets and the oneness of the human race.
- Duty to search for truth with the harmony of science and religion vital for progress.

- Equal rights and opportunities for all and compulsory education.
- Monasticism, priesthood and mendicancy prohibited. Monogamy prescribed; divorce discouraged; obedience to government promoted.

Practices

- Prayer, meditation (twice daily).
- Fasting (19 days: 2–20 March).
- Communal gatherings are in private homes where no centre is established. Calendar: 19 months, each of 19 days. Members meet on the first day of each Baha'i month to read scriptures. Eight feast days per year.
- Ceremonies: Birth naming, marriage and funerals (no cremations)

Buddhism

Key points

- Diverse UK community from India, China, Japan, South East Asia and ethnic European. Founded by Shakyamuni in North India in sixth century BC.
- Cultural, regional and doctrinal differences between adherents mean no assumptions can be made. Two strands: Theravada (way of the elders); Hinayana (small vehicle) in Sri Lanka, Burma, Thailand, Laos and Cambodia. Mahayana (great way) widespread in Mongolia, Korea and Vietnam. In Japan the Zen (meditation) form predominates.

Beliefs

- Cycle of rebirth and death (*samsara*). Life is impermanent and characterized by suffering. The three Jewels are the components of the path to enlightenment. Doctrine of the noble eightfold path (wheel with eight spokes): promoting right understanding, thought, speech, action, livelihood, effort, mindfulness and concentration.
- Submission to Buddha and his teachings (*dhamma*) and the Buddhist community (*sangha*) with its monks, nuns and laity.

Practices

- Meditation.
- Temples offerings.
- Festivals:– Theravada and Mahayana – not fixed except for Zen Buddhists. Commemorate birth, life and teachings of Buddha.
- Diet: Mostly vegetarian – avoiding intentional killing.
- Ceremonies: Birth naming, male temporary ordination, marriage (arranged ones are customary), funeral rituals which focus on rebirth.

Christianity

Key points

- Large number of subdivisions (e.g. Anglicans, Catholics, Methodists, Orthodox [Coptic, Abyssinian, Armenian, Syrian], Presbyterian, Pentecostal and Reformed Churches; Non-Trinitarians are Jehovah's Witnesses, Mormons and Unitarians).
- Practised by the widest variety of minority groups.
- Different understandings of Christianity, its Creeds and Bible are common.

Beliefs

- Jesus of Nazareth was Christ (Messiah) and God incarnate. Second of the three Abrahamic/Semitic religions (Judaism, Christianity and Islam) originating from the prophet Abraham. Few rituals, rules and regulations for life compared with the other two Semitic religions.
- Doctrine of the Trinity: Father, Son and Holy Ghost (3 persons in one).

Practices

- Liturgy – communal worship; Holy Communion/ Mass/ The Lord's Supper/Holy Eucharist is the central sacrament.
- Festivals: Christmas, Epiphany, Lent, Ash Wednesday, Palm Sunday, Maundy Thursday, Good Friday, Easter Sunday, Ascension Day, Pentecost - Whit Sunday, Corpus Christi, The Feast of the Transfiguration, Assumption, Advent, Feast of the Immaculate Conception, Christmas Day and Boxing Day.
- Ceremonies: Christening – naming ceremony; baptism – admittance to church membership; confirmation – reaffirming baptism; marriage, confession; ordination of priests, deacons and ministers: extreme unction for the very sick; burial.

Hinduism

Key points

- Religion at least 5,000 years old and founded in India with significant communities in Mauritius, the Caribbean, South East Asia, Pacific Islands and amongst ethnic UK settlers.
- Many divisions and sub-groups with no cultural or racial homogeneity.

Beliefs

- The eternal way – *sanatana-dharma* is the central tenet. Based on a complex mythology with no real founder but the worship of a supreme being – *Brahman* who comprises the principles of the Absolute and Infinite with three aspects: the Creator (Brahma); the Preserver (Vishnu) and the Transformer (Shiva) in a trinity (Trimurti). The feminine consorts of the Trimurti are the Shaktis.

- Two divisions: Vishnu and Shiva with many deities.
- Concepts of transmigration and *karma* – with each soul destined to multiple births and rebirths and the transmigration of souls from mineral, vegetable and animal states to that of the human. Liberation (*moksha*) depends on one's *karma* – the cosmic chain of action and reaction compared to the saying of Christ 'as ye sow so shall ye reap'.
- The doctrine of *dharma* is the guidance enabling the soul to navigate the cycles of transmigration.
- Four stages of life: youth and celibacy, marriage and householder, state of retreat, total renunciation. Social delineation by caste now abolished in India although jat (tribe/clan) indicates the person's social origin. Traditional four groupings: Brahmin – priests; Kshatriya – warriors; Vaishya – merchants and craftsmen; Shudra – labourers. Dalit, the 'oppressed', were not in the four main groupings.

Practices

- Worship (*puja*) in homes or temples involves contemplation of images (*murtis*).
- Fasting precedes worship.
- Women signal married status with a mark on the forehead. Gold jewellery traditionally indicates social status.
- Pilgrimages are important at the seven annual festivals of which the major one is Diwali, marking the Hindu New Year.
- Diet: Many are vegetarian because Hindus do not believe in killing life. They do not smoke or drink alcohol.
- Ceremonies: Birth naming; the sacred thread ceremony heralds a boy's period of formal education; marriage (not in temples) with many rituals to ensure benediction for the couple; funeral rituals viewed from the perspective of the transmigration of the soul.

Indigenous traditions

Key points

- Customs and traditions vary according to regional and tribal communities ranging from Africa to Australia together with Polynesia and parts of America.
- Adherence to customs and traditions does not prevent the practice of other faiths.
- Difference in understanding about traditions and origins amongst adherents.

Beliefs

- Reliance on 'orality' and the concept of time as ever-present now with attachment to physical surroundings. Life is one continuum of past, present and future and subject to forces of nature. Individuals are tied to their ancestors, responsibilities to future generations and a transcendent power.
- Importance attached to filial and tribal relationships and the key phenomena of nature: earth, rivers, trees, plants and animals. The acknowledgement of ancestors plays a major role in worship and festivals.

Practices

- Depend on the regional origin of the individual and other faith adopted (if any).
- Rituals related to birth, marriage and death vary enormously depending on the region and faith identities of those concerned. African marriages may be polygamous.

Islam

Key Points

- Youngest of the Semitic/Abrahamic religions, originating in Mecca and Medina where the Prophet, Muhammad founded it (570–632 CE).
- UK community is diverse with ethnic English, Welsh and Irish. Other British Muslims span from Albania to Africa, the Middle East to Malaysia and Poland to Pakistan. UK community has been in sea ports for 300 years.
- Cultural diversity of UK members reflect many trends and tendencies so no assumptions can be made about cultural and racial homogeneity.
- Different interpretations of Islam and its creeds available. Qur'an – sacred text.

Beliefs

- Oneness (*shahada*) of God (Allah) with Muhammad the last of the prophets.
- Qur'an determines religious practice, morality and law in Arabic.
- Five pillars (obligations) are: the testimony of belief (*shahada*).
- Five daily prayers (*salat*) at first light, midday, afternoon, sunset and night time.
- Ramadan – fasting (food, drink and sex) from first light to sunset.
- *Zakat* – annual payment of alms – 1/40th of fixed assets to the poor.
- *Hajj* – prescribed pilgrimage to Mecca returning one's inner centre (*ka'ba*) to the shrine.
- God has two equal attributes: feminine (al-Jamal) and masculine (al-Jalal). Muhammad's first wife was an employee in a merchant business but from eighteenth century the place of women was deemed to be at home in line with northern Europe and gender segregation became unfairly enforced.
- Sunni majority adhere to four law schools: Maluki, Hanafi, Hanbali, Shafi'I; Shia minority adhere to a fifth school with flexible rules governing corporate relations.

Practices

- Obliged to cover heads and dress modestly.
- Mosque – main communal worship place but prayers may be said anywhere.
- Festivals celebrated in a strict lunar calendar – a lunar month is 28–30 days and a year has 354 ones so there are no fixed festival dates. Calendar starts in the year when Muhammad migrated from Mecca to Medina.
- Festivals: Ramadan, Eid ul-Fitr, Hajj, Eid ul-Adha or Eid ul-Kabeer, Muharram (1st month of the Islamic lunar year), Milad un-Nabi (Muhammad's birthday).

- Permissible foods (*halal*) and prohibited ones (*haram*) – pork and alcohol. Animals slaughtered according to ritual with blood draining away – *halal*.
- Ceremonies: Birth naming (*aqiqah*) 40 days after birth; female circumcision in African cultures; marriage (*nikah* or *aqd*) with groom providing an agreed sum of money (*mahr*) to the wife; divorce (*talaq*); funerals with ritual ablutions to the body by someone of the same sex with burial within 24 hours of death and 3 days of mourning, which in some cultures extends to 40 days.

Jainism

Key points

- Based in India, older than Buddhism but smaller in size than Hinduism, originating from Gujarat, North West India in 599 BCE with the birth of Vardhamana Mahavira, who abandoned life as a prince at 30 to impart wisdom.
- Four divisions: Shvetambaras (North); Digambaras (South); Shvetambara monks and nuns (white clothes); Digambara monks (naked).
- The UK community has many groups which interpret scriptures differently but follow a basic philosophy.
- Community divides into ascetics, lay, males and females as a fourfold society. Ascetics not allowed vehicles for travel so not found outside India.

Beliefs

- Cyclical time in ascent and descent halves with 24 teachers born in each half-cycle.
- Individuals can transcend human limitations through ascetic practices.
- Everything is either *jiva* (knowing) or *ajiva* (not-knowing). Souls are prevented from realizing pure *jiva* because *karma* (Law of Causality) attaches *ajiva* but this can be transcended through ascetic practices.
- *Ahimsa* – non-injury to others so they observe a vegetarian diet.
- Temple worship with offerings to *Tirthankara* – a teacher.

Practices

- Go into retreat in the rainy season for teaching and worship.
- Pilgrimages at festival times, according to a lunar calendar, celebrating the events and lives of the *Tirthankaras* (teachers).
- Diet: Vegetarian with the orthodox avoiding root vegetables and fruits with seeds.
- Ceremonies: Similar to the Hindus in terms of birth and marriage rituals. Cremated at death but do not perform the *Shraddha* commemorating this because they do not believe in the transfer of merit from the progeny to the departed soul, which is the purpose of the Hindu ceremony.

Judaism

Key points

- Oldest of Semitic or Abrahamic religions established in the UK in the seventeenth century.
- Two UK Groups: Ashkenazi (from Central and Eastern Europe); Sephardi (the majority – from the Iberian Peninsula, North Africa and the Middle East).

- Diverse – divided between Orthodox and Progressive groups exceeding 0.25 million in the United Kingdom. Speak Hebrew (language of worship) and Yiddish (older Ashkenazi).
- Qualify as an ethnic group by the 1976 Race Relations Act because of a shared history. They range from ultra Orthodox to secular non-affiliated Jews.

Beliefs

- Orthodox Jews: Torah *revealed* by God and the Bible determines law, life and religious practice.
- Progressive Jews: Torah *inspired* by God and is open to revision in changing times.
- Atonement of sin is a central tenet.
- Women are important in the Jewish life of festivals and celebrations and play an equal role and become rabbis (leaders) in Progressive Judaism.
- Three Scriptures: Torah (five books of Moses); Nevi'im (books of Prophets); Ketuvim (writings – Psalms, Proverbs and Ecclesiastes).
- Jewish Law: Halacha applied by Beth Din (Jewish Court).

Practices

- Orthodox men wear dark clothes and wide-brimmed hats in the Hasidic tradition and tend to always cover their heads. Orthodox women may not wear sleeveless garments or trousers with married ones covering their hair. They cannot shake hands with adult males and be touched by them, or vice versa, except in the immediate family.
- Synagogue – main place for communal worship (ten males must be present).
- Three daily prayers: Shacharit (morning); Mincha (afternoon); Maariv or Arvit (evening).
- Shabbat – Sabbath begins before dusk on Friday and ends at nightfall on Saturday with the Torah scroll honoured in the Holy Ark (Aron Kodesh).
- Five major and three minor festivals in accordance with a combined lunar and solar calendar in a 19 year cycle. Each month has 29 or 30 days and a year is usually 354 days with no fixed *festivals* which run from evening to evening.
- Diet: Kashrut rules. Animals, birds and fish are Kosher – slaughtered with the blood drained to minimize suffering. Forbidden foods include pig products, shellfish, game and domesticated animals.
- Ceremonies: Circumcision for males at 8 days (*brit mila*); birth naming in the synagogue; *bar mitzvah* – coming of age for boys; marriage; divorce (*get*) – dissolved contract; funerals - body prepared by someone of the same sex and wrapped in white linen. Ritual mourning (*shiva*) lasts 7 days within the home and then a further 23 days. Kaddish prayers are said in the synagogue for 11 months following death and on the anniversary a tombstone ceremony is held.

Rastafarianism

Key points

- Political agenda against slavery and repression of Black people. No centralized, hierarchical structure but several organizations: the Ethiopian Orthodox Church, the Ethiopian World Federation, the Universal Black Improvement Organization, the Twelve Tribes of Israel and the Rastafarian Universal Zion. Only a small number of UK Rastafarians are affiliated to these groups so theology and practice varies as a result.

- Religious components from Christianity, Judaism, Hinduism and African Traditions and inspired by Marcus Mosiah Garvey (1897–1940) who promoted the Universal Negro Improvement Association in the 1920s and the Back to Africa movement in the 1930s. Also inspired by the accession of Haile Selassie I as Emperor of Ethiopia, under his pre-coronation name of Ras (prince) with the name Rastafari dating from his coronation in 1930. Tafari is considered the Messiah of Black people and all 87 books of the Bible are recognized.

Beliefs

- Interpretation from biblical texts that God is Black and they are the chosen people.
- Jah is regarded a transcendent deity present in everybody.
- Language is based on Jamaican patois.
- As God is life, the righteous cannot die and become reincarnated.
- Salvation is only realized through a return to Africa, the Black Zion: after liberation from the evils of the White-dominated western world, referred to as Babylon.

Practices

- Men and women are assigned gender-specific roles. Women's highest role is that of wife and mother.
- Singing and drumming (especially reggae music) communicate the ethos.
- Cannabis (ganja) smoking is an important part of sacramental religious practice, supported by Hebrews, Chapter 6, verse 7.
- Dress code – dread locks, with men wearing distinctive caps (*tams*) made of knotted leather or cloth in traditional red, gold, green and black colours of the Ethiopian flag. For prayer and spiritual gatherings heads are uncovered and some wear African-style dress. Ras Tafari, the imperial lion symbol of the Ethiopian throne, is worn as a medallion and crosses as symbols of life's burden.
- The year is based on the Ethiopian calendar beginning on 11 September with 13 months, the last having only six days.
- Celebrations: Six important days a year with the anniversary of Haile Selassie's coronation treated as the holiest with drumming, hymns and prayers.
- Diet: Vegetarian with natural organic foods to avoid polluting the earth with chemicals. Pork is prohibited because of a susceptibility to disease as well as biblical injunctions. Many members do not drink alcohol.
- Ceremonies: Birth blessings; no formal marriage but those who cohabit are treated as man and wife. No special death ceremony because of the belief that life is eternal but adherents will follow local customs.

Sikhism

Key points

- The United Kingdom houses the largest Sikh community outside India. Religion founded in the fifteenth century in the Indian Punjab by Guru Nanak to emphasize that the lowest equals the highest in race, creed, political rights and religious hopes, freeing members from the inequalities of the existing gender and caste system.

- Main communities in India, UK, East Africa and Canada with a small number of ethnic English followers.
- Many sub-groups exist with different understandings about Sikhism and its creeds.
- Recognized as an ethnic group under the 1976 Race Relations Act because of a long shared history.

Beliefs

- One God, whose divine name is recalled and meditated on.
- Ten spiritual masters (Gurus) and their teachings from the Holy Book (Guru Granth Sahib).
- Salvation and liberation from the cycle of reincarnation is attained through meditation and service to others.
- 1/10th of personal wealth and income (daswandh) is given to people in need.
- The Tenth Guru, Gobind Singh, established the sacrament (amrit) – a ceremonial benediction at the temple (gurdwara) and the concept of the Pure Sikhs (khalsa), identified by Five K's which remain until death and not removed except by the wearer or if medically necessary. These are Kesh (uncut knotted hair symbolizing obedience); kanga (wooden comb symbolising cleanliness); kara (steel bangle on the right arm symbolising the bond with the Guru); kachha or kachhedra (undergarment symbolising discipline); kirpan (sword symbolising power and dignity).

Practices

- Initiation into khalsa gives men the name Singh (lion) and women Kaur (princess).
- Worship at home or in the temple (gurdwara) recognized by a flag-pole (nishan sahib) in saffron with a flag of the Sikh emblem in black or navy blue. The service consists of hymns (kirtan), a discourse and communal prayer (ardas) with readings from the Granth Sahib which are followed by a meal (langar).
- Five Festivals (over three days) are timed with a lunar calendar and vary from year to year except for Vaisakhi on 13 April. Diwali celebrates the release from captivity of the Sixth Guru, Har Gobind.
- Diet: Most are vegetarian and do not smoke or drink alcohol, tea and coffee.
- Ceremonies: Birth naming (Janam Sanskar) takes place in the temple immediately after birth and involves opening the Guru Granth Sahib at random and the first letter of the hymn on the top left-hand page indicates the letter to begin the baby's name; khalsa initiation involves wearing the Five Ks and observing a strict diet; marriage (anand karajb) - the ceremony of bliss - is in the temple. At a death people gather at the bedside for readings by the Guru from the Granth Sahib and afterwards the body is cremated and the ashes sprinkled into flowing water.

Taoism

Key points

- Most UK Taoists are Chinese and adhere to Confucianism (a philosophy rather than a religion) as both systems constitute a moral outlook permitting membership of other compatible faiths such as Buddhism, Christianity and Islam. Lao Tzu (c. 500 BCE) is considered the founder.
- The diverse Chinese community has no cultural or racial homogeneity and a different understanding of Taoism depending on whether members originate from mainland China, Hong Kong or South East Asia.

- Because religion has been repressed in the People's Republic of China the doctrines and traditions survive in oral record only.

Beliefs

- Tao Te Ching (The Way and Its Virtue) is the philosophical and religious text. It concerns Man and his place in the universe with a principle of non-interference with natural laws. Mountains, rivers, trees and all aspects of nature are sacred.
- Yin Yang symbol emphasizes the relativity of values and polar dimensions. Opposite dimensions (male/female, dark/light etc.) are the basis for understanding the mind and body as well as life and death.

Practices

- Ritual practice pays homage to chosen deities representing dimensions of Tao principles and ancestors to encourage health, happiness and prosperity.
- Analects of Confucius as well as writings of Meng Tzu (Mencius) put forward the main tenets of a moral compass to guide conduct.
- Temples are dedicated to one to five deities with resident priests (some celibate) who give regular lessons on the teachings of Loa Tzu.
- Diet: Attention is paid to the Yin and Yang (cooling/heating) qualities of food for balance. Vegan fasts occur on the 1st and 15th day of every lunar month, otherwise there are no restrictions.
- Festivals: These are based on a lunar calendar and an annual cycle symbolising the passing year. There are seven main festivals involving sacrifices to the spirits, ritual cleansings and feasts. The Chinese New Year is the major public holiday in Hong Kong and China and celebrated in the UK with special banquets.
- Ceremonies: Birth, marriage and death are accompanied by rituals which may not be followed in the UK. Marriage is elaborate with six phases: proposal, engagement, bride's dowry procession, marriage vows and a wedding breakfast. Traditional gowns (*kwans*) are red for good luck and white, western style gowns, symbolising purity, are often worn during the celebrations. Funeral rites are extensive with Taoist and Buddhist elements. Ritual ablutions are performed over the deceased and paper money (for the bank of merits in hell), as well as talismans, is placed over the body to protect it from harmful influences. Paper houses are often burnt and flowers, incense and an ancestor shrine presented. The deceased may be interred or cremated. Close relatives wear black and others black or white. A willow branch symbolizes the soul of the deceased and carried to the family altar. The family gather on the 7th, 49th or 100th day after the funeral and there is often a commemoration ritual after the first and third years following death with a priest invoking blessings.

Zoroastrianism

Key points

- An ancient religion based on the teachings of Zarathushtra (1400–1200 BCE), who lived in Iran before the advent of writing. It comprises those in Iran and the Parsees who settled in India.
- Members have a long-established presence in the UK, Europe and the United States from the 1800s.

Beliefs

- One eternal God (Ahura Mazda) who created the world for the forces of good to reign over the evil spirit (Angra Mainyu). The forces of good are the seven Amesha Spentas (Holy Immortals) protecting the seven creations of Sky, Earth, Water, Plants, Cattle, Man and Fire.
- Life is engagement in a struggle to overcome the forces of evil, to promote goodness and bring about the salvation of all. The Saviour (Saoshyant), born of the seed of a prophet and a virgin, will save the world when good will triumph at the Last Judgement.

Practices

- Prayer is performed standing in front of the sacred fire which always burns, taking place 5 times a day (sunrise, noon, sunset, midnight and dawn). A sacred thread (*kusti*) is worn three times around the waist and across the sacred shirt and unwound and re-knotted evoking the origins of the word religion from the Latin, *ligare,* to bind/tie to the Divine.
- Temple devotions focus on ritual purity and incense is offered to the sacred fire with gifts and money to the priests.
- Pilgrimages to sacred fire temples, special sources of water or sacred mountains take place regularly.
- Festivals: Seven of these celebrate the seasons of the year and the seven creations, lasting for five days.
- Diet: No restrictions other than to avoid anything intrinsically evil.
- Celebrations: birth naming; coming of age; marriage (includes ablutions); earth ceremonies emphasize elimination of negative forces and must not be absorbed into the earth by burial. Corpses are enshrouded and carried to walled enclosures on designated heights to be consumed by vultures with bones purified by the Sun. Today electrical cremations, or burial in cement coffins, are adopted. The funeral takes place as soon as possible with prayers said for three days. For the first year there are monthly commemorations, then annually at All Souls Festival between 16 and 20 March.

Appendix 2:
Terms used for minority ethnic communities

Black

The term 'Black' was at one time felt to be derogatory in Britain but now has a positive meaning. This has come about as a result of the political civil liberties movements in the 1960s and 1970s. In political/sociological contexts the term may refer to all minority groups that are not White. However, as a descriptive term, 'Black' generally refers to all people of Caribbean or African descent.

Coloured

This term, which used to be commonly used, is now considered offensive as it assumes an inferiority of those who are not 'White' by focusing on the racial origin of people.

People of colour

This term is used in the United States and only occasionally in the United Kingdom. It also implies a status based on racial and therefore inferior categories and should be avoided.

Visible minorities

The expression 'visible minorities' has gained ground in recent years as an acceptable term whose scope is wider than 'Black'. The problem with this label is that it might imply the existence of invisible minorities.

Minority ethnic/minority cultural/minority faith/multi-cultural/multi-faith

The above words for communities are now in common use and are considered acceptable as the broadest terms to encompass all groups who see themselves as distinct from the majority in regard to ethnicity, culture and faith. For example, groups such as the Greek and Turkish Cypriots, Chinese and Irish. The term 'minority ethnic' makes clear that ethnicity is a facet of all people's identity whether from the minority or majority population. Reference to minority communities as 'ethnics' and the plural terms 'minorities ethnic' or 'minority ethnics' should be avoided. It is important to consider the context of the term used and to be specific. Is it ethnicity, culture or faith that we wish to distinguish and why?

British

Care should be taken to use the term 'British' in an inclusive sense so that it includes all inhabitants or citizens of our multi-ethnic, multi-cultural society. Exclusive use of the term as a synonym for White, English or Christian is unacceptable.

Immigrants

To describe all people of minority ethnic origin as 'immigrants' is inaccurate given the period of time the majority have been living in the United Kingdom. The term is exclusive and liable to give offence other than reference to 'immigrants' in the strict, technical sense. Likewise, expressions referring to 'second/third generation immigrants' is exclusive and offensive as these people are British citizens.

Refugees/asylum seekers

The term 'refugee' refers to those people who have had to escape from persecution in their home country. These are 'asylum seekers' but the term is now associated with people without a genuine claim to be refugees and so is somewhat pejorative. It is important when using terms to be accurate, factual or technical.

Race, ethnicity and culture

Race: delineates personal characteristics such as physical appearance, which are permanent, unchangeable and not a question of choice but other's perception.

Ethnicity: defines those factors which are determined by nationality, culture and religion so to a limited extent subject to the possibility of change.

Culture: is characterized by behaviour and attitudes which although determined by upbringing and nationality are perceived as changeable.

West Indian/African-Caribbean/African

The term 'West Indian' is used in the United Kingdom as an inclusive term to describe the first generation of migrants who came to the United Kingdom in the 1940s and 1950s from the Caribbean. However, in that part of the world people describe themselves as *'Jamaican'* or *'Barbadian'* etc. to denote the island they come from. The term *'West Indian'* is not necessarily offensive but in most cases inappropriate. It has colonial overtones and best avoided unless people are happy to style themselves this way.

The term 'African-Caribbean' (as opposed to Afro-Caribbean) is widely used, particularly in official or academic documents to refer to black people of Caribbean origin although it is not usually used by the people themselves. Where it is important to locate geographical origin, the term is acceptable. However, some people of Caribbean origin are White or Asian.

Young people born in Britain are most likely to refer to themselves as Black when racial identity is required, so it is appropriate to refer to them in this way. However, there is increasing interest among young Black people in their African cultural origins, resulting in them asserting this part of their identity and the terms 'African Caribbean' or 'Black Caribbean' are widely used in some circles. Also, the word 'African' is acceptable although those who come from this continent will refer to themselves in national terms as 'Cameroonian', 'Nigerian', 'Ghanaian', etc.

Asian/Oriental/British Asian

Those from the Indian sub-continent do not consider themselves as *'Asians'* but this is applied for the sake of convenience in the United Kingdom. They would rather identify themselves by national origin – 'Indian', Pakistani', 'Bangladeshi' – or region – 'Gujarati', 'Punjabi', 'Bengali' – or religion – 'Muslim', 'Hindu', 'Sikh'. The term most relevant in the context should be used.

The term 'Asian' may be used when the exact ethnic origin of the person is unknown. It would be more accurate to make a collective reference to those from the Indian sub-continent as South Asian, to distinguish them from the South Eastern Asians such as the Malaysians, Vietnamese and the Far Eastern populations such as the Hong Kong Chinese. The term 'Oriental' is imprecise and considered racist or offensive.

Young people may assert themselves as 'Black' or 'British Asians' and neither of these terms requires great sensitivity.

Mixed-parentage/dual-heritage/mixed-race/half-caste

The term 'half-caste' is offensive and to be avoided. Labelling someone as of 'mixed-parentage' is a neutral for those born to mixed cultural and ethnic parents, whilst 'dual-heritage' is used to denote those with parentage from two origins. 'Mixed-race' is a label that is pejorative as it focuses on the racial identity of parents as opposed to culture or ethnicity.

Appendix 3:
Examples of how
people are named

Chinese names

- Traditionally, the Chinese naming system consisted of a last name/family name followed by personal name(s).
- Most personal names are gender-specific. The importance of the family name is stressed by being placed first in the sequence.
- Many British Chinese have adapted their names to follow the ethnic UK system. In addition to using their traditional Chinese names, many Chinese nowadays use a European personal name.

Main parts: personal name(s) + last name/family name.
Examples: Wen-Zhi Man; Lan-Ying Cheung.

Hindu names

- Generally Hindu names have three parts: a personal name, followed by a middle one and then a last/family name.
- Some Hindus omit the family name.
- Most names are gender-specific.
- Middle names can signify gender: Lal/Bhai (masculine) or Devi/Bhen (feminine).
- A Hindu woman normally takes her husband's last name/family name on marriage.
- Most Hindu names follow the ethnic UK naming system.

Main parts: first name(s) + gender designation + last name/family name
Examples:

Vijay Lal Sharma (personal name (Vijay) + gender designation (Lal) + last/family name (Sharma).
Jyoti Devi Chopra (personal name (Jyoti) + gender designation (Devi) + last/family name (Chopra).
Indira Gandhi (personal name + last/family name).

Muslim names

- Muslim names vary due to the cultural diversity of adherents.
- The personal name may be one or two words, so both must be acknowledged. In the name Abdul Rahman, it would be incorrect to just use one name.
- Most personal names are gender-specific so find out how the person would like to be addressed.
- In some regions of the Indian sub-continent it is common to have a middle name to designate a gender title such as Begum/Bibi (feminine) or Miah/Agha (masculine). The last/family name can designate a clan (Khan) or derive from the father's first name (Habib).
- A name may be preceded by a title such as Hajji (masculine) / Hajja (feminine) to denote someone who has made an obligatory pilgrimage. Shaykh, Sayyed/Sayyeda or Mohammed is used as a title. The gender designation Bibi/Begum (female), Miah/Agha (male) may be titles and all might be spelt differently according to conventions.

Main parts: personal name(s) + gender designation + last/family name.
Examples:

Abdul Rahman Habib = personal name (Abdul Rahman + last/family name (Habib).
Amina Bibi Khan = personal name (Amina) + gender designation (Bibi) + last/family name (Khan).
Hajji Akbar shah = title (Hajji – masculine) + personal name (Akbar) + family/last name (Shah).
Sayyida Nusrat Mohammed Khan – title (Sayyida – feminine) + personal name (Nusrat) + family/last name (Mohammed Khan).

Sikh Names

- Generally Sikh names comprise a personal name, a (religious) gender designation and a last name/family name.
- Sikh personal names are usually gender-neutral and gender can be signalled by the male (religious) epithet 'Singh' or the female one 'Kaur' followed by the last/family name, although this is not obligatory and is becoming less common.

Main parts: personal name + religious gender designation + last/family name.
Examples:

Manjit Singh Dhillion = personal name + male religious designation + family/last name.
Manjiit Kaur Dhillon = personal name + female religious designation + family/last name.
Manjiit Singh = personal name + family/last name.

Thanks to Kirn Saini, at the University of Leicester, who provided these name examples for the MA in Inclusion in the School of Education.

Appendix 4:
Families and diversity

Key points

- The family unit is the cornerstone of communities and source of personal identity.
- Differences in outlook exist amongst families in a diverse society so assumptions must not be made.
- No major religion condones abuse and those against abusive cultural practices should be acknowledged and supported.
- Cultural outlook is based on our own experience, knowledge and understanding.

Families are unique

There are a number of factors that lead to shared understanding:

- Socio-economic background, schooling and employment
- National identities
- Gender composition
- Religious framework
- Cultural outlook (secular of traditional).

Many variables contribute to our understanding of the family. For many of us the 'norm' is the ethnic European White model but statistics suggest a 'norm' does not exist (Sage, 2004). Families share tendencies but have idiosyncrasies. A study by Jhutti Johal and Owen (2003) considered tensions in families:

- If families suffer as a result of racism in terms of employment, housing etc. it adds to the problems encountered at home.
- Migration may cause hardship as families are likely to more isolated, fragmented and deprived of traditional support.

- Positive changes in parenting depend on intervention accounting for the cultural and moral framework of a family.
- Families with more traditional belief systems tend to resolve problems without outside intervention.
- Traditional families are more receptive to change if their differences are acknowledged and respected.
- Families with secular lifestyles have more in common with each other than those with similar ethnic backgrounds regarding discipline and child autonomy.

Understanding cultural difference

When there are forced marriages, female genital mutilation and 'honour' killings, it is assumed these practices are normal within certain communities. No major religion, however, condones them:

- Many community leaders and religious authorities challenge abhorrent practices. For example, the Jordanian royalty demonstrated against 'honour' killings amongst the Nagev tribes in their country.
- Victims of abuse should not be patronized and assumed passive. They must be allowed to accept or reject parts of their culture.
- Violence against women and children is seen in all communities. Support is needed which does not reject basic beliefs and practices.
- Arranged marriages, where parties are free to make choices, are not the same as being forced in to them.
- Female genital mutilation is not religiously acceptable but is invoked as an authority when it is not.
- Honour killing or homicide is prohibited and not the religious norm. Many religions, however, discourage promiscuity and administer sanctions. Complex debates around the application of Sharia law for adultery should account for the fact that murder is not sanctioned.

Same-sex partnerships

- Changes in adoption law and trends in society generally express support for same-sex partnerships and their families. There are obvious dangers in assuming all families are heterosexual couples and differences should be recognized.

Sexual orientation

Key points

- Lesbians and gay men constantly fear unequal treatment in daily living as their experiences have led to concealing their orientation.
- Most homosexuals have been brought up in heterosexual homes.
- Parliamentary law recognizes that a same-sex couple can constitute an enduring family relationship although some feel that alternative forms undermine marriage.

- Research shows that children brought up by lesbian or gay parents do equally well as those brought up by heterosexual ones.
- Most homosexuals feel that their sexual orientation was present from birth and is unalterable – just like most heterosexuals.
- Some research claims a genetic determinant for sexual orientation, suggesting that it is not chosen.
- Gay couples differ from same-sex ones and should not be judged according to heterosexual marriage principles. Life together has no precedent or tradition and they are able to make their own rules.

Homosexuals as a minority group

Most people are heterosexual but other sexual orientations make up a significant minority. Lifestyles, occupations, political and religious beliefs, as well as financial circumstances, will be as diverse and unpredictable as their heterosexual counterparts and only one facet of their identities. However, there is a cohesive sense of identity and community in spite of such diversity. Five core experiences and values are shared by most gay people:

The majority are brought up in heterosexual homes.
Being gay is an unalterable fact and not a matter of choice with no evidence that they are seduced into this behaviour.
Fear results in hiding sexual orientation from others.
Being gay or lesbian is an emotional orientation as well as sexual. It has nothing to do with paedophile desire as some people might assume.
Growing up gay brings feelings of isolation from the majority.

It is difficult to calculate the number of UK gay men, lesbians and bisexuals. The Kinsey Report (1953): *Sexual Behaviour in the Human Male* (1948) and *Sexual Behaviour in the Human Female* found that 14 per cent of men and 6 per cent of women were exclusively homosexual. Other surveys (e.g. *The Janus Report on Sexual Behaviour,* Janus and Janus, 1993) suggest that 8–10 per cent is a realistic figure.

Some with a homosexual identity do not engage in homosexual activity and others decline to be identified as being of any particular or fixed sexuality. As people become more tolerant the number willing to be identified as gay, lesbian or bi-sexual is increasing. The European Court of Justice Advocate, General Elmer, has estimated that there are 35 homosexuals within the European Union fraternity.

There is a history of widespread discrimination against homosexuals. Surveys have shown persistent bullying at home, school and work. Unequal treatment in daily lives is a normal expectation. Stonewall, the gay rights pressure group in a 1998 Survey found that 35 per cent of respondents had been victims of violent attacks and 48 per cent of physical ones. Many more said they were frequently verbally abused. Tolerance is superficial and not manifested in schools. At work, 94 per cent concealed their sexuality because they feared loss of promotion in jobs and harassment by colleagues.

HIV positive people and AIDS

AIDS and HIV-positive status are not necessarily indicative of homosexual activity. It is heterosexual activity, worldwide, that is responsible for most new HIV infections as well as intravenous drug abuse. HIV treatment can prevent the symptoms of AIDS indefinitely and is available in the United Kingdom to all who need it. Without drugs AIDS develops and death is likely. HIV infection results in a gradual erosion of the body's immune system and treatment becomes necessary when a person's CD4 count has dropped to around 300 which may take 5–10 years from the start of infection. Medical progress has dramatically changed and lengthened the lives of HIV-positive people but the fear and stigmatization resulting from misunderstanding of the issues is still prevalent.

Gender inequality

Gender equality for women remains important in private and public life in spite of what has been achieved in recent decades. Women have been legally subordinate to men until well into the twentieth century and voting rights in national elections were not equalized until 1928. Historical inequality is reflected in traditional ideas about the role of women and men and although they have shifted over time, assumptions and stereotypes are deeply rooted and persist. It cannot be assumed that all women will have children, look after them and take a break from paid work to raise a family. This view disadvantages women and assumptions about their primary role as bearers and carers of children and of men as breadwinners do not reflect the real life experiences of most people.

Family issues

Non-conformist families are increasingly common in the UK. There is no evidence that children are excessively teased or bullied because their parents are unmarried or gay. Increasing numbers of lesbians and gay men, who are secure in their sexuality, are wanting children and taking steps to have them. Some lesbians ask gay or straight male friends to act as sperm donors and others place advertisements in the gay press. Others opt for an anonymous donation through a sperm bank or informally through friendships. Whether the biological father will be involved in the upbringing is a matter of agreement. Confidence in dealing with life evolves from a loving, supportive, secure home with good communication. Most competent families, whether hetero or homosexual, equip their children to deal with the ups and downs of life by talking through issues.

Appendix 5:
Glossary of disability and social exclusion

Information on a comprehensive range of disabilities is available on the website: www.enablelink.org. This section gives a brief overview and more information is available in Sage (2004).

Alzheimer's disease

The common symptoms of this progressive disease involve memory lapses, difficulty in word-finding and mood swings. There is also a loss of inhibitions, with individuals adopting unusual behaviour, such as becoming lost, undressing in public or making inappropriate sexual advances. There is much repetition seen in questioning, phrases and movements. Although most sufferers are over 70 years of age, there are increasing numbers of younger people with this distressing condition.

Attention deficit hyperactivity disorder (ADHD)

ADHD defines overactive, impulsive children and adults who have difficulty paying attention. If attention is more evident, the description 'attention deficit disorder' (ADD) is used. Associate factors are neurological damage or underdevelopment, diet and poor socialization. About 1:100 children may be affected and five times more boys than girls are reported with the condition.

Autism, Asperger syndrome and specific language disorder

Autism is a life-long developmental disability which hinders ability to communicate and relate socially with others. Problems are aggravated by stress and it is difficult for sufferers to cope with school and work. A less severe form is Asperger syndrome and further down the continuum lies Specific Language Disorder, with speech, grammar and/or syntax, semantics, pragmatics and prosody problems. Pervasive types include all of these elements and lesser ones demonstrate just one of more of them.

Cerebral palsy

Individuals with cerebral palsy experience disorders of movement, posture and communication often accompanied by hearing and sight difficulties. Communication problems present as the most pressing problem and technical aids, such as a speech synthesiser or word board, are often required. Those with learning difficulties are easily confused by questions with fatigue affecting concentration and co-ordination of movement. Frequent breaks in activities are required.

Cerebral vascular accident (CVA)

CVAs result from a clot or haemorrhage in the brain which suddenly affects an apparently healthy person in many different ways. These include weakness or paralysis of a limb on one side of the body, twisting of the face, loss of balance, disturbance of vision, swallowing difficulties, problems in receptive and expressive communication, speech and language disturbance and loss of bladder and/or bowel control. The greatest problem is not being able to pronounce words or put them in the right context or order as well as not being able to put words together to make meaning. Stress and fatigue exaggerate symptoms and children who suffer the effects of this condition find it difficult to cope with school pressures.

Chronic obstructive pulmonary disease (COPD)

COPD refers to a number of disorders that obstruct airways. Examples include asthma, chronic bronchitis, bronchiectasis, emphysema and pulmonary fibrosis. The main symptom is shortness of breath accompanied by coughing and wheezing so sufferers may need inhalers at regular intervals to relieve discomfort. These take time to work and can cause palpitations and slight dizziness, so a break in activity is necessary. Children increasingly suffer from asthma and must be taught to always have their inhaler with them as severe attacks can be fatal.

Diabetes

Diabetes arises when insufficient insulin is secreted by the pancreas to control or process the sugars in the blood stream. It can be controlled by diet alone, tablets or insulin through injection. Some diabetics need to test blood sugar levels every two hours. If these fall below normal the person suffers a hypoglycaemic attack including palpitations, sweating, irritability and speech slurring. It is treated by taking sugar to restore blood sugar levels as fast as possible. Loss of consciousness means an ambulance must be called immediately.

Down's syndrome

Down's syndrome results from a genetic defect and an extra chromosome (47 instead of 46). There are around 300 distinguishing features of which the most recognisable are a flat nose, small mouth, protruding tongue and reduced stature. Some individuals have limited or no speech and communication with low intelligence. They frequently suffer from heart problems, bowel malformations and predispositions to infections, leukaemia and learning problems.

Dyslexia

People with dyslexia have difficulty with information processing, particularly the matching of sound and sight symbols necessary for reading. They have problems organising information so fail to understand and answer questions. Dyslexics require extra thinking time and repetition of information. Visual prompts should be given and word processors used for writing with spell checkers to reduce stress. They are often intelligent individuals who find a range of coping strategies. However, energy is diverted into operating these systems leaving them few extra resources to call upon when they have to deal with situations that fall within their areas of weakness.

Epilepsy

Epilepsy is a very individual condition but sufferers will experience seizures or fits where they black out, lasting for a few seconds (petit-mal) or a few minutes (grand-mal or tonic-clonic). The former causes the individual to stop what they are doing, stare, blink or look vague. The latter brings unconsciousness and after coming around, a period of drowsiness, confusion and headaches with no recall of what has just happened. A minority of individuals have neurological symptoms, learning disabilities and behavioural problems. Stress may exacerbate the condition and should be avoided if possible.

Hard of hearing (deaf)

There are three main categories of hearing impaired people who can be referred to by the term deaf. The capital 'D' in 'Deaf' defines those who use sign language and identify with the Deaf community. The lower case 'd' is used for all other deaf people who have usually acquired an impairment post-lingually and employ a mixture of communication forms. Deaf/blind forms the third group and these rely on touch, taste and smell to understand and communicate with the world. According to the degree of deafness, speech may be difficult to follow with a monotonous voice tone. Sufferers can feel very isolated and their use of theatrical gestures is often interpreted as a sign of rudeness. Background noise is very stressful. Those who are deaf in one ear will cope normally in one-to-one situations but in a large group will find it difficult to judge sound source so that following what is said is a problem.

Heart disease

Heart disease affects the heart muscle or blood vessels and examples include congenital and coronary artery heart disease, angina, hypertension and heart valve pulmonary stenosis. Shortness of breath is a common symptom, aggravated by activity or stress as well as fatigue, weakness and mental confusion.

Incontinence

An inability to control natural functions may be exemplified by fidgety behaviour, inattention or general unease. It often accompanies conditions such as cerebral palsy or other muscular disorders. A sufferer must arrange a signal so that they can leave the room quickly without disturbance.

Inflammatory bowel disease

This is known as Crohn's disease and ulcerative colitis comes under this heading. The main symptoms in the former case are stomach pain and diarrhoea whilst in the latter bleeding occurs. The general ill-health resulting from this leads to a short temper, anxiety and depression. Children often miss significant periods of schooling.

Mental health problems

Around 50 per cent of those attending doctors' surgeries in some areas suffer from mental health problems and an increasing number of children are sufferers. When these are long-term this becomes a disability and made worse by prolonged stress. A wide spectrum of conditions is covered by the term and includes depression and manic depression, post-traumatic stress, anxiety and schizophrenia. Sufferers behave in ways that are distressing to themselves and others and may have hallucinations, delusions and thought disorders. However, it is a myth that they are dangerous and violent and are more likely to harm themselves than others. They need a calm, caring environment as they tend to be highly sensitive. Medication may lead to embarrassing side effects such as tics and excessive sweating.

Spina bifida and hydrocephalus

Most people born with spina bifida (a malformation of the spine) have hydrocephalus (water on the brain). They have sustained some impairment of the brain function but may have normal intellect and can learn successfully, hold down a job and have children. Evidence of brain impairment lies in slow thought processing and delays in answering questions. Memory processes take longer to record information and there is a tendency to take things literally. The range of mobility is wide from unaided to wheelchairs but now that the spine malformation is repaired very early in babies there are few with severe walking difficulties. Change can provide considerable stress for some individuals.

Spinal cord injury

Spinal cord injury can leave a person with paralysis below the point of injury. Sufferers often perspire profusely and have spasms as paralysed limbs move at odd times and in strange ways. Severe cases need a breathing machine which results in soft, fragmented speech and gulping breaths. Individuals fidget a great deal to relieve skin pressure but most are independent despite being in wheelchairs.

Thalidomide sufferers

People who are thalidomide sufferers usually have limb disabilities. They either have no arms or very short ones and this can apply to legs, which puts them in wheelchairs. Some have hearing impairments.

Visual impairment

There are over one million UK people who have become blind or partially sighted. Some with impaired vision can see enough to read slowly and hesitantly but they may have difficulty crossing the road and judging the speed of traffic. Aids such as Braille, large print, audio tape, screen readers and disks are available to help communication.

Mental disability

Mental disability may arise because of mental ill-health, learning disability or brain damage. There is a fundamental difference between a mental health problem and learning disabilities. The latter were previously referred to as 'mental handicap' and in an educational context are referred to as 'learning difficulties'.

Mental ill-health

People become mentally ill through life experiences. Some respond to medical treatment and recover from their symptoms. The condition takes many forms including *neurosis* (a functional derangement such as a phobia) and psychosis (a severe mental derangement involving the whole personality as in paranoia or schizophrenia). There are increasing numbers of older people who are classified as having acquired organic brain syndrome (a neurotic disorder generally due to vascular changes) as in dementia and Alzheimer's disease).

Learning disabilities

Individuals are learning disabled when their brain will not develop or function normally. There is no cure although education and training, together with a disability awareness culture, helps people to become accepted and valued members of society who can fulfil their potential. The causes are varied and often unknown but include:

Genetic abnormalities such as Down's syndrome. There are hundreds of genetic abnormalities and some can lead a near normal life with appropriate medical intervention at an early stage. Others, such as dyslexia, require adjustments to educational methods so they can use their abilities fully. External factors comprise *diseases* such as German measles, *toxins* as in substances taken in pregnancy, vaccine damage or food allergies and *trauma* like birth injury or accident.

Non-specific abnormalities

This comprises the largest category and includes unrecognised conditions. These individuals are at the lower end of the normal intelligence range and may not require extensive specialist services so often go unidentified. Environmental and social factors play a part and the medical label is *idiopathic* being part of the normal distribution. Until recently, identification was based on intelligence identified by IQ score (intelligence quotient). Such assessment has not proved functionally useful and there is now a preference for classifying people according to their degree of independence, such as eating, dressing, communication and social skills.

Brain damage

The care and treatment of those with brain damage differs from that of mental health or learning disabilities. If the damage occurs during the developmental; years (e.g. during childbirth) this will be classified as a learning disability. Being diagnosed within one or more of these categories does not necessarily result in lack of mental capacity. For example, not everyone with cerebral palsy due to brain damage will be a *'patient'*. Even if someone has grown out of their condition, the history of an invisible disability still entitles them to the provisions of the Disability Discrimination Act, 1995. Stress can trigger old symptoms previously overcome.

Terminology

Words to describe mental conditions or limitations have changed usage and meaning since the Acts of Parliament that were enacted to protect those involved. Terms such as *moron, idiot* and *imbecile* are no longer used in professional practice. There is a continual search for terms that do not carry a judgemental stigma but there is no consistency in those adopted and medical and educational professionals often use a completely different set of words to define conditions. For example, in medical circles developmental speech problems may be called dyslalia whereas in education they will be referred to as speech defects.

Learning disability

In England and Wales the legal term for learning disability used to be 'mental sub-normality' whereas in Scotland it was 'mental deficiency', in the United States 'mental retardation' and in Ireland 'mental handicap'. In 1983 the term 'mental impairment' was adopted in England but the following year the Scottish legal system chose 'mental handicap'. 'Learning disability' and 'intellectual impairment' are increasingly used but may not yet adequately convey the meaning in society.

Many voluntary groups concentrate on particular types of learning disability and it is convenient and reassuring to parents to identify impairment by means of a recognised name or 'label'. This enables them to achieve social and economic support. Therefore, it is helpful to be aware of the common names, although they may not represent a precise medical classification and have no legal significance. The largest single category is Down's syndrome but other identified conditions are cerebral palsy, autism, hydrocephalus, meningitis and encephalitis. Some children are referred to as 'hyperactive' although this condition generally subsides as they grow up. Sometimes reference is made to the individual being 'mentally *retarded*', indicating the effect of the condition rather than its cause.

Mental disorder

The term 'mental disorder' is defined by the Mental Health Act, 1983 as: 'mental illness, arrested or incomplete development of mind, psychopathic disorder and any other disorder or disability of mind' (sl (2)). The term is thus extremely wide, describing any identifiable disorder or disability of mind and including the categories above. Being irrational, immoral, eccentric or under the influence of drink or drugs will not itself be sufficient to be classified as mental disorder and the term is often used as a screen to exclude these behaviours. In cases of dispute a medical diagnosis is required to confirm its presence.

Social exclusion

The term 'social exclusion' refers to a situation of economic or social disadvantage. It is broader than concepts such as poverty or deprivation but includes these dimensions. The term includes disadvantage, which arises from discrimination, ill health or lack of education, as well as that arising from limited material sources. Many individuals from this group are drawn into criminal activity which further marginalises them. There is no legal definition of social exclusion and a range of definitions are used by academics and politicians according to their disciplinary and ideological perspectives. However, there are some core features which most definitions share:

- Someone who is unable to participate in key activities in society is socially excluded and these include:
  - o *Consumption* – ability to purchase goods and services which are customary in society.
  - o *Production* – ability to contribute to society through paid or unpaid work.
  - o *Social interaction* – having access to emotional support and friends with opportunities for cultural expression.
  - o *Political engagement* – experiencing some individual autonomy and able to take collective action with a say in local/national decision making.
- Social exclusion is a matter of degree rather than a situation of *'us'* and *'them'*.
- Complex cause and effect situations lead to social exclusion and operate at many levels: *individual personality and characteristics, family background, neighbourhood or peer group effects, the local economy and services, national policy and economic systems plus national, international and global trends.*

Deprivation, unemployment and low literacy levels make the United Kingdom one of the most poverty-stricken countries amongst the developed nations. Only the Republic of Ireland and the USA suffer higher levels of poverty than the United Kingdom, ranked 14th behind Germany, Japan and Australia in the United Nations Development Programme poverty index. Between one-fourth and one-fifth of UK adults are considered functionally illiterate while 13.5 per cent were living below the poverty line, defined as half the median personal disposable income (United Nations Report, September, 1998). A decade later the situation has not improved and many would consider has worsened.

Refugees and asylum seekers

Migrants make up around 10 per cent of the UK population with roughly a one-fourth each coming from the European Union, Indian sub-continent, Africa and the Americas, according to National Statistics. However, figures are not reliable due to the lack of systematic counting and there are a growing number of refugees and asylum seekers from Iraq, Zimbabwe, Afghanistan, Somalia and China. In the village where I live, near to an MI motorway service station and mainline railway, it is common to see groups of immigrants that have been dropped off from lorries coming from the continent. They do not speak English and the police are not interested because of the problems of processing them. If this is happening on a regular basis in one area it must surely be common elsewhere.

References

Sacks, J. (2002) *The Dignity of Difference; How to Avoid the Clash Of Civilizations*, London: Continuum.

Sage, R. (2004) *A World of Difference*, Stafford: Network Educational Press.

Index